Australian Cricket Scandals

Australian Cricket Scandals

Ball tampering, bets, bribes, blow-ups!

KEN PIESSE

Published by:
Wilkinson Publishing Pty Ltd
ACN 006 042 173
Level 4, 2 Collins Street
Melbourne, Vic 3000
Ph: 03 9654 5446
www.wilkinsonpublishing.com.au

Copyright © 2018 Ken Piesse

All rights reserved. No part of this publication may be reproduced, stored in a retrieval system or transmitted in any form by any means without the prior permission of the copyright owner. Enquiries should be made to the publisher.

Every effort has been made to ensure that this book is free from error or omissions. However, the Publisher, the Author, the Editor or their respective employees or agents, shall not accept responsibility for injury, loss or damage occasioned to any person acting or refraining from action as a result of material in this book whether or not such injury, loss or damage is in any way due to any negligent act or omission, breach of duty or default on the part of the Publisher, the Author, the Editor, or their respective employees or agents.

 A catalogue record for this book is available from the National Library of Australia

Planned date of publication: 09-2018
Title: Australian Cricket Scandals
ISBN(s): 9781925642575 : Printed - Paperback

Internal Design by Bruce Godden
Cover design by Tango Media

Contents

Author's Introduction		vi
1	Sandpaper Saturday	1
2	A great injustice	15
3	Bring Back Deano	25
4	Throwing a Test match	35
5	Singapore sling	47
6	500-1	59
7	Underhanded	71
8	Packer's raid	83
9	Thrown out	99
10	Watering the wicket	113
11	Supreme Court	121
12	Don't cross Don Bradman	135
13	Endangering an Empire	143
14	Bradman v The Board	157
15	Boardroom brawling	163
16	Outcast	171
17	Sydney riot	177
18	Kidnapped	183
Further reading		188
About the author		192
Acknowledgements		193
Index		194

AUTHOR'S INTRODUCTION

The full Monty

I didn't consider the bans to be excessive.
The trio had shamed the game and themselves…

We were all mortified and embarrassed. For the first time I was almost ashamed to admit I'm Australian. The atrocities of 'Sandpaper Saturday' in Cape Town in the autumn of 2018 were numbing, our adventure in paradise undermined by just one stunning misjudgment, still reverberating around the cricketing world — a bigger scandal than the underarm, matchfixing, even Warnie popping the wrong pills before a World Cup.

The booing and jeering for Australia's captain Steve Smith at Newlands as he walked in *and* out was loud and prolonged. It came from every direction, not only those in the cheap seats.

By so flagrantly abusing the spirit of cricket, Smith and the others discredited themselves, the game and 450 other Australian Test players who'd so proudly worn the baggy green cap.

Millions of shocked Aussies watched the events in horror. Our Australian Cricket Society tour group had flown in just 24 hours earlier to South Africa's most popular coastal playground. All of us were eagerly anticipating the deciding Tests. Under brilliant blue skies and with the majestic Table Mountain as a backdrop, being there 'live' was akin to being in paradise. We revelled in the contest, the new 'wunderkid' Martram, the mid-pitch argy-bargee between Pat Cummins and AB de Villiers and all the colorful sights of 'Dress-Up' Saturday from the Marines to the young fellas from home wearing Hawthorn jumpers.

But it all went pear-shaped shortly after the 2 pm drinks break on Saturday, March 24 — the exact halfway mark of the game. Cameron Bancroft had been seen tampering with the ball. There was a torrent of booing when a close-up of Bancroft trying to conceal something he had in his hand was shown on the big screen. The vision was re-played again and again and the booing reached a crescendo as the umpires Nigel Llong and Richard Illingworth, tipped-off from the sidelines, bailed Bancroft up and insisted he turn out his pockets.

Smith later said Bancroft had been using nothing more sinister than some tape. In fact it was a small thin piece of sandpaper, aimed at scuffing one side of the ball hoping it would misbehave.

Introduction

It was found that Bancroft had been 'entrusted' with the job of tampering with the ball to enhance the chances of Mitchell Starc and Co. running through the South African top-order while the ball was at its hardest and Australia still had half a chance of winning. Starc, Josh Hazlewood and Patrick Cummins, the likely beneficiaries, were said to have had no part in it.

With the Australians in position for a new over, Smith ran 40 metres to join Bancroft and the umpires to the side of the pitch. The rookie opener had been caught by the cameras. And like the instigator, team vice-captain David Warner, known for years as (the loose) 'Cannon', he had nowhere to run and nowhere to hide.

In one mindless, renegade act, the trio had disgraced cricket's 'brand' and the nation's most prestigious sporting XI.

No amount of provocation – and there was plenty – could be blamed for the crazy decision taken by Australia's team leaders. How they would have loved to have had that five-minute lunchtime conversation all over again. On the Saturday night, having heard a crestfallen Smith try to downplay the severity of the afternoon happenings, it was clear the strongest possible action had to be taken. It was such a shame that Smith, the finest batsman since the Don, wasn't strong enough to say 'no' to his vice-captain. The Australian press wanted scalps, especially coach Darren Lehmann's, but I was certain had Lehmann known about the unsavory happenings about to unfold, he would have stopped it then and there. He's too good a cricket person to have allowed it. I wrote as much for **sportshounds.com.au** and was the first of the on-the-spot media pack to predict severe sanctions of 12-months each for the errant three.

I didn't consider the subsequent bans to be excessive. The trio had shamed the game and themselves.

A week later during the lack-lustre final Test in Johannesburg I offered some spare tickets on the final morning to a woman walking down to the ground with her three young children. Hearing my accent, she asked: 'Where are you from?'

As soon as I said 'Melbourne', one of her boys, aged seven or eight, started taunting me: 'Sandpaper, Sandpaper...'

So dispirited were the Australians at the Wanderers it was a miracle the game lasted five days. Later South Africa's opening batsman Dean Elgar said he'd never played in a quieter Test match.

Lehmann resigned within a week, unfairly tarred by many as being 'in the know' about the whole sordid affair. And by early June, the scandal proved to be one of the last major public appearances by James Sutherland, Cricket Australia's chief executive who had flown into Johannesburg to co-ordinate and deliver the sentences.

As scandals go, it was the Full Monty. Sent home in disgrace Smith admitted he'd cried for four days. So had we all.

THE MOMENT: Having been given an impromptu woodworking lesson at lunch, Cam Bancroft tries to conceal a thin piece of sandpaper inside his trousers. Fox Sports

1
2018 CAPE TOWN

Sandpaper Saturday

The condemnation of the best batsman since Bradman was fierce, frenzied and unrelenting. No Australian cricket captain had ever been so shamed. Steve Smith was immediately sacked after his 'guilty' admission to ball tampering on Black Saturday at Newlands. Two other culprits David Warner and Cameron Bancroft were also sent home in disgrace. Their five minutes of madness was to cost millions of dollars in withdrawn contracts and sponsorships and trigger more resignations. Smith and Co. had derailed the integrity of the game. It was all so very un-Australian. We were all stunned. Our most iconic cricketers were cheats.

Player power has always imperiled cricket. Liberties are taken and the good of the game and its fans often ignored. In 2018, less than 12 months after the elite Australian cricketers went on strike and won, a bursting, narcissistic confidence emanated. Some senior players felt themselves untouchable and above the law.

The results were calamitous, Australia's culture of disrespecting opponents and win-at-all-costs arrogance bubbling out of control during the autumn-time Tests in South Africa.

Rarely before had the spirit of cricket been so flagrantly abused as in the opening two Tests between two of the world's elite XIs. It was war without weapons. In Durban where the ball swings according to the time of the tides, Australian vice-captain David Warner's reaction to the run out of AB de Villiers for a duck was vulgar and insulting. In the excitement of the moment, clean-skin Nathan Lyon all but dropped the ball on de Villiers' chest as he lay prostrate and crestfallen at the non-striker's end, victim of his own slip and Warner's reflexes. Relations between the teams, always terse, zeroed out of control, the vilification of Aiden Markram, South Africa's opener in his first series against the Australians, rude and relentless. Those manning the pitch microphones were astonished by Australia's brazen attitude. This wasn't mental disintegration. It was

NEW LOOK: After the disgrace of Cape Town, Australia went to Wanderers without either David Warner or Steve Smith for the first time in a Test home or away since 2013. Susan Piesse

abuse of the highest order, guaranteed to upset and divide. The Australians asked for the microphones to be turned down. And the abuse became an uncontrollable torrent. It seemed little had changed in four years since Faf du Plessis likened playing against Australia to opposing a pack of wild dogs.

At teatime on the penultimate day at Kingsmead, Warner and South Africa's Quinton de Kock traded personal barbs in the player's stairwell before Warner was corralled inside, the South African having disparaged Warner's wife Candice, a mother-of-two.

Earlier, South Africa's champion de Villiers was the only one to survive Mitchell Starc's high-speed reverse swing which decimated South African middle-order. His 71 not out was worth a century every other day. Late in Starc's irresistible spell, de Villiers accosted Warner, claiming the Australians were 'doing something to the ball', so devilishly late was Starc's swing.

'Are you accusing me of cheating "AB"?' Warner was alleged to have said.

With his thumb and index finger heavily bound in adhesive tape, his exaggerated, ultra-vigorous shining of the ball had triggered suspicions way beyond South Africa's homeroom.

In Port Elizabeth where South Africa squared the series, its headstrong fast bowler Kagiso Rabada shouldered Australia's captain Steve Smith and was duly suspended for two matches – only for the ban to be reversed on appeal. The Australians were amazed and dismayed. Rarely before had cricket got so physical or tempers veered so dangerously out of control. And those in charge seemed powerless to stop it. Warner again attracted unwanted headlines after two South African Board executives allowed themselves to be photographed with three patrons who'd entered the ground wearing Sonny Bill Williams masks – a reminder of a messy night years earlier involving the rugby superstar and Candice Warner, when she was single. The two executives were immediately stood down.

SANDPAPER SIGNAGE: *South African supporters dined out on Australia's nefarious tactics in Cape Town.* David Beames/australiancricketsociety.com.au

Our Australian Cricket Society tour group had landed in Cape Town just 24 hours before the start of the Test. We were thrilled to be attending the two deciding games of the series. By the time several of us arrived at the nets in Newlands, less than a handful of the Australians were still practising. Coach Darren Lehmann nodded and said 'G'day'. He appreciated some Aussie support. Warner was in the nearest net and playing chancily, his short-arm jabs through midwicket, punctuated by nicks to second slip and gully. Something seemed amiss. He was trying hard enough but he would have been out three times in 20 minutes. Given the enormity of the Test match, we would have liked him to be more Lawry-like. Down a few nets was Smith, facing the left-arm slows of back-up spinner Jon Holland and throw-downs from Lehmann. Having been dismissed in three of his first four Test innings on tour by left-arm finger spinners he was working on his shot selection, particularly his sweep shot, looking to paddle it fine and beat the fielder on the '45'. Both bowled from wide on the return crease, mimicking the South African Keshav Maharaj. If Holland or Lehmann struck his pads, he was consistently asking: 'Where did it pitch? Was it on line?' It was reassuring to see Australia's two leaders and batting champions spending extra time in the nets, even if Warner's feet seemed unusually leaden. When Smith finally was satisfied, Tim Paine took his place and played with immediate balance and poise. Six months earlier, having been excluded from Tasmania's first Sheffield Shield XIs of the summer, he'd seriously considered taking a desk job in Melbourne. Now he was living his dream, batting at No.7 and keeping wickets again for his country.

We'd arranged to have a group dinner with Barry Richards at the nearby Kelvin Grove Club compliments of our host, DMC Sports Travel's Dusty Miller. Barry was keen to do some media work during the match but had been denied a press pass. Of

AUSTRALIA TEAM SHEET
2018 SOUTH AFRICA TEST TOUR

versus

Match:	4th Test Match
Date:	Friday 30th March to Tuesday 3rd April 2018
Venue:	Bidvest Wanderers, Johannesburg

#	C	WK	Players (Batting Order)	Age	Cap #	Test #
1			Matthew Renshaw	22	449	11
2			Joe Burns	28	441	14
3			Usman Khawaja	31	419	33
4			Peter Handscomb	25	447	11
5			Shaun Marsh	34	422	32
6	■	■	Mitchell Marsh	26	438	28
7	(c)	(wk)	Tim Paine	33	414	13
8			Patrick Cummins	24	423	14
9			Nathan Lyon	30	421	78
10			Chadd Sayers	30	452	DEBUT
11			Josh Hazlewood	27	440	40

12th Man				Age	Cap #	Tests
12			Mitchell Starc	28	425	43

Emergency Fielders				Age	Cap #	Tests
13			Glenn Maxwell	29	433	7
14			Jon Holland	30	444	2
15			Jhye Richardson	21	NO CAP	NO CAP
16						

Captain: Tim Paine   Signature: _[signature]_

CAPTAIN BY DEFAULT: *The official team sheet showing for the first time Tim Paine as captain and Australia's XII for the fourth and final Test in Johannesburg in April. Was Mitchell Marsh the original intended captain, or was it just a clerical error?*

THE SOUTH AFRICAN 'RICHIES': 'The Marines', the Kepler Wessels Appreciation Society, who gather in ever-increasing numbers on the hill on Test Saturdays in Cape Town

all of South Africa's past champions he is the most embittered by the new regime's refusal to recognise anyone who had played prior to 1993 and the implementation of the country's multi-racial quota system. 'It's as if we don't exist,' he says.

Nothing beats being at a much-anticipated overseas Test 'live' and under brilliant blue skies and with the majestic Table Mountain as the backdrop, it was simply wonderful to be part of such a vibrant scene. The local Newlands trains all crawled ever-so-slowly into the nearby station, their drivers hoping to see a ball or two. One of the other Aussie tour groups, all resplendent in their multi-colored wattle shirts, were ideally positioned on their bean bags on the grassy mounds at fine-leg. A few young fellas in Hawthorn AFL jumpers were also a long way from home. It was a working Thursday but the crowd was lively and animated. The donut sellers were doing a thriving trade, as were those running the souvenir stalls.

When Markram fell for a duck to Josh Hazlewood from the press box end, the Australians had an immediate ascendancy. Seeing de Villiers motor to a classic half century was worth all the hours in the air. He'd been welcomed onto the ground like he was Don Bradman. We all hoped he'd get going. Seeing such a master at work was a privilege. Opposed by Pat Cummins, he caressed a trademark boundary wide of mid-wicket. So crisp was his timing he didn't even have to run. Anything pitched full and on the stumps was fodder.

Dean Elgar was slower and less showy. But without him South Africa could never have made anywhere near 300. He'd been dropped by Lyon at backward point at 53.

Australian Cricket Scandals

SEVEN EXAMPLES OF BALL TAMPERING

1994: England captain Mike Atherton *(pictured)* is fined $3700 for using dirt, taken from the pitch, to try to keep his hands less sweaty while working on the ball during a Test against South Africa at Lord's. The match referee, Australian Peter Burge, had seen close-ups of Atherton using dirt on the ball via TV replays.

2000: Pakistan's Waqar Younis is found guilty of trying to alter 'the composition of the ball' during a limited-overs match against Sri Lanka. He is suspended for a match and fined 50 per cent of his match fee.

2006: Pakistan refuses to take the field after tea on day four of The Oval Test in England following ball-tampering accusations levelled by umpires Darrell Hair and Billy Doctrove. Hair and Doctrove call the match off, awarding England the win via forfeit. Pakistan attempts to re-take the field to continue saying it was only a 'short protest' but the umpires refuse to resume. The London *Independent* calls it: CRICKET'S DARKEST DAY.

2010: Pakistan's Shahid Afridi is banned from two Twenty20 internationals after being found guilty of ball-tampering during an ODI in Perth. Standing in as skipper, Afridi is caught on cameras trying to bite and chew the seam.

2013: Having rubbed the ball on the zipper of his pants pocket, prompting umpires to award Pakistan a five-run penalty against the Proteas, Faf du Plessis pleads guilty to the charge of ball tampering and is fined 50 per cent of his match fee. South Africa's manager Mohammed Moosaje insists it is 'harsh' to call it tampering. AB de Villiers says 'we are not cheats'.

2014: South Africa's Vernon Philander is captured on cameras using his fingers and thumb to scratch the ball during a Test in Sri Lanka. Philander digs his nails into the rough side of the ball. He accepts the charge and is fined 75 per cent of his match fee.

2016: South Africa's du Plessis loses his entire match fee but avoids suspension after being found guilty of using a mint to shine the ball against the Australians in Hobart.

SANDPAPER SATURDAY: The entry ticket to the most talked about day in South Africa-Australia Test history, March 24, 2018, Newlands. Andrew Miller/DMC Sports Travel

By the spinner's high standards, it was a sitter. Had the catch been taken, Hazlewood would have had three for 19 from his first 12.

Australia and Warner started like they were in a Twenty20. Tucked up and struck midships second ball by Rabada, he crunched three 4s in a row, two through the off and one wide of mid-on. Rabada's first two overs cost 18. His easy approach belied his high pace. His radar was just a little off. In between overs, South Africa's captain Faf du Plessis put his arm around Rabada and walked with him down to fine leg, reinforcing the tight line he wanted. At the start of his next over, Rabada pitched on the stumps, but it was short and Warner flicked the ball over the fine leg ropes where it was wedged on a corner of a first floor canopy of the Western Province CC members' stand. Rabada's next, fuller and wider, was smoked wide of point. Four more. Warner was throwing his arms at everything. He'd made 30 of Australia's first 43. But few of us were convinced. He was playing like a prize-fighter, behind on points, desperate to score a knockout before the bell. Rabada bowled again, faster and straighter. Warner flailed at an attempted square drive. His footwork was minimal and he was bowled, his off stump cartwheeling almost all the way back to wicketkeeper de Kock. It was the definitive dismissal of the match, maybe the entire series. Warner had been castled again… for the third innings in a row. In the stands, a black couple were dancing in the aisles holding a sign: 'Take a bow, King KG (Rabada)'.

Warner trudged off face down, looking ruefully at the face of his bat. As he reached the gate one of the patrons in the WPCC members stood up and walked towards the fenced-off player's race and hurled abuse at him. Warner momentarily stopped, eyed the man before continuing up the stairs. The agitator was immediately ejected. Apparently he was a guest of a member who was away buying more beers.

The extra lift was disconcerting many of the Australians. Smith made just five before being beaten by Morne Morkel's height and bounce. His scores for the summer had a consistent downward theme: 56, 38, 25, 11 and 5. One delivery from Rabada to Paine took off like a super ball. Any sort of lead was going to be golden. Paine hung in bravely and found an ally in Lyon who made some breezy hits, but South Africa's lead was still 56. By lunch on dress-up Saturday it was 121 and steadily increasing…

KING 'K.G': *Having conceded 18 runs from his opening overs, Kagiso Rabada skittled David Warner sending his off stump almost to the feet of wicketkeeper Quinton de Kock standing 20 yards back.*
Wayne Ross/australiancricketsociety.com.au

Among the guests I'd spent time with on the opening days was Dr Ali Bacher who had been the prime mover in South Africa being re-admitted to world cricket in the early '90s. A former South African captain and administrator he had championed the rise of black fast bowler Makhaya Ntini and taken the game to trouble spots like Soweto. He loved watching Rabada and felt he could become the most feared express bowler in the world. He'd been watching the entire 2018 series with growing sadness, believing the players from both sides had forgotten that they were playing a sport and not engaging in war. Bacher had an ear to the rooms. The South Africans claimed the sledging of Markram was happening almost 'every second ball'.

Prior to Cape Town he'd written to du Plessis, saying the constant sledging and lack of respect being shown by both the South African and Australian players had left him stunned and seriously worrying about the game's future. He hadn't expected a reply, but received one almost immediately.

'Faf and I talked about all this chirping, as it is called,' he said. 'I suggested to him if he was being sledged he should consider seeking out the opposition captain and tell him unless it stops immediately, he would walk off.'

In two series and nine Tests against the Australians, including four as South Africa's captain in 1970, Bacher said not once did the teams exchange even one swear word. 'And our cricket was tough and hard and just as competitive as it is now with all the fast bowlers around, Graham McKenzie for the Australians and "Prockie" (Mike Procter) and Peter Pollock for us.'

Bacher said future captains at a summer start should broker an agreement on what is acceptable and what isn't. Australia's request for the pitch microphones to be turned down had triggered 'open slather sledging' which totally flaunted the spirit of the game. 'It simply has to stop, for cricket's sake,' he said.

The Test was slipping away from the Australians. Sometime during the 40-minute luncheon break, Warner concocted the plan to scuff the ball to aid the swing of Starc and Co. The ball was still hard and new and one quick wicket could become two. He sought out his junior partner Cameron Bancroft to discuss a plan. Cameras were sure to be on him and not necessarily on Bancroft. Smith was party to it all. Lehmann was deliberately not consulted.

Bancroft re-took the field with a cloth to keep his sunglasses clear and clean. Also in his pockets was a thin piece of sandpaper. Smith later admitted the decision to tamper with the ball had been made by the 'leadership group'. He refused to name names. Bancroft, as the junior member of the side, had agreed to carry out the group's instructions.

Had Usman Khawaja taken a catch diving full tilt to his left before Markram had scored, the Australians may not have considered anything so desperate.

Shortly before mid-afternoon drinks, close-ups of Bancroft shining the ball were repeatedly shown on the big screen. There was muffled booing when further investigation showed him with something small and yellow in his right hand *(Smith later was to say it was nothing more sinister than tape, when in fact it was a carefully cut thin strip of sandpaper... not only was he party to the cheating, he was now lying about it).*

The vision was damning. It was played and re-played and the booing became louder and more concerted. There were more than 10,000 watching on, the biggest attendance

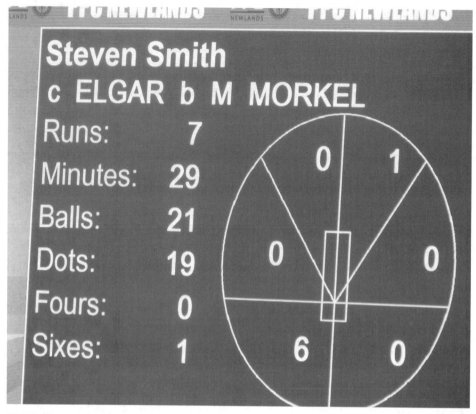

SMITH'S LAST STAND: Steve Smith was booed to and from the wicket as Australia lost all 10 second innings wickets in a single session at Newlands. Wayne Ross/australiancricketsociety.com.au

of the match. Lehmann rang downstairs to Australia's 12th man Peter Handscomb: 'What the fuck is going on?' he asked.

Bancroft had been caught on the big screen. Whatever he had in his pocket he needed to hide it or get rid of it. Handscomb, like the rest of the team, had no idea what had transpired at lunchtime. Had Lehmann known, he would have stopped it there and then.

By now, every available camera from every angle was trained on Bancroft. Taking the sandpaper strip from his pocket, he tried to conceal it inside his trousers.

Within minutes he was bailed up by the on-field umpires Richard Illingworth and Nigel Llong who asked him to turn out his pockets. It wasn't a casual request. They stood either side of the Australian, ever so close, wedging him in. Starc was at the top of his run-up ready to bowl. Wicketkeeper Paine and the slips were all in place. To more boos and jeers, Smith ran 40 metres from second slip to support Bancroft. Replays continued to be shown on the giant screen confirming that Bancroft was trying to hide something down the front of his trousers. At tea-time Lehmann demanded answers. He was ropable.

By stumps South Africa was safe at 5-238, a lead of almost 300 with two full days to play.

At the highly charged press conference Smith admitted the Australians had deliberately gone outside the laws. It had all been pre-meditated. 'The leadership group knew about it. We spoke about it at lunch,' he said. 'I'm not proud of what's happened. It's not within the spirit of the game. My integrity, the team's integrity, the leadership group's integrity has come into question and rightfully so. I'm not naming names, but the leadership group talked about it and "Bangers" (Bancroft) was around at the time. We spoke about it and thought it was a possible way to get an advantage. Obviously it didn't work. The umpires didn't see it change how the ball was behaving, or how it looked or anything like that. (It was) a poor choice and we're deeply regretful for our actions.'

Quizzed late in question time about his own position, Smith was defiant: 'I won't be considering stepping down. I still think I'm the right the person for the job. Obviously, today was a big mistake on my behalf and on the leadership group's behalf as well. But I take responsibility as the captain, I need to take control of the ship, but this is certainly something I'm not proud of and something that I can hopefully learn from and come back strong from. I'm embarrassed to be sitting here talking about this. We're in the middle of such a great series and for something like this to overshadow the great cricket that's been played and not have a single cricket question in here, that's not what I'm about and not what the team's about. We'll move past this. It's a big error in judgment but we'll learn from it and move past it.'

Under the spotlight of question time, Bancroft also made a hash of it, sugarcoating what he had been using. Initially he claimed it was nothing more than a piece of adhesive tape, very sticky on one side enabling him to take some granules from the wicket area to scuff the ball. 'It didn't work,' he said. 'The umpires didn't change the ball. Once being sighted on the screen I panicked and tried to shove it (the tape) down my trousers… We have this yellow tape in our kit and it is connected to some padding but the sticky stuff is very sticky and I felt like it could be used to collect some stuff from the side of the pitch.'

It was all a lie. But both had insisted on fronting the media that very night. Neither mentioned Warner by name or that it was he who had suggested how Bancroft could use the sandpaper. Peter Lalor of *The Australian* termed it: 'An impromptu and infamous woodwork class.'

When play resumed the following morning, there were multiple signs around the ground: 'Free Sandpaper Here'. *(They were soon to be confiscated by security staff)*.

On the Sunday morning the Australian rooms were hushed. Lehmann walked up to Paine and said: 'You're captain'. Smith and Warner had been stood down.

Our dinner guest the night before, Barry Richards sent a text: 'Shameful way to treat the game. Feel sorry for all in your tour group. A long way to come to see this. What a let down.'

Smith had batted for 35 hours in the Ashes series. Not even Don Bradman had done that *(and only one Australian, Mark Taylor, 38 hours, had ever batted longer in an Ashes series. That was in 1989 when a sixth Test was played).*

Despite a week off leading into the match, Smith was mentally and physically exhausted. Out on his feet. Nothing left in the tank. Like Greg Chappell a generation earlier, he was not fit to be Australia's captain that game. He was almost beyond caring. How he wished he could have had those lunchtime moments with Warner all over again.

The condemnation from home lasted for weeks. Justin Langer talked about the team being full of spoilt brats. Ricky Ponting thought the whole affair catastrophic. Even the Prime Minister Malcolm Turnbull described the events as 'a shocking disappointment'.

Senior Cricket Australia staff seemed as stunned as the public. Three, including Iain Roy, the Board's head of integrity, were enlisted immediately to mount an investigation and determine the damage. Just how many in the 'leadership group' were involved? Did Lehmann know about it all? Surely he must have... so the newspapers columnists claimed.

SHOCKED: Two of the Sunday newspaper headlines back home in Australia

Within days a stern and distraught James Sutherland, the Board's chief executive, announced penalties: 12-month suspensions for Smith and Warner and nine months for Bancroft. Warner was not to be given any sort of leadership role in the future. None could play any cricket in Australia, except on Saturday afternoons for their clubs. One hundred hours of community service was also to be served. *(originally the International Cricket Council had suspended Smith for the following Test and stripped him of his entire match fee. Bancroft was fined 75 per cent of his match fee but avoided suspension. At that stage Warner's lead role in the affair was not known)*

1 Sandpaper Saturday

DINING OUT: South Africans loved their team's breakthrough series victory against Australia

In announcing that only three were involved, Sutherland was stony-faced: 'Australian cricket fans expect certain standards of conduct from cricketers representing our country,' he said, 'and on this occasion these standards have not been met.'

Would all this have happened if Cricket Australia had insisted months earlier on playing 'hardball' with its players over money distribution issues? The admissions by Smith and Bancroft — and later by Warner — told of a desperate outfit, out-of-tune with reality. They were willing to do anything to keep up with the South Africans. And Smith had rubber-stamped it all.

The Johannesburg Test proved to be an even bigger travesty. Within days Lehmann was gone. Sutherland soon followed. And most of it due to a tiny piece of sandpaper… and inflated, out-of-control egos. What a sorry, outrageous business it was.

- Australia collapsed in a session late on the fourth afternoon at Newlands. Set 430, it lasted less than 40 overs. The three cheats Smith, Warner and Bancroft were all booed to and from the wicket. Only once all summer had the Australians batted even 80 overs. A cricket match which had promised so much and included Morkel's 300th wicket had ended in farce. Smith and Warner were jostled and jeered at Cape Town Airport. They took separate flights home, their reputations scarred forever. Our tour party spent the following day at the Cape of Good Hope, glad for once to talk about anything but the cricket.

    Weeks later just as Justin Langer was being formally announced as Lehmann's replacement as coach, the vastly experienced Cameron White, a 142-game Australian representative across all three formats, was discussing the scandal at one of our Australian Cricket Society luncheons. He was asked as a young player starting off in the team, would he also have 'done a Bancroft'?

    'Yes,' he said. 'If Ricky Ponting had asked me… yes.

    'But,' he said, 'he would never have asked me…'

MILESTONE: Brad Hodge doubles it up against the South Africans in Perth in December 2005

2 BRAD HODGE

One of the great injustices

Brad Hodge ticked all the boxes. He possessed indomitable confidence, a rare cricketing intellect and skillset and built a simply awesome Sheffield Shield record. His long-time coach Greg Shipperd regards him as the finest Victorian player of his generation and says his exclusion from Australia's XI in 2006, just two Tests after making a breakthrough double century remains 'one of the great injustices in Australian sport'.

'I can't explain it. It's one of the great mysteries,' Shipperd says. 'He was a sensational player with a rare "x" factor and deserved to play (for Australia) many, many more times.'

Was Hodge too chirpy on the field? Did those he looked to unsettle carry a grudge? Why did his otherwise stellar career include just six Tests?

Cricket is all about meeting challenges head-on and being the best you can be under the most pressure-cooker of situations. For all his stellar, most exhilarating moments in the game, Brad Hodge flunked the most important of all, a Boxing Day Test in front of his own adoring home fans. So giddy was he from all the backslapping he received walking down the ever-so-long race from the Australian viewing area that he reckoned he was seeing 'three Shaun Pollocks' as he took guard and tried to unscramble his eyes. He'd taken Ricky Ponting's advice and hastened to the middle, trying to ignore his hometown nerves. But he was still far from composed as the South African seam master began his approach.

Having left the first delivery alone, he swatted at the second, a bouncer directed at his right shoulder and top-edged it unconvincingly over wicketkeeper Mark Boucher's

PROLIFIC: *A young Brad Hodge once made nine centuries in a junior season… and celebrated each time with hamburgers from Hungry Jacks*

head. It could have ballooned anywhere. Almost 72,000 breathed a collective sigh of relief. Hodge's immediate thought was that he was 'four off two… that's good'.

Within half an hour he was out, nicking one to Graeme Smith at slip. He'd never looked comfortable.

Captain Ponting made a century, as he so often did in big matches in Melbourne and the Australians won convincingly both in Melbourne and in the New Year Test which immediately followed in Sydney.

With four scores of under 25 (one was not out), Hodge had failed the most intense of cricketing examinations. And despite his mid-December 203 not out approaching the two glamor holiday-time Tests, he was dropped — never to play another Australian-soil Test.

Playing elite, big-time sport was all about the challenge and your reactions, Hodge said. 'You get one chance and you need to put your best foot forward. I played in an era where it was very, very tough to get into the Australian Test team. The very fact that I was able to do it on six occasions is something I'll always treasure… yes it's damning when you make runs and are not selected. But it was never in my nature to give up. I'd always compete.'

Conspiracy theories abound at his continuing absence from Australia's Test XI. One persistent rumour had him in a fierce slanging match with Ponting during a particularly-competitive Sheffield Shield match at the MCG. There were cross words, both telling each other to 'fuck off', Ponting standing up for his young teammates and Hodge refusing to back down. But it was not taken any further. Certainly it never got physical. Ponting may have been Australia's captain, but their cross words had nothing to do with Hodge's absence from the international stage.

Victoria always played aggressively, looking to isolate and unsettle the newcomers. Hodge often told big-name opponents what they could do. Ever since the Chappell-era, sledging had been an inherent part of the game.

He and Ponting have been mates ever since their days together at the Australian Cricket Academy in Adelaide. They worked with each other for hours in the WACA nets approaching the mega-moment in Hodge's career in 2005. Hodge always had the highest regard for Ponting's work ethic and abilities.

Academy head Rod Marsh's way of inducting Academy newcomers was often to turn the bowling machine up to express speeds and gauge the reactions.

'There was no-where to run and no-where to hide,' said Hodge. 'A couple of the boys were caught in the headlights and struck. Rod had that machine going at close to 160 km/h (100 mph). We all put on extra padding and soon worked out the safest option was just to duck under the bouncers. The ball would thump in an instant into the back canvas. Bang. Ricky came in, with just a cap on, no helmet like the rest of us and started smashing them from the first ball. You could tell he was going to be unbelievably good. We all shook our heads (in wonder) at the things he could do. And he was only 16 or 17 at the time.'

TWENTY20 EXPERT: Hodge at the Indian Premier League. He is now part of Channel 7's T20 commentary team

Brad Hodge was always a young man in a hurry. He walked at eight months and according to his mother Val was 'running around the (Cheltenham) house from 18 months on'.

Invariably he would be armed with a bat or ball, practicing his shots or perfecting his action. Dennis Lillee was his hero and he even learned to mimic Dennis' trademark two fingered appeal.

He loved all sports, cricket, football and baseball his particular favourites. Two of his uncles Des and Fred Cole played League football with St Kilda and a cousin, Susie Baker offered a golfing scholarship to America.

Those walking their dogs past the Dane Rd. Special School in Moorabbin on summer Saturdays had to stay alert as a young Hodge and his Under 12 Moorabbin teammate Ian Hewett would try and outdo each other with their six hitting.

They'd open both the batting and the bowling, Val Hodge often telling her son to 'keep the ball down.'

'The team's coach Graham Stewart came up after the first game and told us we should have Brad coached. He thought he was a natural.'

Hodge was 12 when he made the first of more than a dozen 100s at Dane Rd. Years

MEETING HIS HERO: Hodge with Dennis Lillee at the Punt Road Oval. Hodge family archives

later, driving past the ground, he couldn't believe how short the boundaries were. 'The boundary would have been no more than 30 metres,' he said, 'but then again I was only about four foot high back then. They were big hits to me at the time.'

As a 13-year-old he amassed nine centuries in one season with the Moorabbin under 14s. Once he made 99, having been told his score by coach Graham Croft, who was umpiring at square-leg. 'I just about froze and was bowled in the very same over!' he said. 'Back then you didn't have to retire. I wanted to make at least 50 every time as that meant Dad buying Hungry Jacks for us!'

Before joining Melbourne and beginning his first steps at the big-time, he made another six or seven 100s in the Under 16s.

Val Hodge hardly missed a ball. 'I was always driving him around to games,' she said. 'I loved it. I could sit and watch cricket each and every day.'

Once Mrs Hodge took Brad and a friend into Australia's training session at Richmond's Punt Road Oval. In-between collecting autographs, she took Brad's picture standing beside Dennis Lillee. 'I ended up talking with people like Dennis, Rod Marsh and AB (Allan Border) for four or five minutes,' said Hodge. 'It was pretty big at the time.'

Going home that night Hodge was so excited at meeting some of his heroes that he kept repeating: 'I'm going to play for Australia one day… I'm going to play for Australia.'

WITH WARNIE: *Playing Test cricket alongside some of his long-time mates like Shane Warne was an extraordinary thrill*

In a massive career which was to last almost 25 years thanks to the ballooning popularity of Twenty20 cricket, Hodge's mega calendar year came in 2004 when he was 30.

He and his sweetheart Megan Allen married and enjoyed an extended honeymoon in the UK. Hodge played his 100th match for Victoria, amassing a career-best 1300 runs in a Pura Cup title-winning year.

In English county ranks with Leicestershire he made five 100s including a record three doubles. In the opening home game against Glamorgan and his mate Matty Elliott, he made 105 and 158.

When Ponting broke his thumb slip fielding during a one-day international in England on the eve of Australia's tour of India, Hodge made a phone call home to confirm his availability. He was immediately enlisted, but other than a solitary game at Mumbai on the eve of the first Test, he wasn't required. It was still a thrill to be involved and at Nagpur he fielded for 10 minutes as a substitute for Jason Gillespie. He wore a white floppy hat rather than the baggy green he so coveted.

Having rejected overtures to shift interstate to Sydney, Hodge intended returning to Australia for Victoria's opening ING Cup match of the new season in Adelaide.

However, just hours before his international flight, from Mumbai, he was recalled to Nagpur after Darren Lehmann injured a hamstring. His stand-by status was continuing. The Sydney prodigy Michael Clarke had created immediate headlines by making 151 on his debut in the first Test at Bangalore, but Hodge could see opportunities opening elsewhere in the order.

After a quieter beginning when he admitted he was probably trying too hard, an unbeaten double century for Victoria against the South Australians was the first of three hundreds in a row, guaranteeing him a place as Australia's reserve batsman on the autumn-time tour of New Zealand and to England in 2005.

In one of the great series of them all, Hodge was to be Australia's 12th man

BEST EVER: Hodge made 20 centuries for Victoria at Fifty50 level and more than 50 tons in all. Cricket Victoria archives

three times. At Old Trafford he fielded for most of the match after Clarke injured his back just minutes in the game. He played only one first-class game, in-between the first and second Tests at Worcester. Having switched counties from Leicestershire to Lancashire, he passed 12,000 first-class runs. Only Tasmania's Jamie Cox had made more first-class runs without playing a Test.

Some would consider touring England without playing even one Test a body-blow. But Hodge said it was a grand experience and thousands would have loved to have been in his place, watching, learning and building towards future opportunities.

'If I had got in I would have deserved it as it has been such a strong period for Australian cricket,' he said.

Every day under Victoria's 'baggy blue' was special, he said, especially the opportunity to play alongside some of the greatest of the modern era from Dean Jones, Shane Warne and Paul Reiffel through to Elliott and Darren Berry. They played tough, competitive, aggressive cricket. He liked their on-field chat.

Another near-miss followed when he was made 12th man for a one-off 'Test' back home in springtime between Australia and the Rest of the World.

But finally his moment came when Simon Katich was discarded after failures against the World XI and in the opening Test against the West Indies in Brisbane.

Hodge was named for the second Test in Hobart. And this time he played, becoming Australia's 393rd Test cricketer. Australian cricket legend Bill Lawry presented Hodge

HIGHEST ALL-TIME VICTORIAN RUN-MAKERS

First-class cricket

	Mts	Inns	NO	Runs	HS	Ave	100s
Brad Hodge	147	265	25	11,350	286*	47.29	33
Dean Jones	124	217	17	10,412	324*	52.06	33
Matthew Elliott	107	204	16	9684	203	51.51	32
Bill Lawry	99	164	16	7618	266	51.47	20
Bill Ponsford	55	87	7	6902	437	86.27	26

* denotes not out

One-day cricket

	Mts	Inns	NO	Runs	HS	Ave	100s
Brad Hodge	139	137	16	5597	144	47.03	20
David Hussey	103	98	16	3557	140*	43.37	6
Matthew Elliott	78	76	6	2640	118*	37.71	6
Dean Jones	57	54	11	2256	139*	52.46	4

* denotes not out

with his cap on the morning of the game. It had been Lawry who had led the fast-tracking of a teenage Hodge direct from Cricket Academy ranks into Victoria's XI in 1993.

The Australians fielded first, Hodge spending much of his time under a helmet at short-leg, taking several catches in the process from the bowling of Stewie MacGill. Everywhere he looked he saw stars. Adam Gilchrist was keeping. Warne and Ponting were in the slips. Matthew Hayden was in the gully. It was a who's who of golden greats.

Coming in at No.5, Hodge scored a polished 60 on debut.

A week later, in Adelaide, he missed out with 18 and 23. But ahead was Perth and his greatest moment in cricket.

When Brad Hodge reached 150 on his way to a Test double century against the South Africans in Perth in mid-December 2005, Gilchrist congratulated him in mid-pitch and said he just saw a monkey run off Hodge's back and jump back into the West Australian zoo.

Thanks to the generosity of Ponting who delayed his declaration until tea-time, Hodge was able to turn one century into two in the solo moment of his all-too-brief Test career.

MOST VICTORIAN 100s		MOST VICTORIAN GAMES	
33	Brad Hodge	147	Brad Hodge
33	Dean Jones	138	Darren Berry
32	Matthew Elliott	124	Dean Jones
26	Bill Ponsford	114	Ray Bright
		107	Matthew Elliott
		105	Tony Dodemaide

HIGHEST SCORES BY VICTORIANS SINCE 1950	
324*	Dean Jones v. South Australia, MCG, 1994-95
286*	Brad Hodge v Queensland, Brisbane, 2007-08
271	Dick Maddocks v. Tasmania, MCG, 1951-52
266	Bill Lawry v. New South Wales, Sydney, 1960-61
264	Brad Hodge v. India, MCG, 2003-04
261	Brad Hodge v Queensland, MCG, 2008-09
261	Ian Redpath v. Queensland, MCG, 1962-63

* denotes not out

Tables: Ken Williams

He'd been 91 not out at stumps on day 3 before reaching his 200, on the point of tea break when Ponting finally closed with Australia 450 runs ahead. Rather than revelling in Hodge's showstopping double-ton, some of the critics launched into Ponting for days after the South Africans batted 126 overs to save the game.

Hodge, 30, was the first Victorian to score a Test double century since his hero Jones more than 15 years previously.

Having batted two hours for 41 in the first innings, Hodge batted almost eight hours for his 203, helping Australia to build an impregnable position. It was a wonderfully, focused hand, Hodge constantly reminding himself of the words of Allan Border five and six years earlier to make the most of a start and really 'cash in'.

He'd worked for hours in the lead-up with Ponting and felt as confident as at any time in his career.

Only four other Australians had turned their first Test 100 into a double:
- Syd Gregory (201, in 1894 in Sydney),
- Sid Barnes (234, 1946, Sydney),
- Bob Simpson (311, 1964, Old Trafford)
- & Dean Jones (210, 1986, Madras).

Afterwards, at the press conference, Hodge said years of frustration had been lifted in just one afternoon's cricket. 'It has been a long road to this day. I didn't have a great deal of sleep last night (being 91 not out). It was a massive moment for me to get 100 and to turn that into 200 is surreal. I didn't think it would happen.'

Within a month or so, after he under-achieved in Melbourne and Sydney, Hodge was back on the fringes, Damien Martyn taking his place on the autumn-time tour of South Africa. And other than a one-off Test in the West Indies in 2008, he never played again.

Rather than being miffed by all his selection disappointments, Hodge was proud to be selected six times for Australia when its top six was as strong as at almost any time in history. He's chuffed that Ponting believed him capable of playing 100 Tests in any other era.

The competition for middle-order places in the first decade of the new Millennium from the likes of Michael Clarke, Mike Hussey, Andrew Symonds and Martyn was always a roadblock.

HIS LIFE STORY: Brad Hodge: The Little Master *was published in 2010 for a tribute luncheon run by the Australian Cricket Society.* australiancricketsociety.com.au

Australia's loss was Victoria's gain and with 11,350 first-class runs Hodge remains the highest run scorer in Victorian history, ahead of all the icons from Armstrong and Ponsford through to Lawry, Jones and Elliott.

His long-time state coach Greg Shipperd dubbed Hodge 'The Little Master' saying his famed confidence gave the Victorians an air of invincibility and led to countless titles and trophies. He'd coached only one finer batsman in all his years in Tasmania and Victoria: Ponting.

'Brad had a hunger and drive for runs and a will to win that few possess,' he said. 'He showcased his strengths magnificently for such a long period of time. His was the wicket the other teams always celebrated the most. He deserved to play many more times for his country.'

- Hodge's flair for white-ball cricket saw his representative career extend past his 40th birthday. He played 40 times for Australia at Fifty50 or Twenty20 level, his last ODI for Australia coming at the age of 32 and his last T20 appearance at 39.

DEANO-FITS: Dean Jones was a walking contradiction, amiable and chatty one day and inward and brooding the next. Patrick Eagar/Cricketer magazine

3 DEAN JONES

Bring back Deano

Few polarised opinions quite like Dean Jones. Proud, brash and opinionated, he was a walking headline, a trailblazer loved and revered by the public, yet sent to Siberia while still in his prime, having upset his captain, the national selectors and team-mates. In South Africa in 1994, Jones shunned an official commitment to go out on the town by himself. 'He's not one of us, is he?' said captain Allan Border to a group drinking at the bar as Jones departed. Dropped from the final ODI in Bloemfontein, Jones announced his international exit. At 31, he was in the prime of his batting life. No amount of back-pedalling or mega scores could convince the selectors that Victoria's finest batsman since Hassett and Harvey was anything but retired.

Was Dean Jones' dismissal purely a cricket decision? Or were those in the corridors of power simply less prepared to accept all of the contradictions?

His 'Deano-fits' created controversy and inner angst yet he numbered among his supporters tens of thousands of Melburnians and dozens of Test legends from Dennis Lillee and Rod Marsh who played in his testimonial game through to Ian Botham, who said once he'd trust Jones with his life. 'Bring back Deano' banners are still seen at the MCG, testament to the enduring respect and love for 'The Legend' – a nickname he bestowed on himself.

An assured and aggressive stroke-maker, one of the first to quit Monday-to-Friday work and become a fulltime cricketer, Jones' skill and adventure triggered fresh fortune for his teams. His double-century in cricket's second tied Test in Madras remains one of the all-time Test epics. Both his Test and one-day international averages are well above 40. He sprinted between wickets with daredevil flair, was the first to use sunglasses when outriding and had so much confidence he even demanded Curtly Ambrose take off his pearly-white wristbands one crazy night in Sydney. Ambrose was enraged and tore through the Australians.

Long-time Test team-mate David Boon says Jones had a heart of gold and believed he was capable of playing many more Tests. The legendary Bill Lawry called him a talisman for international cricket. Celebrities Elton John and Greg Norman called him a mate. Yet after South Africa in '94, the door wasn't just closed on his career — it was slammed.

No player with Jones' profile or sheer weight of runs was so snubbed. Even those who toured South Africa with Kim Hughes' rebel teams in the mid-'80s were soon forgiven. In five golden summers after being dropped from the Test XI, Jones made more than 4000 runs in a dazzling set of domestic performances which cemented his standing alongside Armstrong, Ponsford, Harvey and Lawry as Victoria's greatest batsman. 'I've always been a confidence player,' declared Deano. 'When I get on a roll, it's hard to stop me.'

HAPPIER TIMES: Dean Jones (foreground) with Victorian teammates Darren Berry and Jamie Siddons at the Junction Oval in 1990-91

His record in 52 Tests of 3631 runs significantly exceeds Ricky Ponting's total through his first 52 Tests — and Jones played in a less-dominant Australian team against the finest and fieriest West Indian fast bowlers in history. His tally was also marginally ahead of Allan Border and Ian Chappell at the 52-Test milepost, further ahead again of Boon and a long way in front of Steve Waugh. In time he was to term the Waugh twins 'the Koalas'. He regarded them as a protected species.

Deano's axing, at the start of the 1992-93 series against the Windies, remains one of the most statistically contrary in Australian cricket history. It was just about the worst week of his life. The raw statistics show he had made 433 runs from his previous four Tests at an average of 70-plus.

Just as significantly, Mark Waugh's Test form had been disastrous. He'd been dropped late the previous summer, then fleetingly earned the nickname 'Audi' for scoring four consecutive ducks in a three-Test series in Sri Lanka. Waugh made 61 runs at an average of 10 per innings in that series. Jones topped the averages with 276 runs at 55. Only one other made more runs.

Yet, when the Australian XI was named for the series opener in Brisbane, Jones was demoted to drinkwaiting duties. Both Mark and Steve Waugh were included,

Steve for the first time in 18 months. West Australian Damien Martyn, 21, was also named, on promise rather than returns, even though he'd captained Young Australia and had performed marvellously well for one so young in the Sheffield Shield.

The integrity of the selectors — West Australian Lawrie Sawle, Victoria's Jim Higgs, NSW's John Benaud and coach Bobby Simpson — was questioned. As a panel, however, they had made some extraordinarily far-sighted decisions, Ian Healy's elevation from unknown stumper to his country's 'keeper and the fast-tracking of Shane Warne being masterstrokes.

Conspiracy theories were floated, but Jones was simply a victim of circumstance, someone who for reasons beyond his own control had not had the same match

MASTER BLAST: Dennis Lillee forecast Jones' dismissal from Test cricket in his column in the Melbourne Sun News-Pictorial

practice as other top-order contenders. He'd also consistently struggled to make runs in the tropics. Only one of his 35 first-class centuries had been scored in Brisbane. And in five 'Gabba Tests, his average was 17.

The selectors also felt that a less predictable Australian front six may cause the world champion West Indians problems. Jones might have played outstandingly well in Sri Lanka, but his performances the previous summer had been poor (bar an unbeaten 150 at the close of the summer in a 'dead' Test against an undistinguished attack).

The pro-Jones lobby points to his deeds in Sri Lanka as being indisputable evidence that their man was unfairly cut off at the knees. After all, only 10 weeks had passed since Jones' match-saving deeds at Colombo's Khettarama Stadium when he made 77 and 100 not out to be man of the match.

Had he been part of the second-innings collapse, which saw Tom Moody and Mark Waugh out to successive balls from 20-year-old debutant off-spinner Muthiah Muralidaran, Australia (after narrowly winning the first Test) could have been sorely embarrassed. Even the street-fighting Border succumbed cheaply and left Australia at 5-149 in its second innings, an overall lead of just 138 with Jones the last of the batting specialists. In scoring an unbeaten century, his 11th in 52 Tests, Jones was fortunate to survive two grassed catches; one a real soda. Despite this luck, in the context of a rain-affected draw it was an absolutely crucial knock.

He had been given more responsibility, too, at No. 4 after the selectors ruled that Border, while still inspiring, was not in the form of old and should bat lower. Ever since the '89 tour of England, Jones had been Australia's virtual full-time No. 5. His promotion and the use of Tom Moody at the head of the order replacing fellow Sandgroper Geoff Marsh, was part of the team's biggest batting revamp in years.

Jones liked No.4. He'd averaged 88 there. Included among three Test centuries was his mammoth career-best 216 against a triple-A West Indian attack including Malcolm Marshall, Patrick Patterson, Curtly Ambrose and Courtney Walsh in Adelaide in 1988-89.

RETIREMENT DAY: Jones at Victorian cricket headquarters at Jolimont

In Sri Lanka, Jones averaged 55 and made more runs that any of Australia's batting specialists. While he missed out in the final Test at Moratuwa, so did Mark Waugh, who became the most notable batsman in Test history to score four ducks on end.

Jones had every reason to believe he should remain among Australia's first-choice batsmen, but the demise at age 33 of Border's long-time deputy Marsh earlier in the year left him uneasy. Jones was only two years younger. Clearly, the Academy kids such as Warne, Martyn, Michael Bevan, Justin Langer and Michael Slater were emerging.

On the eve of selection, the legendary Dennis Lillee suggested in his syndicated Australia-wide column that the West Indies could be beaten without Dean Jones. Under a heading in the Melbourne *Herald Sun*, DUMP DEANO, Lillee wrote, 'He [Jones] might be a fine one-day player, but that's perfect for him when there are no slips or gullies. He's the one to go if new blood is to be injected, which it should.'

Jones sensed he was vulnerable. An uncommonly wet Melbourne spring had seen hardly a ball bowled (other than indoors) during the entire month of October and in his only two Sheffield Shield matches preceding the opening Test he had missed out, scoring 24 runs in three digs. Conversely Mark Waugh, so out of sorts in Sri Lanka, had made a double-ton against the touring West Indians in Sydney, while Martyn started the season brilliantly with twin centuries against the Queenslanders at the 'Gabba.

Breaking with tradition, the selectors named an extra pace bowler in their XII and included a seventh batsman in Martyn, who they believed had the flair and inner confidence not to be intimidated by any pace attack, even one from the Caribbean. Most expected the youngster to be 12th man, but Jones wasn't so sure. Leading into the game he played golf with Border and when he asked where he would be batting, Border was strangely noncommittal.

In his autobiography, *My Call*, Jones reported an 'animated discussion' between Border and coach/co-selector Simpson on match-eve. 'I don't know what was said but I sensed it was no good for me,' he said. 'At the team meeting, there was no discussion of the batting order, which was just ridiculous and very unprofessional. We were about to play a Test match, for goodness' sake.'

The Australian selectors felt the West Indians could be vulnerable without Viv Richards, Gordon Greenidge and Jeff Dujon and wanted to telegraph as few of their pre-match moves as possible, including the composition of their top order. At 10 pm Simpson rang Jones and asked if he could see him for a chat. When Simpson offered him a drink, Jones knew he was gone.

'Dean was finding new ways of getting out, which suggested his powers of concentration were deserting him,' said Simpson in *The Reasons Why*. 'Concentration is the first thing to go, not eyesight, mobility or courage.'

As 12th man, Jones ensured he was far from forgotten, especially during a mid-match hailstorm when he sprinted onto the 'Gabba with an armful of helmets to protect ground staff from the hailstones, some of which were as big as golf balls. Only Deano would have done that.

Some Jones supporters suggested that had a second national selector been Melbourne-based, Deano would have maintained his place in the top six. But the two from NSW had for years been Jones 'devotees'. Simpson was the first to suggest that Jones, then 22, use a lighter bat in India in 1986-87, leading to his breakthrough double century. Twelve months earlier, Benaud, a skilled and experienced journalist, had 'ghosted' Jones' best-selling first book. He liked Jones' flair and his refusal to allow bowlers to dictate.

So what happened? In a game renowned for its bonhomie and happy associations, Jones and many of his former teammates still don't talk. 'Deano,' said long-time teammate Darren Berry to him one day, 'you may be the best player Victoria ever produced but you're going to retire without a friend in the world.'

From the time Jones exited as the highest runmaker in the history of Victorian cricket, he was rarely again welcome in the Bushranger dressing rooms. And when he found himself in the same Australian Broadcasting Corporation commentary box as Berry, with whom he had been warring for years, even the MCG's electronic scoreboard operator recognised the unease. Within seconds, up flashed the message: 'Temperature at the MCG: 30 degrees. Inside the ABC commentary box: 40 and climbing!'

Jones passed Paul Reiffel in the street one day, and when Reiffel didn't respond to his 'G'day', Jones exploded, wishing him a &#@*ing horror day. Even Merv Hughes, as benign now off the field as he was aggressive on it, has never forgiven Jones for deliberately belittling him in a scratch match one pre-season at suburban Frankston. 'We used to hang out together a lot, too,' said Hughes.

At the height of the Hansie Cronje cash-for-favours scandal in 2000, ABC television's Geoff Hutchison of the *7.30 Report* sought to interview Jones, only to walk away when Jones asked that the camera angle include the sign outside his Port Melbourne restaurant. It caused quite a how-do-you-do, with the ever-quotable Jones laughing at the irony of a reporter's deliberate retreat. He was working for the ABC at the time. Surely the rules of protocol could have been bent just a little?

On the third morning of a match against Western Australia during his final interstate trip as a Victorian player, Jones sat out for the best part of an hour in the dressing rooms after an altercation with Berry and state coach John Scholes. His place in the field was taken by Victoria's 12th man Shawn Craig.

| DEAN JONES' RUN BLITZ AFTER BEING DROPPED ||||||
Age	Season	Runs	HS	100s	Ave
31	1992-93	383	72*	-	31.91
32	1993-94	918	158*	4	76.50
33	1994-95	1125	324*	4	69.50
34	1995-96	974	145	3	51.26
35	1996-97	521	152	2	40.07
36	1997-98	896	151*	3	52.70
* denotes not out					

Jones' age seemed inconsequential as he unleashed a phenomenal run spree in the mid-'90s, including his memorable triple-century in Melbourne's first ever day-night Sheffield Shield match in 1994-95 — an awesome innings of power and nonchalance in which he made a South Australian attack which included two Test-standard spinners in Tim May and Peter McIntyre look like novices. SA wicketkeeper Tim Nielsen said he hardly had to take one ball, so dominant was Jones over the first day and a half of the high-scoring game. In four full sessions, using his favourite Super-Legend Kookaburra bat, he made 71, 83, 64 and 77 before declaring on 324 not out, the highest score at the MCG in 30 years.

In interstate cricket, only South Australia's Darren Lehmann and Queensland's Matthew Hayden were anywhere near as prolific – and neither had the same hero-worshipping following as the publicity-pushing Jones, who combined playing with radio commitments and a newspaper column. The media work ensured his high profile but also miffed officials, several saying privately that Jones' campaign of self-promotion was grating. When he threatened to quit the captaincy in favour of a TV career he claimed was on offer, some on the executive were all for letting him go. They were further riled several months later when Jones broadsided the administration, saying they were responsible for the parlous condition of cricket in Victoria.

Jones played big shots on and off the field and cornered the news even ahead of the emerging Shane Warne. Often abrasive and outspoken, he simply wore out his welcome. Even his long-time captain Border admitted Jones had offended too many, too often. His Bloemfontein axing was all about Jones' fading focus, Border claimed. Jones told Boon that he simply wasn't prepared to be a nondescript any more. He didn't like being a reserve batsman on tour. Not when he was Dean Jones.

By rights, as Victoria's most distinguished player and one of Australia's all-time most-capped, he should have departed a hero and been given every good wish: Dean Jones, master runmaker, the leading one-day player of his time — thanks for the memories. But instead of free-flowing tributes, much of the copy was coloured. As formidable a player and personality as he was, the consensus from dressing rooms, from Derbyshire to his beloved MCG, was that Deano had shot himself in the foot. He had overstepped team boundaries, divided opinion and, for some, become unmanageable. He told cricket writer Ron Reed one day: 'If you want the good qualities of Dean Jones, you have to be prepared to put up with the bad ones.'

Jones' emotional farewell at VCA House in 1998 was an admission that he no longer held the numbers in the corridors of power. In reality he beat the axe only by days, the selectors having decided that, as good a player as he still was at 37, team harmony was as important as performance. Even institutions have a use-by date.

Jones was never prepared to stand aside for anyone. He told Reed: 'I don't care what they think about me as a bloke as long as they say: "I wouldn't mind him in my team".

'I don't play sport to be liked. I play sport to win. I don't worry about what people think, only about what I can do... sometimes honesty is a little bit too hard for some people to handle.'

DEAN JONES IN TEST CRICKET – GROUND BY GROUND							
Venue	Mts	Inns	NO	Runs	HS	100's	Ave
Adelaide	6	11	1	603	216	3	60.30
Brisbane	5	8	1	121	38*	-	17.28
Hobart	1	2	1	121	118*	1	121.00
Melbourne	6	10	0	251	59	-	25.10
Perth	5	7	1	488	150*	2	81.33
Sydney	6	10	2	460	184*	1	57.50
Total	29	48	6	2044	216	7	48.66
Overseas	23	41	5	1587	210	4	44.08

As a 17-year-old, Jones opened the bowling for a Melbourne mid-week team, the Plastic XI, and would curse and abuse the opposition, many of whom had been playing top-level club cricket for years. Even then he was a 'one-off', brazen and cocksure, with an unpredictability that amazed us all.

It mattered little to Jones that he consistently ignored protocol. So what if he used a mobile phone in the Victorian team bus or called himself 'Legend'? The public condemnation of his teammates, however — among them Mark Taylor — was treated more seriously. Taylor hadn't played even one game on Australian soil as Australia's just appointed new captain when Jones took aim, saying Steve Waugh was more suited to dual captaincy of the Test and one-day sides. 'My biggest problem with Mark is his fitness and whether he can bat 50 overs,' Jones wrote. 'And then I wonder if he's got the firepower at the death. I doubt whether he can hit big 4s and 6s. He can probably say the same thing about me in the last couple of games. But at least I've done it — and I've never seen him do it.'

WHITE BALL KING: *No one commanded more respect at limited overs levels than Deano*

Jones continued to dominate for Melbourne and Victoria, but comments like these were never going to win friends or favour. In his column in the *Sunday Age*, he also was critical of some former Australian players who he reckoned 'had forgotten how hard the game is'.

'In the Australian [one-day] team we've got to the stage of wondering who is next on the hit list,' he said. It was good provocative copy and spoken from the heart, but it was guaranteed to test friendships. The further his dream drifted of being picked again for Australia, the more outspoken he became.

Jones admitted he was mercurial and moody, but that all came with the territory. He had never wanted to be loved, only respected. Maybe he was too honest and passionate for his own good at times, but why should he apologise? If people were happy to applaud his hundreds, they could accept his warts, too.

Plenty of Jones' mates were totally supportive of him. ODI allrounder Ian Harvey said his own first-class career was stalling badly before he had a full-frontal dialogue with Jones in Perth in the mid-'90s. Having played only 10 state games in three years, Harvey knew another failure against the Warriors would be final. 'There were still four or five games to go and Deano [then captain] told me I'd be playing no matter what. It was a big turning point. I went out and got 50 in the second innings [against Western Australia], 85 at Bellerive in the next game and then 136 against the Redbacks. Only then did Deano confess had I made a duck in that second dig, I would have been dropped! But it was his way of giving me some confidence to go out and play my natural game. I'm very grateful to him. If I'd got dropped after that game I might never have made it back.'

England fast bowler Devon Malcolm, whom Jones captained at Derbyshire for a year and a half until Jones' mid-season walkout in 1997, said he may have been a tough talker but few possessed his spirit or strut. 'Dean was a very hard man,' he said in his book *You Guys Are History!*, 'but he was still a fine batsman who led from the front. He'd never ask another batter to do what he couldn't do. All of us admired his positive approach. Winning popularity contests didn't bother him as much as winning cricket matches … Jones and [Les] Stillman [Derbyshire's Australian-born coach] kept boosting me throughout the 1996 season, telling me I was still the fastest bowler in England. Whenever I took a wicket, they'd say "That's another one for [Ray] Illingworth" [England's selection chairman].'

Bobby Simpson called him frustrating, exciting, reliable, unreliable, selfish, unselfish, a mug lair and a team player — and truly believed that Jones' unpredictability was an inherent part of his charm. Hughes, once one of his closest friends, says their infamous spat in the Frankston trial game spilled over at St Kilda's Junction Oval a week later. According to insiders, punches were almost thrown. 'I thought he was trying to take me down,' said Hughes in *Merv: The Full Story*. The pair didn't speak again for three months. Deano could be his own worst enemy.

- In retirement Jones is now as nice as pie; amiable and relaxed and still working as a commentator. He wishes the bloke with the Bring Back Deano sign can attend every Christmas Test in his home-town Melbourne.

TARGETED: Shane Warne (above) and Mark Waugh accepted monies from Mukesh Gupta (alias John the Bookmaker) in the mid-'90s

4 1994 KARACHI

Throwing a Test match

The adulation reserved for Australia's most celebrated cricketers can be head-turning. Many, like Shane Warne, lived in a bubble, protected from the realities of life. While others around him did all the mundane tasks from paying bills to picking up the bread and milk, megastar Shane only had to turn up on time and keep ripping his signature leg-break past the world's best. He was idolised everywhere, especially on the sub-continent where cricket's elite are treated like royalty.

Had he been more street-smart and aware, never would he have accepted a $US5000 gift from a little Indian he'd only just been introduced to in a downtown Colombo casino. Within weeks Warne and teammate Mark Waugh were entangled in a sinister trail to match-fixing which all but railroaded their careers.

It was September 1994. Shane Warne was at a beachside casino in Colombo playing roulette — and losing. Heavily. Red 23 wasn't proving as lucky as usual. He was down $US5000, serious money, even for Australian cricket's latest millionaire-in-the-making. His team-mate Mark Waugh had tossed a chip onto the table and told the croupier: 'Wherever it lands mate'. His number came up and Waugh headed for the cashier's window, immediately cashing in on his good fortune.

Returning the following night, Warne's entourage soon included a man named John who had been introduced 24 hours earlier by Waugh 'as a man who bets on the cricket'. John was from New Delhi. They spent half an hour together. He loved cricket and the company of cricketers. Having witnessed Warne's earlier misfortunes, John had asked Warne to his room and told him he was his favourite cricketer. He'd seen him lose heavily the previous night. Would Warne accept a token of his appreciation? In his hand was a very fat envelope containing $US5000 in greenbacks. 'No strings,' said John. 'I don't want anything in return.'

Thanks to Warne he'd won on Australia many times in the past. This was the least he could do.

Warne's immediate instinct was to say 'thanks, but no thanks', but when John said he would be offended if Warne didn't take the envelope, he accepted it – so accustomed was he to handouts and privileges accorded the world's most feted cricketers. Naively he believed the money to be nothing more than a gift from a benevolent stranger with loads of spare cash. He was a long way from home, or reality. He shook John's hand, went back down to the tables and blew most of it. Again.

Soon the spin sultan was to join Waugh as an unwitting informant to the sub-continent's illegal billion-dollar cricket gambling industry. And, within a month, he was to be targeted for the biggest sting of all — the throwing of a Test match.

BARELY SHAVING: A young Warnie before the NZ tour in 1993

Few had been so fast-tracked into international ranks ahead of their time. As a teenager Warne had been bypassed from the best schoolboy squads and even been told by his first senior captain that he'd be better off concentrating on his batting.

But there was something about the confident kid from the Melbourne bayside who could make the ball turn square. One of his mentors Shaun Graf first noticed him at St Kilda pre-season training. 'What did the blond kid say he did again?' he asked of the Saints' practice captain Noel Harbourd. From 1993 to 1995, Warne became the outstanding strike bowler in the world, another Richie Benaud, only better. Almost everything he touched turned to gold. He was the matchwinning flipperman, the kid who could spin it on ice. Through a myriad of endorsements and contracts, Warne suddenly had access to more monies than he had ever dreamed about — or needed. His name was on every important celebrity 'A-list' in Melbourne. Instead of driving around in his old, hotted-up Cortina, he bought a blue Ferrari and paid almost a $1 mill. for a house right on Brighton's exclusive Esplanade.

He was living his dream — playing cricket for his country, staying at the most luxurious hotels and mixing with the rich and famous.

John the bookmaker stayed in touch, ringing Warne two or three times before important matches asking for weather and pitch information and, on one occasion, the likely make-up of the team. In another call, he wished Warne a merry Christmas. The calls continued into the 1994-95 Australian season and the one-day internationals, as well as the short tour of New Zealand in early 1995.

ACADEMY RETURN: Warnie with Channel Nine's Ray Martin celebrating the first 10 years of the Australian Cricket Academy. Commonwealth Bank

While the Australians were in Colombo, John also gave Mark Waugh money: $US4000 in his case. Waugh owned racehorses, loved punting and dealt regularly with bookies. He saw no problem with providing John with general information. He likened it to doing a radio interview. Only selection was a 'no-go' zone. During a five-month period, in five different countries, John (whose real name was Mukesh Gupta) rang Waugh on the eve of games at least 10 times. The calls stopped in Kingston, Jamaica, early in 1994-95, when Waugh told John they could no longer talk. By then, both Waugh and Warne had been interrogated and fined by the Australian Cricket Board.

At no stage in their liaisons with John did either Warne or Waugh divulge team tactics or policy. Nor did they suspect that he might have been involved in match-fixing. For them it was just easy money.

Colombo was a prelude to Australia's next major tour — to Pakistan in September and October 1994. Expectations were sky-high under new captain Mark Taylor. Although the first Test was to be played at Pakistan's cricketing citadel, Karachi, where Pakistan had been unbeaten for four decades, Australia had developed a bowling arsenal so formidable they believed they could win anywhere in the world.

By the fourth night of the Test, at Karachi's National Stadium, the locals knew just how serious the Australian threat was. Having already conceded a first-innings lead, the Pakistanis were set 314 to win. At stumps they were 3-155, the match fortunes having swung again in the final minutes with the wicket of Pakistan's captain Saleem Malik to the big West Australian Jo Angel.

THE SULTAN OF SPIN: Warnie on the attack against Pakistan in the controversial Test in Karachi in which he was approached to bowl badly. Australian Cricket magazine

Saleem, with Saeed Anwar, had threatened to assume control of the game before edging one to slip. His dismissal was greeted joyously by the Australians. Saleem was one of the leading players of spin in the world and it was a bonus to have him back in the pavilion rather than expertly negating the dual spin of Warne and Tim May on the fifth day.

Late that night, around 10.30, Warne and May were relaxing in their hotel room at the Pearl Continental when the phone rang. Saleem wanted to talk to Warne urgently.

The Pakistanis were also staying at the Pearl. 'Wonder what he wants?' said Warne. 'Do you want to come too?'

'It's too late for me,' said May, who was dozing. 'I'm buggered. You go.'

Curious and not wanting to offend, Warne went to Saleem's room. Known as 'The Rat' to the Australians because of his long face, Saleem had been a regular visitor to Australia and had played at Essex, the same English county club as Mark Waugh. Warne respected him as a player but thought him aloof. Why would Pakistan's cricket captain want to talk to him? And at 10.30 pm?

The conversation revolved around the intensity of the first four days before Saleem looked at Warne in the eye and said that Pakistan couldn't afford to lose the match.

WARNE: 'Don't know about that, mate. We can still do it.'

SALEEM: 'No, you don't understand. We cannot lose. Our pride is at stake. Everything is at stake. We can't lose this first Test. '

WARNE: 'Well, mate, our pride is at stake, too. I'm sorry to tell you this, but we are going to whip you blokes tomorrow.'

SALEEM: 'I don't think you understand what I am asking of you. What I want is for you and Tim May to bowl wide of the off stump and bowl poorly, so that the match is a draw, and for that I will give you and Tim May US$200,000. I can have it in your room in half an hour.'

WARNE: 'What the hell is going on here? What do you mean? What are you talking about? I don't understand.'

SALEEM: 'I'm serious. You must get back to me.'

Warne was staggered. Pakistan's captain, one of the finest cricketers in the world, was asking him to throw a game. And for huge money — twice Warne's then annual wage as an Australian cricketer and enough for him to pay cash for a double-fronted Victorian villa back home in plush South Yarra.

Turning on his heel, Warne said: 'Go and get fucked.' Returning to his room, Warne was white as a sheet. 'What did the Rat want?' asked May. When told of the bribe, May made a joke of it before telling Warne to ring Saleem back and tell him he also said piss off and how the Aussies were going to 'nail them tomorrow'.

'We'd heard rumours [of match-fixing] since the '93 tour of England, but had no idea how it worked,' he was to say later.

'At the time [in 1993] we thought it was just a joke. Now we thought, shit, it really does happen. It was pretty scary. You realised it wasn't just the local chicken shop behind it.'

Only days before making his offer to Warne and May, Saleem had called a press conference to denounce persistent chat that his team was involved in gambling. Calling the rumours 'malicious', he said the conspiracy against him and his team was affecting performance and morale. 'The players are under tremendous tension,' he said. 'The batsmen are afraid if they got out they would be said to have been bought by the bookies. The bowlers are afraid because if they have got hammered they will be labelled as bought by the bookies.'

In a titanic finish the next day, Pakistan won the Test, but only just. With two runs needed to tie and three to win, Warne's dipping leg-break to an advancing Inzamam-ul-Haq all but bowled him. Instead it went for four byes, skidding straight past wicketkeeper Ian Healy. As Pakistan's No.11 Mushtaq Ahmed fell to his knees, kissed the ground and thanked Allah, Healy looked back at the ball and the boundary, hung his head and furiously kicked over the stumps. Mushie claimed it to be 'one of the easiest stumpings ever' and that Healy was so distraught that he had to be picked up by a teammate and led from the pitch to the dressing room. Pakistan's last two batsmen had scored a world-record 57 runs for the final wicket to steal a remarkable win. It was the closest any team had come to defeating the Pakistanis at the National Stadium and continued Australia's hoodoo on the subcontinent. On the podium Saleem hissed at man-of-the-match Warne, 'You should have taken the money'.

SO CORRUPT: Saleem Malik dined out on the Australian bowling in the 1994-95 Test series in Pakistan. Cricketer magazine

After Taylor attended a post-match disciplinary hearing, Warne notified Taylor of the offer made by Saleem the night before. Given the circumstances of Pakistan's extraordinary victory, he believed he had little choice.

Australia's win in the subsequent ODI triangular tournament — which also involved Hansie Cronje's South Africans — was only some consolation given the spectre of match-fixing, which none of the Australians had ever experienced before.

Halfway through the tournament, at a reception in Rawalpindi, Saleem again made an approach. This time it was to Mark Waugh, when Saleem offered him and three others a $US200,000 inducement to lie down. Given his own hard-line response to Saleem's first approach just weeks before in Karachi, Warne (who had been standing in a group with Waugh when the offer was made) was amazed at the temerity of the Pakistani captain as much as at the magnitude of the offer. After the Pakistanis won an extraordinarily fast-scoring match by nine wickets with 10 overs to spare, Waugh, who had made a century, came into the rooms and flippantly declared: 'Ah, would've been better off taking the bribes, guys.'

At that stage only a few players — and coach Bob Simpson — even knew of the offers. Manager Col Egar wasn't told until the very last game of the tour, a week later in Lahore. 'Col, sit down. I've got something to tell you,' said Simpson. Egar listened in amazement and said, 'Righto, let's get hold of the match referee [John Reid] straight away and see what can be done.' The Australian players decided to keep the issue in-house. Even Egar wasn't briefed by Taylor until they were back in Sydney. 'It was all very hush-hush,' said Egar later.

Having read about the ruthless practices of the subcontinental Mafia, some of the players feared physical reprisal and believed the bribery offers to be a matter for Jolimont. Saleem, with a double-century and 143 in the last two Tests, had bullied Australia at every turn on the field and was central to Pakistan's 1-0 series victory. The Australians couldn't comprehend how a player so gifted and at the height of his form could be so corrupt.

The scandal remained cricket's best-kept secret until the following February, when the *Sydney Morning Herald's* Phil Wilkins exclusively reported that an ICC inquiry was pending and that Waugh, Warne and May had all provided sworn statements to say that approaches had been made. As Warne said in *My Own Story*: 'Why would anyone make such serious allegations knowing they were false? Inventing something like that would cause more trouble for us than the accused.'

The following morning Mark Ray of the *Sunday Age* said Dean Jones had also been approached to lie down four years earlier. Match-fixing and big cricket was a huge issue, especially in India and Pakistan.

Having studiously maintained a conspiracy of silence, the ACB immediately launched its own inquiry during the short tour of New Zealand, via team manager Ian McDonald. McDonald asked every player if he had had any dealings with bookmakers. Only then was the liaison uncovered between Warne, Waugh and 'John', the well-heeled Indian cricket lover. With the team about to depart for the West Indies, the ACB discussed the matter with visiting International Cricket Council officials, including president Clyde Walcott. They decided to keep the matter silent in the belief that it would be an enormous embarrassment for the players and a public relations disaster for the game given the fall-out from the Saleem allegations and continuing doubt over the legitimacy of matches on the subcontinent. The Board did, however, fine both players heavily: on 28 February, just days after the Australians had won the Centenary series in New Zealand, Warne was fined $8000 and Waugh $10,000 — five times the penalty handed to the South Australian Wayne Phillips for calling the selectors 'idiots' in 1986.

It was four years before the cover-up finally reached the public domain. The story was told in intricate detail in *The Australian* by cricket writer Malcolm Conn and broadcast on Melbourne radio station 3AW by former Test cricketer David Hookes, who had received a late tip-off while playing golf earlier that day. Conn had spent two months investigating claims that Mark Waugh had been involved with an illegal bookmaker. He had seen a letter sent to the Pakistan Cricket Board's legal advisers during the Pakistan High Court inquiry in Lahore. 'I didn't believe at the time that it could be true,' said Conn. 'But he [Waugh] was a punter so I didn't dismiss it completely. I was thinking only in terms of match-fixing.'

In Brisbane two days before the first Test against England in early November 1998, the Australian Cricket Board held its official season launch. Later, a large group of media people, sponsors, officials and players gathered at Ian Healy's sports bar, Adrenalin. 'I mentioned Mark Waugh to an associate of mine involved in Australian cricket and he confirmed that Waugh had indeed been involved. I nearly fell over,' said Conn. 'He pointed out that it was not match-fixing — but for giving information. He knew Waugh had been fined but couldn't be more specific. I rang many people to try and confirm it and went to Malcolm Speed [the ACB's chief executive] and put it to him. To each question, Speed, a former lawyer, said, "I can neither confirm nor deny."'

Conn knew that the story was 'on'. He checked and double-checked his sources and a few days later rang Speed to tell him he was writing what he knew and the Board could comment if it liked. Speed said to give him an hour. When he rang back, he not only confirmed Waugh's involvement but said that another player was involved too: Shane Warne. Until then, Conn had had no inkling of Warne's involvement. But Speed's options had run out. He had no choice but to confess everything. The question, 'Is there anybody else?' would undoubtedly have been asked.

The Australian ran the exposé as its front-page lead under a major heading: CRICKET STARS HUMILIATE NATIONAL GAME. The piece provoked extraordinary comment. It was the biggest cricket news story since World Series Cricket and won Conn a Walkley Award, the highest distinction in Australian journalism.

Having been anything but transparent in the previous three and a half years, the ACB moved quickly. A press conference was held at the Adelaide Oval in December at which Warne and Waugh, looking like truant schoolboys, publicly admitted to receiving secret payments from illegal bookmakers. Their involvement, as innocent as it had initially seemed, seemed to be a prelude to a bigger sting. Both read prepared statements and refused to answer questions.

'I realise I was very naive and stupid. I've always strived to do the best I can for my country and I think that the way I play and conduct myself on the field shows I'm a cricketer with integrity who has never given anything but his best,' said Warne.

'In the period since I was fined the full implication of the possibility that I may be linked to actions much more sinister than those I innocently undertook in 1994 have become very clear to me. I realise and accept that my actions were naive and stupid,' said Waugh.

BAGGY GREEN SHAME headlined the *Sydney Morning Herald*, while *The Australian* said $11,000 PRICE OF DISGRACE. 'Their carefully worded but banal statements yesterday should have included words such as greedy and selfish,' said Patrick Smith in the Melbourne *Age*.

Until that time, the Australians had been considered cleanskins in the match-fixing scandal that was bubbling away on the subcontinent and touching even apparent white knights like Hansie Cronje. While the ACB was at pains to say that neither Warne nor Waugh was guilty of anything more than offering general weather and pitch information, the Board's long-running silence — which almost certainly would have continued but for the inquiries by Conn and other journalists — was damning in itself and fuelled suspicions that there must be more unsaid. THE UNVEILING OF A DIRTY LITTLE SECRET said *The Australian* the day after the press conference. The paper's Letters to the Editor column was full of the scandal. 'A new day, a new word: Hypocricket', said Philip Glaister from Brisbane. 'Naive and stupid, definitely, but they left out "greedy"', said Bruce Hogan of Cloisters Square, Western Australia. Ted Gallop from Kalamunda said, 'Memo Warnie: is the Australian Cricket Board pay so bad that you have to do a little moonlighting?', while Gareth Davies of Maylands lamented, 'I thought I'd never see the day where I would say "It's not cricket" about cricket.'

ASTONISHING: Mushtaq Ahmed shared a match-winning last-gasp 10th wicket partnership with Inzamam-ul-Haq in Karachi

Cricket-loving Prime Minister John Howard was also indignant. 'I would imagine, given the great passion Australians have for cricket, there's an intense feeling of disappointment about the whole issue,' he said. One of Don Bradman's Invincibles, Neil Harvey, said a two-year ban should be imposed on both Warne and Waugh. Richie Benaud asked why the issue had been covered up for so long.

The ACB went to extraordinary lengths to keep the fines in-house. There was no mention of the scandal or the fines in its minutes. 'There was a majority decision taken to carry out the action which was carried out,' Malcolm Gray, current ICC chairman and then a Board member, told the ABC's *Four Corners* reporter Liz Jackson. 'It was wrong and it was silly ... there's a totally different environment today.' The-then ACB chief executive Graham Halbish said that the silence had been the decision of the

KEEN PUNTERS: *Mark Waugh (left) with Ricky Ponting at the races in Barbados.* Gordon Brooks/ Australian Cricket magazine

entire board, not just one or two members. Furthermore, Walcott and David Richards, the ICC's executive director, had been informed.

It was widely felt that neither Warne nor Waugh should ever be allowed to hold any future leadership roles in the Australian XI. However, most cricket lovers baulked at further disciplinary action, as both players had already been fined years earlier.

The controversy weighed heavily. In the *Australian Women's Weekly*, Warne's then-wife Simone said, 'I told Shane to give up cricket. What he was going through, all the talk of bribery, just wasn't worth it.' In the third Test, which started almost immediately after the press conference, Waugh was booed by sections of the large Adelaide Oval crowd while walking to and from the wicket on the opening day. Warne, still rehabilitating after shoulder surgery, was back in Melbourne representing Victoria. Only 773 attended on the first day and it was impossible to truly judge the crowd's reaction to his latest impropriety. However, at nearby Jolimont Terrace, the home of Victorian cricket, receptionists were fielding irate phone calls demanding Warne's immediate resignation as the state's captain.

A few months later the ACB showed its hand by giving both players interim leadership roles. It seemed past misdemeanours had little or no relevance. Warne was to lead the Australians for much of the one-day summer in 1998-99 after Steve Waugh twice injured a hamstring and could play in only two of the 12 matches. With Taylor stepping down as captain on the eve of the West Indian tour, Warne was also made Test vice-captain behind Steve Waugh. For a player unsure if he would be able to play cricket again after shoulder surgery just nine months previously, it had been a traumatic, roller-coasting time for the master leg-spinner, soon to be recognised alongside Sir Donald Bradman as one of *Wisden's* Five Cricketers of the Century.

Warne had wrestled with his form and his detractors all summer. Most were prepared to forgive and forget, but unfortunately for Warne, never the sharpest tool in the shed, more misdemeanours were to follow and at such rapidity that the Board announced that no longer could one's genius as a cricketer override the ambassadorial faults and controversies ever-present in his life.

Warne had consistently struggled with living life in a goldfish bowl, his every movement monitored.

Not long after he and his family moved into a prestigious double-storey property on millionaire's row on Brighton's Esplanade, a bus pulled up outside. Warne started chatting to a man from the bus before bolting back inside when he realised he was one of a group of tourists on a sightseeing tour of the houses of the rich and famous.

The Australian Test captaincy should not only be a role for the best cricketer, but for one whose diplomacy skills and CV are flawless. In June 2000, during a season with English county side Hampshire, Warne was accused of harassing 22-year-old Donna Smith, a nurse and single mother from Leicester. Warne admitted the contact but denied anything more than some 'dirty talk' on the phone, which the woman had reciprocated. He said had the incident remained unreported, it would not have been a mistake.

'The journey of life is something you live and fully enjoy,' he told Channel Nine's *A Current Affair*. Warne confessed that the spotlight on high-profile international sports-people made his life a soap opera. He couldn't even light up a cigarette without creating a stir.

Asked what happened on the night he met Ms Smith after Hampshire's match against Leicester, Warne said, 'She came up to me and said, "I heard you're famous. Can you sign my back?" She bent over in front of me and wanted me to sign her back. I said no. She tried to lift up my shirt and said, "Well, I'll sign your chest." [I said,] "No, I'm not doing that, thank you." She kept on trying.' Warne said his wife Simone was dismayed, but that like all married couples they 'had their ups and downs'.

The episode with the nurse was an example, he said, of how the Australian media seemed to delight in exposing his misdemeanours. 'In Australia unfortunately it [the publicity] was like a runaway train,' he said. He conceded that his captaincy prospects had nosedived, a position confirmed soon afterwards by the ACB when it sacked him from the Test vice-captaincy. For every 10 letters received by the ACB on the issue, nine were anti-Warne. He'd worn out his welcome.

Mark Waugh, too, was never to lead his country.

- Pakistan remained the centre of all sorts of match-fixing innuendo and allegation. No one knew when the real Pakistan would show up. Or just who had been got at.

WHERE DO I SIGN?: Just-married Melburnian Rod McCurdy was able to provide some immediate extra security for his wife Donna and young son Ryan

5 REBELS TO SOUTH AFRICA

Singapore sling

At first glance, it seemed to be little more than a fortnight of goodwill, a one-day tournament to celebrate the Golden Jubilee of the Ranji Trophy, India's stellar first-class competition in the spring of 1984. But when key members of the victorious Australian team stopped over in Singapore, to join others just arrived from the south, it suddenly assumed fresh significance. Another raid was being made on Australia's playing elite.

It was 11 pm and the receptionist at Singapore's Paramount hotel was working overtime. 'Dr Ali Bacher's suite? Yes sir,' she said.

She'd had inquiries all day, all of them from strong, athletic types with broad accents.

Upstairs in the biggest room in the complex, Bacher, the recruiting power behind the South African Cricket Union's rebel tours, was fine-tuning a two-year agreement for an unsanctioned Australian visit to the Republic. He'd gone close in 1983 before his cover was blown and negotiations stalled. This time he had a $3 million budget, with large advances payable to the 14 or 15 top-notch players prepared to commit.

South Africa had been a 'no-go zone' for sportsmen for years. While its cricket administration had a reputation for its indefatigability and was much admired by outsiders for at least trying to maintain a profile for cricket via international tours it seemed a hopeless, uphill fight.

Attitudes were hardening. The South Africans had been denied a hearing by the game's rulers, the International Cricket Council and Bacher and two other key administrators refused visas to even enter Australia.

When three countries broke ranks and toured South Africa in the early 1980s, Australia's cricket-loving Prime Minister Bob Hawke met leading Australian players at The Oval during the 1983 World Cup and reminded them of the Government's

REBEL SPRINGBOKS: *Back row, left to right: Henry Fotheringham, Corrie van Zyl, Brian McMillan, Brett Matthews, Hugh Page, Jimmy Cook, Dave Richardson, Kevin McKenzie. Front: Ken McEwan, Clive Rice (captain), David Pithey (team manager), Graeme Pollock, Garth le Roux. Insets: Roy Pinaar, Omar Henry*

continuing stand against South Africa. Until the abolishment of Apartheid he wanted total isolation and no sporting associations whatsoever with the Republic. He reminded the players of the last two lines of their passports: THIS PASSPORT REMAINS THE PROPERTY OF THE AUSTRALIAN GOVERNMENT, a not-so-veiled threat of Government intervention should anyone consider turning renegade.

Almost the same week, across town in a swish apartment in Mayfair, Bacher was having a series of meetings with the Aussies, who were showing genuine enthusiasm for a tour and tax-free monies — if not for South Africa's politics or the potential bans they faced.

While Australia's top-ranked 16 players were enjoying increased security via a newly implemented three-tiered contract system — the best on $65,000 — the rest were still playing for peanuts.

Seasoned trio and prime targets Graham Yallop, Rodney Hogg and Carl Rackemann were Test regulars. Others, like Melburnian Rod 'Puppy' McCurdy were on the fringes, having worn only the canary yellow uniform of the Australian one-day team. Like everyone else he knew there would be a backlash and sanctions for any who broke rank. Graham Gooch and his English team had been outlawed for three years. At 24, McCurdy had age on his side should Australian authorities also outlaw any Australian pirates. But the money was impossible to ignore: $200,000 for two seasons, including an upfront signing fee. Any tax would be paid by the Union. 'The Pup' couldn't sign quickly enough.

THAT'S OUT: Henry Fotheringham is trapped lbw to Terry Alderman for 19 in the third Test at the Wanderers

His judgments weren't clouded by politics or the fact that Nelson Mandela was still imprisoned on Robben Island. He didn't want to know about all the internal unrest, the whites-only beaches and trains, the brutality and murders. He was working as a storeman on basic wages in the eastern suburbs. Suddenly there was this white knight from faraway South Africa prepared to pay Monopoly-type monies for his services. McCurdy's priority was his wife and young son. Australian players on the 1984 tour to the Caribbean had grossed little more than $10,000 each. The wages at Sheffield Shield level were still abysmal, despite the World Series revolution. The Australian Cricket Board's contractual hold on their leading players extended only 12 months. From November 1 1985, they were free agents.

The meeting in Singapore with Bacher went for five hours and after a break at 4 am, resumed again at 10 am. The former South African cricket captain was eloquent, determined, persuasive — and cashed-up. The night before, he'd hosted the New South Wales contingent at Raffles, Singapore's most famous hotel, and shared his dream of a 'new' South Africa in which a truly multi-racial game could thrive in the townships and black communities. In time some of the blacks would play for South Africa, he believed. And only then could South Africa ever again hope to re-win favour with its international brothers.

At the time, the rebel tours were intrinsic in promoting the game's continuing profile. Bacher feared an entire generation of South Africans being lost to cricket. The

1986-87 REBEL AUSTRALIANS: Back row, left to right: Lorne McGee (physiotherapist), Peter Faulkner, John Maguire, Tom Hogan, Terry Alderman, Carl Rackemann, Michael Haysman, Rod McCurdy, Kepler Wessels, Trevor Hohns. Front: Rodney Hogg, Greg Shipperd, Steve Smith, Kim Hughes (captain), Steve Rixon, John Dyson, Mick Taylor, Graham Yallop

Australians would not only be handsomely rewarded and play against some of the world's best at some of the game's most-esteemed venues, they would be challenging Apartheid by direct contact rather than ostracism.

Alongside him was his Australian agent Bruce Francis from Sydney, a former Test opener, who for years had been advocating sporting links with the Republic. It was Francis who'd made the initial contacts with players just weeks earlier during a training camp in Canberra. He'd worked for the South African Rugby Board and in 1973 he toured with Derrick Robins' XI, the first multi-racial cricket team to visit South Africa.

Before the meeting started, Bacher took David Hookes aside and offered him the captaincy. Events were to preclude Hookes' eventual involvement — his trip resulted only in the embarrassment of him being late to the South Australian Cricket Association's Bradman Medal night, despite rushing to the count direct back from Adelaide airport.

The assembled players were keen and attentive. In what was a very informal gathering, many of the players were stretched out on the carpeted floor. At one stage Francis pointed out that the higher profiled, those with considerable Test experience, should receive more than others. He suggested a sliding scale of payments. But Bacher intervened, saying it was untenable. He spoke of the problems a similar system had caused when Lawrence Rowe's West Indians toured two years earlier. Asked by Carl Rackemann what guarantee the Australians had of being paid, Bacher, for once, was lost for words. 'I had no answer,' he said. 'Nobody had ever asked that question before.'

With Bacher and Francis out of the room, the players took a vote and agreed that fees of $200,000 each were fine — if they could be guaranteed. On Bacher's return, they also emphasised the importance of an upfront component.

When Jeff Thomson's solicitor, Andy Hewlett, expressed concern that Thomson's sizeable provident fund monies may be at risk, lessening his client's enthusiasm for the tour, Bacher called a 10-minute interlude and immediately telephoned Terry Alderman in Perth. It was midnight and Bacher said he'd like Alderman to get on the next available plane. If one of his frontline fast bowlers was going to be a dissenter, he wanted to know that a more-than-able replacement was standing by. Alderman assured Bacher of his interest — he was receiving only match payments from the ACB — but it wasn't practical for him to leave straight away. He asked to be kept informed.

Bacher left Singapore truly believing for the first time that an Australian tour was not only feasible — it *would* take place.

SIDELINED: Springbok champion Graeme Pollock had his right hand broken by rebel speedster Carl Rackemann

The players returned to Australia, determined that the arrangement was 'one-in, all-in'. They agreed to keep the arrangements hush-hush. Many of the players aspired to one last Ashes tour. If there was a leak, it would blow everyone's cover. In 1977, all but four of the chosen 17 had signed with Kerry Packer and were well into their tour before the story was revealed. Maybe they could be as lucky, tour England and if necessary, fly down to South Africa afterwards.

Nine of those present in Singapore were shortly to be named in Australia's first Test team in Perth. Kim Hughes was another of the rebels — not that he knew it at the time. He was to resign his captaincy in tears just two Tests into the summer. Having also being omitted from the 1985 touring party to England, he was grateful for the invitation. With Hookes' withdrawal, he was the natural choice as captain.

For much of the home summer, there were veiled hints that another major revolution might be brewing. Senior players seemed particularly anxious to check their provident fund balances. Hughes' entitlement was $75,000. Others also had substantial amounts due. By early March, just after the touring team to England had been announced, the rumours were confirmed when the ABC's Jim Maxwell broke the story on national

> ### REBEL TEAMS TO SOUTH AFRICA 1981-90
>
> **1981-82, ENGLAND** *(toured in March 1982)*: Graham Gooch (captain), Dennis Amiss, Geoff Boycott, John Emburey, Mike Hendrick, Geoff Humpage, Alan Knott, Wayne Larkins, John Lever, Chris Old, Arnie Sidebottom, Les Taylor, Derek Underwood, Peter Willey & Bob Woolmer.
>
> **1982-83, SRI LANKA** *(October to December 1982)*: Bandula Warnapura (captain), Ajit de Silva, Bandula de Silva, Flavian Aponso, Hermanthe Devapriya, Lanthra Fernando, Mahes Goonatillake, Nirmal Hettiaratchi, Susanthe Karunaratne, Lalith Kaluperuma, Tony Opatha, Bernard Perera, Anura Ranasinghe & Jerry Woutersz.
>
> **1982-83, WEST INDIES** *(January to February 1983)*: Lawrence Rowe (captain), Richard Austin, Sylvester Clarke, Colin Croft, Herbert Chang, Alvin Greenidge, Bernard Julien, Alvin Kallicharran, Collis King, Everton Mattis, Ezra Moseley, David Murray, Derek Parry, Franklyn Stephenson & Ray Wynter.
>
> **1983-84, WEST INDIES** *(November 1983 to January 1984)*: Lawrence Rowe (captain), Hartley Alleyne, Faoud Bacchus, Sylvester Clarke, Colin Croft, Alvin Greenidge, Bernard Julien, Alvin Kallicharran, Monte Lynch, Collis King, Everton Mattis, Ezra Moseley, David Murray, Albert Padmore, Derek Parry, Franklyn Stephenson & Emmerson Trotman.
>
> **1985-86, AUSTRALIA** *(November 1985 to February 1986)*: Kim Hughes (captain), Terry Alderman, John Dyson, Peter Faulkner, Michael Haysman, Tom Hogan, Rodney Hogg, Trevor Hohns, John Maguire, Rod McCurdy, Carl Rackemann, Steve Rixon, Greg Shipperd, Steve Smith, Mick Taylor & Graham Yallop.
>
> **1986-87, AUSTRALIA** *(November 1986 to February 1987)*: Kim Hughes (captain), Terry Alderman, John Dyson, Peter Faulkner, Michael Haysman, Tom Hogan, Rodney Hogg, Trevor Hohns, John Maguire, Rod McCurdy, Carl Rackemann, Steve Rixon, Greg Shipperd, Steve Smith, Mick Taylor, Kepler Wessels & Graham Yallop.
>
> **1989-90, ENGLAND** *(January to February 1990)*: Mike Gatting (captain), Bill Athey, Kim Barnett, Chris Broad, Chris Cowdrey, Graham Dilley, Richard Ellison, John Emburey, Neil Foster, Bruce French, David Graveney, Paul Jarvis, Matthew Maynard, Tim Robinson, Greg Thomas & Alan Wells

radio. He'd been at a dinner with a former Test player, privy to the offer. Within 36 hours, it was front page news around the world. It was like a bomb going off. World Series Cricket all over again — except this time Kerry Packer was in bed with the ACB. Believing they'd been undermined by cricketers too mercenary for their own good, the Australian Board threatened 10-year bans on prospective rebels who refused to sign statutory declarations saying they wouldn't tour South Africa. They also denounced the South African Cricket Union, saying it was as culpable as the players.

CENTURION: Graeme Pollock started the series with 108 at Durban. Fiery paceman Rodney Hogg (also pictured) took five for 88

The politicians stoked the controversy, Prime Minister Hawke accusing the rebels of so prejudicing the future of cricket in Australia, that other Test-playing countries may consider their own boycotts. Accusing the players of having blood on their hands, an angry Mr Hawke promised that every rebel's personal finances would be investigated and extra income tax payable — if he could force the legislation through in time. There was no such inquisition on trade with South Africa, of course. That was considered an entirely different matter. In the first 11 months of 1984, exports had soared 80 per cent to more than A$200 million. Mr Hawke also conveniently ignored public opinion polls. Eighty per cent were in favour of the link with South Africa — even if it was an unofficial tour.

The Government's Immigration Minister, Chris Hurford, initially blocked entry visas for Bacher and fellow Union heavyweights Geoff Dakin and Joe Pamensky, who needed time in Australia to prepare their defence of writs issued by the ACB against Francis and eight of the players. Several days later the Foreign Minister, Bill Hayden, countermanded the order, saying it was undemocratic and contravened natural justice.

Meanwhile seven of the 17-man Ashes squad were confirmed as having signed with Bacher. In a day of drama, Dirk Wellham, Wayne Phillips, Graeme Wood and Murray Bennett did an about-face, signed the ACB's declaration and withdrew.

But Rackemann, McCurdy and Alderman stood firm, Rackemann charging those who had withdrawn with disloyalty and endangering the entire operation. He told Trevor Grant of the Melbourne *Age*: 'By bailing out they have made it harder for the

UP-AND-COMER: *Hugh Page bowls Tom Hogan in the fifth ODI at Johannesburg*

other guys ... it seems they have been bought out. If it is true it is interesting to note that the people who run Australian cricket consider there are some players worth buying out and others who are not. None of the four consulted with the others or the organisers before they reversed their decisions. When we originally signed, we all pledged we would stand firm, no matter what. We have had to depend on the South Africans honouring their side of the bargain. In fact, one thing which worried us was if the going got tough, would the South Africans stand by us? But the net result is that a few of us haven't stood by the South Africans.'

Wellham was one of five promising young cricketers rewarded with a $45,000 three-year scholarship from Kerry Packer's promotional arm PBL Marketing. Another was Victorian Dean Jones, who had initially also received a South African tour offer.

Undaunted by the drop outs, Bacher immediately determined to go recruiting again, opening bat Greg Shipperd among the beneficiaries. 'I would have had to have played for another 25 years well into my 50s to have got the monies we were paid,' said the diminutive West Australian.

'Ali Bacher worked assiduously across the entire country and within all communities, blacks, whites and coloureds using sport as a vehicle to change society.

'It's a magnificent country South Africa and our cricket was a unifying force. There was high security at all the grounds of course, but we helped to break down some barriers and help change society. We went into the townships, we saw, we entertained and we inter-acted.

'They had an amazing team, guys like Le Roux, Rice and of course Graeme Pollock. It was a shame that here in Australia we didn't get to see them play much. Pollock was simply breathtaking, as awesome a player as any of us had ever seen. He'd come in and the whole field would scatter. None of our plans worked against him and our attack was highly rated with Hoggie, Alderman, big Carl Rackemann and Rod McCurdy. One day at Wanderers he batted against us one-handed (his right hand was fractured and in plaster) and still made a score. He was unbelievably good.' (In 16 unofficial Tests from 1982 to 1987, Pollock scored five centuries and averaged 65, including 143 on his last appearance, in home town Port Elizabeth at the age of 43).

Victorian Sheffield Shield player Mick Taylor was another late call-up. He was earning $75,000 a year as an AMP agency manager and while his business career was to take a step backwards, he had no regrets. 'Almost everyone was very supportive of me,' he said. 'Only two or three said I wasn't doing the right thing. I'm not so sure, though, they'd walk away from an opportunity like the one I had. I was 29 at the time and hadn't played for Australia. There were no state contracts in place. I had nothing to lose. The opportunity to go on a tour like this was a career highlight. I would have gone for free.'

So paranoid were officials at news of the rebel tour being leaked, most of the players had to train solo, away from their normal official club environments. Taylor spent hours at Dav Whatmore's indoor centre in Mt Waverley. (He was to make 109 at Kingsmead in the very first unofficial Test late in 1985)

While bans were to be imposed, they were only for three years from Test cricket and two from the Sheffield Shield. Given that the rebels were unavailable anyway for two of the years, they were being thrashed with a feather. Several of the World Series players who had been ostracised in 1977 were amazed at the leniency.

One was to accuse the ACB of hypocrisy when one of the rebels, Queenslander Trevor Hohns, later became Australia's selection chairman.

Much of the doings of the patched-up and under-achieving 1985 Ashes squad in England were given scant treatment as newspaper editors concentrated on the rebel tour scandal. The headlines continued right through until August when lawyers agreed to an out-of-court truce. After weeks of legal manoeuvring, the South Africans agreed to pay $120,000 of the ACB's legal costs and promise no more raids. Two more players outside the ACB's contracts list were allowed to join-up: South Australian Michael Haysman and Tasmania's Peter Faulkner.

Of the 16 rebels to South Africa in 1985-86, Alderman, Hohns and Rackemann were the only players to represent Australia again in Tests, Hohns for the first time.

In a nine-year period, seven touring teams visited from four countries, England, West Indies and Australia twice and Sri Lanka once. All players were banned from

KINGSMEAD: South African all-rounder Alan Kourie on his way to 44 against the Australians in the first rebel Test in Durban at Christmas 1985. Wicketkeeper Steve Rixon and Trevor Hohns are also pictured. The match was drawn

official Test cricket, the Englishmen and the Australians for three years, the Sri Lankans for 25 years and the West Indians for life.

The teams not only figured in some stellar cricket, they acted as ambassadors, involving themselves in multi-racial games. The selection of Cape Coloured spin bowler Omar Henry in two Tests against the Australians in 1986-87 further softened world opinion. When first told of his selection, Henry thought it a hoax. 'The moment of glory wasn't just for me,' he said in *The Man in the Middle*, 'it was for the non-white community of South Africa. If cricket, by then, was open, in everyday life there remained a gulf between the whites and non-whites.'

In a giant public relations exercise to celebrate its centenary year of Test cricket in 1989 and further promote the advances cricket was leading towards a new Apartheid-free South Africa, the South African Cricket Union invited former players and journalists from around the world to share in the gala occasion. Hong Kong was a popular stopover point, spending-money even being provided. When my wife Susan and I had to delay our travel plans for 24 hours, Bacher arranged an alternate flight and even came to Johannesburg Airport himself to pick us up. He whisked us through customs in an instant — quite a feat for those familiar with the workings of the O.R. Tambo.

Among the assembled guests were ex-Test captains 87-year-old Bob Wyatt and Tony Greig from England, Lindsay Hassett, Ian Craig, Ian Johnson and Neil Harvey (Australia) and Walter Hadlee and John Reid (New Zealand). Bacher was particularly impressed by the statesmanlike Johnson. 'You could tell why Bradman had made him captain (in the mid-1950s),' he said.

Members of the Australian Cricket Board declined their invitations, some most reluctantly. 'Our international critics ignore the glaring defects around the world and direct their venom at us,' said South African Cricket Union president Pamensky. 'We can never be satisfied with the pace of change in South Africa, but surely only the most cynical would dare to deny that sweeping change is taking place here, especially in the world of cricket.'

Evidence of this was the dozens of games going on in a huge clearing in Soweto and the passion for the game in other black townships like Alexandria. While the whites-only facilities were eye-opening, all-race cricket teams were being promoted and it was clear that cricket was a pacesetter in much of the bridge-building slowly reunifying South Africa, after the shunning of black and coloured communities for years.

- Approaching the first Test in Kingsmead, Kim Hughes' Australian squad boasted 230 Test caps and 353 ODI caps. Facing the first half-pace overs from opening bowler Rod Hogg, South Africa's opener Jimmy Cook was unimpressed by his speed and told his partner Henry Fotheringham that South Africa might make 600. The first ball of Hogg's third over fizzed past Cook's nose and he immediately called for a helmet. 'For the next four or five overs we experienced the fury that this man could unleash when it suited him,' Cook said. The Australians lost two and drew five of the Tests from 1985-87. South Africa's isolation from world cricket ended in 1991.

IRRESISTIBLE ODDS: Dennis Lillee won a small fortune betting against Australia

6   1981 LEEDS

500-1

As tour pranks go, it was the grand-daddy of them all. But so irresistible were the 500/1 odds that Dennis Lillee felt compelled to have an interest, even if it did mean betting against Australia.

England was to win one of the most dramatic of all Ashes Tests and Lillee and his mate Rod Marsh pocketed winning worth more than than $40,000 in today's currency.

Lillee's confession, 12 months later, prompted an extraordinary reaction, Rick McCosker saying the bet was a poor example to young people and reflected badly on the game. Neil Harvey wanted the maverick paceman banned for life.

Dennis Lillee had never been anything but a small-time gambler. The son of a long-distance truck driver, his first serious job was as a bank teller in Perth. The pay was modest and he soon learnt money was not to be squandered. But like many of his Australian team-mates, the betting tents dotted around the Test and county grounds in England were alluring. You could bet on anything, from the smallest regional race meet through to the big Ashes Tests.

At a one-dayer in Bradford, during Lillee's first tour in 1972, most of the Australians contributed to a team kitty, believing the 5/1 odds to capture five Yorkshire wickets before lunch was highly achievable. 'With about half an hour to go in the session we had our five wickets and Dennis was running around and jumping up and down with excitement,' said wicketkeeper Rod Marsh. 'He went to the tent to collect only to be told that the session hadn't finished and if we got any more wickets it would be a lost bet. Dennis yelled out not to take any more, so we proceeded with caution. A few minutes before the end of the session we were almost home and hosed when Bob Massie at fine leg took an absolute screamer of a catch. We all raced down to kick his backside!'

NEW RECORD-HOLDER: During the match Dennis Lillee created a new record for most wickets in Ashes Tests

At Leeds in 1981, Kim Hughes' Aussies had taken total charge of the third Test and betting agency Ladbrokes, looking to initiate some late-match interest, posted the extraordinary odds of 500/1 on a series-squaring English win. Dour Yorkshiremen dismissed the odds as ludicrous and went back to their fish and chips and Tetley's, believing the game in all likelihood would finish in four days, so dominant were the Australians.

Sixteen thousand kilometres away in Prahran, just south of the Melbourne CBD, it was almost midnight and I was putting the finishing touches to the sports section of next day's *Sunday Observer* newspaper. I was also convinced that only one team could win — and it wasn't England. In those days we'd do three and even four editions and happily work through until 2 am and even later on Saturday nights when Wimbledon was on. It meant the latest news going out to a few extra thousand readers — anything to give us an edge over our direct competitors the *Sunday Press*.

When the seventh wicket fell with England still almost 100 runs behind, we changed our front-page banner to ASHES COME HOME. Australia was already leading the series 1-0. Soon it would be 2-0, so we all believed. We ran the latest odds from Ladbrokes: 1/4 Australia, 5/2 the draw & 500/1 England.

Back at the game, in the Australian dressing rooms, Lillee couldn't believe his eyes. He called teammates to the window:

PLEASE EXPLAIN: An unhappy Greg Chappell with Dennis Lillee after an out-of-sorts Lillee bowled a bouncer with wicketkeeper Rod Marsh standing over the stumps

'Have a look at that [scoreboard],' he said. 'Five hundred to one! Surely those odds can't be right.'

On a high, having just broken the record for most wickets in Ashes Tests, he reached for his wallet and pulled out a brand new 50-pound note which had only just been reintroduced. 'Who else wants some of the 500 to one?' he called.

The room was silent. There were no other takers. Even Marsh reckoned his mate was throwing his money away. 'All right,' said Lillee. 'Have 10 with me then.'

Marsh was still reticent, but minutes later, as the Australians were re-taking the field, Marsh walked past the Australian bus driver, Peter Tribe, and with a raise of his hand indicated he'd have five. Spinner Ray Bright also said he was in, but just as quickly changed his mind. 'The punter in me told me you only have a bet if you have a chance of winning,' he said. 'Basically it was a giggle bet.'

At 7-176 in their second innings, having followed on, the Englishmen was still 51 behind and facing an innings' defeat. Several of their XI — including Ian Botham, who

INFAMOUS: Cricket gets physical at the WACA Oval... the clash between Dennis Lillee and Javed Miandad. Popular umpire Tony 'TC' Crafter didn't realise just how much danger he was in...
Cricketer magazine

was not out — had booked out of their hotel on the fourth morning, believing there was little chance of the game going into a final day. 'Most of us had given up the Test for dead,' he said in *The Incredible Tests 1981*.

The tea-to-stumps session remains one of the most memorable in Ashes annals with Botham and England pulverising the Australians with a 175-run session at almost seven an over. Most of these runs came from Botham in the innings of his illustrious career. He'd made a pair at Lord's and been replaced as captain by Mike Brearley. He had nothing to lose and kept throwing haymakers like a modern-day Twenty20 hitter. Against all odds, England rapidly clawed their way back into the contest.

After Marsh had indicated he also wanted five quid at the extraordinary odds, Tribe briefly debated keeping the 15 quid and handing it back to Lillee and Marsh at the tea break. But in the end he duly went around to the tent and laid their bet.

Twenty-four hours later, thanks to Botham's thrill-a-minute 149 and an astonishing onslaught from Bob Willis, England won the closest Ashes Test in more than 50 years. It was only the second time in more than 100 years and 905 Tests that a side following on had won. Tribe said he felt sick in the stomach watching the Aussies capitulate.

Lillee and Marsh's 'collect' was 7500 pounds ($15,000, or the equivalent of more than $40,000 today). Bright, who was rooming with Lillee, still remembers the money being delivered to their hotel room. It was all in one-pound notes. Soon it was strewn all around the room like confetti. It was to assist in the buying of many extra pints of full-strength lager and secure for Tribe a new set of golf clubs and a return trip to Perth to visit his mates. 'Ladbrokes didn't have [all] the money at the ground,' Bright said. 'The rest arrived a few days later.'

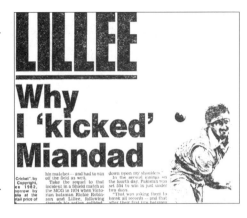

There was no suggestion that either Lillee or Marsh had not played with their normal focus and ferocity. Lillee's fifth-day stand of 35 with Bright was the second highest in Australia's total of 111 all out. And one Test later, at Edgbaston, Marsh broke down when Australia squandered another winning position to again lose narrowly.

News of the bet somehow remained 'in-house' until 12 months later with the release of Lillee's autobiography *My Life in Cricket*. Australian authorities immediately inserted a clause into the players' match contracts, banning them from betting on games in which they were involved. Ex-players were shocked, the legendary post-war left-hander Neil Harvey leading the dissenters.

'I never lost a moment's sleep because of it,' said Lillee. 'I didn't regard it as betting against my team or my country. I just thought the odds of 500/1 were ridiculous. I'd flatten anyone who ever suggested I threw a game. I have a completely clear conscience over it. I believe my integrity, as far as playing to win every game I played, is unquestioned.'

Marsh said both he and Lillee felt they were betting against the English bookmakers, 'trying to show the Poms how silly they were for offering such stupid odds'.

'I couldn't see the harm in it,' Marsh said. 'Nobody would have known or cared about the bet if we had won. It wasn't until after the game when someone said that we had won a quid that it dawned on us. But I don't believe we did the wrong thing because we didn't consider it a bet against Australia. That was never the intent.'

Overnight, Botham became English cricket's new folk hero. He'd bullied the Australians in a savage display of power not seen from an Englishman since Ted Dexter in his prime. With almost 200 runs and six wickets, Botham not only saved the match and the series, but established himself, once and for all, as one of the finest all-rounders in cricket history.

The betting scandal was just one of the many controversies to embroil the maverick fast bowler during his fabulous, headlining career.

While universally respected for his commitment and his (then) unequalled wicket-taking exploits, Lillee is also regarded as one Australian cricket's most notorious bad boys — his only real rival David Warner.

From the time 'DK' knocked Geoff Boycott's cap from his head with his first delivery in an international against the 1970-71 Englishmen at the WACA Ground, Lillee generated news like few Australian cricketers before or since.

LEEDS 1981: England had no chance – so the bookmakers reckoned…

His lack of love for cricket administrators came a close second to his hatred of opposing batsmen. He had a maverick streak and blued at times even with his captains, especially if they happened to dare prefer someone else with the new ball!

Lillee's spitfire speed from a rocking, energetic run-up was timed in excess of 90 mph (145 km/h), just fractionally behind the wild one, his pace partner Jeff Thomson. Lillee's frank admissions that he bowled his short deliveries to scare and, if necessary, hurt opposing batsmen were part of his intimidating persona. He revelled in his role as Australia's enforcer and refused to slow down to a change bowler's pace. Ian Chappell had never met a cricketer with such an iron will or such a passion for running in fast and causing mayhem at the opposite end.

As the all-star fast bowler of the 1970s, Lillee was feted everywhere he went. He made such a remarkable recovery from his severe spinal injury of 1973 that officials, glad to have him back, allowed him to consistently overstep the bounds of sportsmanship and flaunt the spirit of the game.

Unwittingly, those who tended to forgive and forget and gloss over Lillee's indiscretions ultimately did him a disservice. Initially a shy man, bordering on introverted, Lillee developed a supreme ego. Had he been subject to discipline earlier, he may not have become quite as big a rogue.

Wisden editor John Woodcock claimed to be sickened by Lillee's antics. 'Some say it is money that has caused this collapse in the ethics of the game, others that it is the reflection of a graceless age. In Australia, I am afraid, it is partly the result of weak government. For too long, the Australian Cricket Board have been over-tolerant of indiscipline and actions of dubious intent. True cricket lovers have been as sickened by Lillee's antics as they have been spellbound by his bowling.'

SUPREME EGO: Had Dennis Lillee been disciplined earlier in his career, surely he would not have been as provocative later... Patrick Eagar/Cricketer magazine

Lillee's lead role in the Javed Miandad kicking controversy, the aluminium bat affair and the vandalism of a dressing room at Launceston's NTCA Ground during his comeback half summer with Tasmania in 1987-88 were other serious indiscretions.

Rarely before had there been a more provocative 10 seconds in Test history, or as open a display of on-field aggression, as his infamous tangle with Miandad at the WACA Ground in Perth in 1981-82. As Javed menacingly brandished his bat, having been ankle-tapped, Lillee clenched his fists and shaped up like an old-time bare-knuckle boxer. The cricket world held its breath.

From slip, Australia's captain, Greg Chappell, yelled 'Dennis!' and sprinted down the wicket to intervene. Umpire Tony Crafter had already stepped between the pair, trying to shepherd Lillee away. It was an extraordinary, never-to-be-forgotten display of petulance that resulted, amazingly, in just a two-match ban.

In his book *Over and Out*, Lillee says this incident is the only one he *truly* regrets. 'Javed jabbed me in the rib cage with his bat, but nobody wanted to know about that,' he said. 'I'm not saying I was right in what I did, even though I gave him only a slight tap on the pad. I'm sorry thousands of kids saw it, but I'm also sorry the incident wasn't fully shown in television replays.'

THE GREAT 'DK'

'Few fast bowlers have had finer physique or temperament, or such a gloriously flowing action. He added edge to it; with a hostility to his opponents often theatrical and sometimes offensive. He would have been greater still without that,' — JOHN ARLOTT

'Dennis was a captain's dream and a batsman's nightmare,' — IAN CHAPPELL

'Dennis Lillee is very plainly the finest pace bowler of my era, if not of any era. Lillee has everything. He frequently bowls well within himself for four balls of an over, slipping in two exceptionally quick deliveries from an action which scarcely seems to deviate from normal. He does exactly what he wants with the ball, swinging it either way but bowling the outswinger with control and consistency,' — KEITH FLETCHER

'Of all the great fast bowlers I have faced — Roberts, Holding, Hadlee, Marshall — I would have to place him as the best ... given the combination of his natural talent and a ferociously competitive nature, he was as complete a fast bowler as there can ever have been,' — DAVID GOWER

'Dennis Lillee was the complete fast bowler with a magnificent action and superb control and variation. He and "Thommo" (Jeff Thomson) made a perfect combination,' — MICHAEL HOLDING

'At times he becomes a little hard to handle when he becomes too hot under the collar. When he loses his cool Dennis is inclined to swear and carry on towards the batsmen, but that's only because he is so determined,' — ROD MARSH

'He is a bowler of great endurance. He does so much with the ball and it is always a worry which way he is going to go and just what he is going to do next. Lillee is after you all the time,' — VIV RICHARDS

'As a competitor he was fierce. The sort of guy that, if the time came, would slit your throat with a smile on his face.' — AUSTIN ROBERTSON snr

'It was Dennis' snarl and piercing, flashing glance which had the most effect. His statistics for wickets in Test matches cannot do justice to how he achieved them and in what circumstances,' — DIRK WELLHAM

The first weeks of the 1979-80 season — the first of the cricket compromise — were almost as stormy, with Lillee accused of petulance and ignoring the spirit of the game.

The first black mark came as the opening West Indian Test in Brisbane was petering out to a draw. Relegated on the final afternoon to first-change duties behind Thomson and Rodney Hogg, Lillee angered Chappell and wicketkeeper Marsh by deliberately sending down a bouncer while Marsh was standing over the stumps. Having seen Lillee bowl a slow off-break from just three paces, Chappell called to him, asking whether he was bowling fast or spin. 'Spin,' said Lillee, riled at the no-ball calls being made by umpire Robin Bailhache. Chappell changed the field to suit a slow bowler, thinking Lillee intended to finish his over, which was to stretch to 11 balls, as quickly as he could.

Instead, from just five or six paces, he delivered a short-pitcher at close to top pace. It whistled past an astonished Collis King and fairly thumped into Marsh's gloves. Marsh fumed and cursed at Lillee, who was already storming back to his mark without even half an apology. Chappell was clearly unimpressed and strode 60 metres from slip to near the members' pavilion to admonish his fast bowler.

Ten days later Lillee was headline news again, this time over his revolutionary Combat aluminium cricket bat in the opening Test against England at the WACA Ground. Lillee had first used the bat, without even a ripple of protest, in the Test in Brisbane, but given that he had batted less than 10 minutes and faced just seven balls without scoring a run, the lack of attention was hardly surprising. However, his continued use of the bat caused a furore and triggered action from the game's rule-makers, the Marylebone Cricket Club.

ALL-ALUMINIUM: Dennis Lillee's Combat bat

In a bizarre start to the second day of the Test, Lillee, who was not out overnight, resumed with the bat he had been attempting to market into schools at two-thirds of the price of normal English willow. After four deliveries from Ian Botham, one of which Lillee drove through mid-off for three, England captain Mike Brearley complained to umpires Don Weser and Max O'Connell that the ball had been damaged.

An unscheduled 10-minute break in play ensued while Lillee argued over the legality of his bat. Australia's 12th man, Rod Hogg, came out and offered Lillee a wooden bat but Lillee refused and marched back into the rooms with Hogg before re-emerging, still with the offending blade. 'I wanted to introduce the bat to the public,' Lillee said afterwards. 'We wanted the bat to get some exposure for Christmas sales. Mike Brearley stuck his nose in when he shouldn't have.'

Lillee was hooted by sections of his home crowd over his antics, which included hurling his bat 20 metres towards the pavilion in apparent anger. Many, like English wicketkeeper Bob Taylor, felt that Lillee was grandstanding and making a fool of

PUBLICITY SEEKER: Dennis Lillee with Mike Brearley at the WACA Oval in December 1979. Patrick Eagar/Cricketer magazine

himself. 'It was a totally theatrical performance for the benefit of the cameras and Lillee had the cheek to feign a loss of temper,' said Taylor.

The umpires refused to re-start the game until Lillee swapped bats, so Chappell ended the fiasco by taking a conventional Duncan Fearnley blade out himself. It was an extraordinary stand-off in which Lillee openly challenged the authority of the umpires. He escaped official censure when he produced a letter from the ACB saying it neither approved nor disapproved of the revolutionary bat. At the time, the laws of cricket did not demand that bats be made from wood.

The aluminium bat now takes pride of place among Lillee's array of memorabilia at his luxury home in Perth. While Combat bats are now sometimes auctioned, Lillee says he would never part with the original, which is signed by both teams and includes a message from Brearley: 'Good luck with the sales, Dennis.'

Lillee's standing as the greatest fast bowler of all time is rarely questioned. He smashed through opposing batting line-ups, intimidation and passion central weapons. He bullied, taunted and berated batsmen. Some critics considered him headstrong and callous; but no one dared say it to his face.

Lillee was also one never to be intimidated by formality. He said 'G'day' to the Duke of Edinburgh and during the Centenary Test in 1977, even asked Her Majesty the Queen for her autograph. Months later, a personally signed photo of the Queen arrived from Buckingham Palace!

Lillee's bowling partnership with Jeff Thomson in 1974-75 revived memories of Bodyline. It seemed inconceivable that any pair could have bowled faster. In response the MCC's team physiotherapist, Bernard Thomas, prompted the Englishmen to wear across their chests made-to-measure foam-rubber 'armour'. 'Never in my career have I witnessed so much protective gear applied to individuals before they went out to bat,' said captain Mike Denness. 'On the plane flying from Australia to New Zealand, the players were clearly more than relieved that they had all left Australia intact and without fatal injury.'

Recalled veteran Colin Cowdrey rated Lillee and Thomson the most difficult and unpredictable pair he had ever faced. He said they were ahead of the very best from around the world he had opposed in his prime years, from Lindwall and Miller and Hall and Griffith to the Springbok tearaways Adcock and Heine.

In the Sydney Test, Lillee's first ball to Dennis Amiss soared over Amiss' and Marsh's heads before thudding one bounce into the sightscreen for four byes. Another bouncer, to tailender Geoff Arnold, just missed the batsman's ear and again soared out of Marsh's reach to the boundary. Even Lillee looked relieved that the ball had missed Arnold. The English man seemed frozen by fear and had hardly moved from out of his stance.

In the second innings, John Edrich, England's acting captain, had a rib broken by the first ball he faced from Lillee. With huge black storm clouds gathering and Lillee charging in to chants of 'KILL, KILL, KILL', the atmosphere was unforgettable. A record 180,000 attended the five days.

EXHAUSTED: Greg Chappell looks across to the players' gate and sights the strapping figure of All Black Brian McKechnie… years later Chappell admitted he wasn't fit to be captain of Australia that day. Cricketer magazine/Ken Piesse collection

7

1981 MELBOURNE

Underhanded

Greg Chappell had never felt so exhausted. It was one of those blisteringly hot February days in Melbourne, 30-degrees plus and so steamy that you could fry an egg on the footpath. A wicket fell and instead of joining the group in the centre, Chappell stretched out at long-on, hands on his knees assessing the equation. There was one ball to go. New Zealand needed six to tie and extend the best-of-five World Series into one final showdown. Out of the corner of his eye he sighted the strapping frame of NZ's incoming batsman, All Black Brian McKechnie striding to the wicket for one death-or-glory swipe. If anyone looked capable of hitting a six first-ball, it was this fella. Panicking, he stood and marched into the centre making a beeline for his brother. 'Trevor,' he called…

Maybe we should blame the West Indian Wayne Daniel. Just minutes before midnight one January night in 1978, his mighty six down the ground triggered an incredible victory with just one ball to spare against the WSC Australians at Melbourne's VFL Park. There wasn't a more exciting or memorable finish in the two years of the rebel movement — and the scars were lasting.

Greg Chappell had been involved in some stoushes and scandals — like the time he announced his abdication to Kerry Packer's World Series rebels while still captain of traditional Australia in 1977. But none are as remembered, or as infamous as the underarm he ordered to end the third one-day final against Geoff Howarth's New Zealanders on February 1 1981.

The best-of-five finals series was tied 1-1 coming to Melbourne. After an exhausting summer of five Tests and 10 lead-up World Series games, Chappell didn't want to extend the finals any longer than was absolutely necessary. He was virtually out on his feet, desperate to get off the field and forget about cricket in a week which not only included at least one more World Series showdown, but yet another Test match.

Earlier, in Australia's innings, he'd been brilliantly caught in the outfield by lawyer Martin Snedden, but neither umpire could confirm the catch and Chappell advanced his score from 58 to 90, the bonus runs being all-important in Australia's thrilling win. The Kiwis were livid, especially Mark Burgess, who had been close to the catch, and Snedden, who castigated Chappell for not taking his word and walking. 'It was the most brilliant catch I've ever seen,' said the bowler Lance Cairns. 'Greg watched it, then turned away. He simply didn't want to believe his eyes.' But umpire Peter Cronin, at the bowler's end, wasn't absolutely sure if the catch had been taken. He consulted his partner, Don Weser, in one of his first internationals, but he'd been watching the batsmen running between wickets and could only guess. With no official access to replays Cronin felt he had no option but to rule Chappell 'not out'. Snedden had taken the catch of the summer. He was furious. So much for cricket being synonymous with sportsmanship.

Thanks to opener Bruce Edgar's unbeaten century and some sloppy Australian fielding, the Kiwis clawed their way towards the 236-run target. As Trevor Chappell began the final over, 15 runs were still required. In the run-chase, Richard Hadlee and Ian Smith fell and with one ball remaining, seven were needed to win and six to tie. Captain Greg Chappell sat down in the outfield, at the foot of the MCC's cigar stand. He was exhausted. Finally the game seemed safe.

But as soon as he saw NZ's No. 10 McKechnie enter, picture-perfect flashbacks of Daniel's amazing 11th hour six against Mick Malone in the same city three years earlier raced through his mind. Surely it couldn't happen again, could it? Forgetting his physical discomfort, he rose to his feet and started walking towards his brother, looking over his shoulder at the old manual scoreboard and double-checking the equation.

McKechnie, a rugby and cricket dual international, didn't have the air of a man who intended just to pat the last ball back to the bowler. He'd come to party. A first-ball six at the expansive MCG was a big ask, but he fully intended giving it a try. As he made his way from the players' viewing area and out of the shade down the race and onto the field, there was a roar of anticipation. Few of the world-record ODI crowd of 52,990 had left. It had been a highly dramatic and entertaining game. Mathematically, a glorious tie was still possible, even if the odds were astronomical.

As he was walking out, McKechnie was already focusing on the most likely area for hitting sixes. The huge square boundaries were out of the question. Even Lance Cairns with his trusty Excalibur bat would struggle to clear the east or west fences. Going straight was the answer. He reasoned that Chappell would try to bowl a yorker at leg stump and restrict the room in which to swing his arms. He would therefore step away at the point of delivery and swing as hard as he could, hoping to lift the ball over the mid-on fence and into the members — a hit of 80-85 metres (approximately 90 yards).

As he reached the centre square, the only players in his immediate vicinity were Rod Marsh standing near the stumps and the Chappell brothers at the far end. Everyone else had scattered.

7 Underhanded

THE MOMENT: Trevor Chappell delivers the underarm to Brian McKechnie. A disgusted Rod Marsh watches on in horror. Peter Bull/Cricketer magazine/Ken Piesse collection

Calling Trevor over, big brother Greg said: 'How are you at bowling your underarms?' 'Oh… I dunno… why?'

'Well, you're about to find out.'

Turning to umpire Don Weser, Chappell said, 'Don, Trevor is going to bowl the last ball underarm.'

'I beg your pardon?'

'The last ball will be bowled underarm.'

'Hang on, I'll inform the batsman… and the other umpire.' Weser conferred with Cronin. When he told McKechnie, the New Zealander dropped his bat in amazement.

'It didn't enter my mind to say no,' said the younger Chappell. 'I actually didn't consider it to be a yes/no type of question. It was the captain of my team asking me to do something that was, at the time anyway, within the rules of the game. It seemed like a good idea.'

Hundreds of kilometres away in Adelaide, the Chappells' father, Martin, was watching on TV. He instinctively knew what was about to happen. 'Trevor is going to bowl an underarm,' he told his wife Jeanne. In the commentary box, Bill Lawry was incredulous. 'Surely not,' he said, 'can you believe it?' Behind the wickets, Rod Marsh was shaking his head. 'No, mate, don't do it,' he yelled, trying to be heard above the din. Trevor shrugged his shoulders, looked back at Greg at long-on and, from a two-step run-up, delivered a slow grubber. Even 'the Bradman of Bowls', Glyn Bosisto, would have approved of his style, but this was a cricket match. It had been almost 60 years since an underarm had been bowled at the MCG.

TREVOR CHAPPELL: 'It didn't enter my head to say no'.

McKechnie blocked it, threw his bat up the wicket in disgust and stood in mid-pitch arms akimbo, defiantly glaring at Trevor. 'I thought to myself: "They must be joking". I couldn't believe they'd stoop so low,' he said afterwards. At the non-striker's end Edgar stuck his two fingers up in a defiant gesture at the bowler before consoling McKechnie and, seeing the fans storming onto the field, running for the rooms.

Neither umpire had noticed that Dennis Lillee was outside the fielding limitation line and that technically it was a no-ball. An angry Howarth was one of the first to reach the harassed umpires. He was furious. 'Underarm bowling has been banned. You shouldn't have allowed the delivery,' was the printable part of his high-octane serve.

Afterwards he learnt that the ruling applied only in England, where he was a regular county player. In the Victorian Cricket Association's room, match referee Bob Parish was called to the phone. It was long-distance: Adelaide. Like everyone else, Sir Donald Bradman was incredulous.

Marsh approached Howarth and apologised. 'I don't want it to go any further,' he said, 'because if the team hears that I'm saying it, it doesn't do the team situation much good… I was not in agreement and told Greg so. Please accept my apologies.'

Chappell admits that everything got to him this day: the heat, the pressure, the schedule and especially McKechnie. Chappell was unfit to be Australia's captain that oppressive Sunday afternoon.

Greg's crazy, shameful decision ensured Australia a win but violated the spirit of the game. So incensed was New Zealand's Prime Minister Robert Muldoon that he dubbed

ANOTHER ANGLE: Having defended the grubbing ball, Brian McKechnie threw his bat in the air in disgust.

it 'an act of cowardice ', and said it was further proof of his theory that Kiwis had higher IQs than Australians. It may have only been grandstanding rhetoric but even the most patriotic Australian was appalled. The incident remains an indelible black mark on one of the most peerless careers of all.

If Chappell could change one moment of his career, this would be it. If he had any idea of the furore the ball would cause, he would have backed down. But at the time, he was beyond reason. He had spent six and a half hours on the field and, as he told biographer Adrian McGregor, knew the action wasn't going to be well received. 'I expected a lot of people would say, "Tch, tch, not cricket", but quite honestly I didn't give a rat's tail. I was quite prepared for a rap over the knuckles if it saved us from an extra game.'

Umpire Weser said: 'He seemed the normal Greg Chappell to me. He didn't seem any different.'

The Australians sprinted off to widespread boos from all sections of the ground, even the members. Soft-drink cans and paper cups were thrown in their direction. One young girl ran at Chappell and said he was a cheat. The Kiwi players stood at their open door, grim-faced. Watching from the VCA Delegates' Room, a teary Sam Loxton, one of Bradman's Invincibles, made his way down the stairs and told Chappell he'd just lost a lot of his friends. 'It's a helluva way to win a cricket match son,' he said.

No one spoke in the Australian dressing rooms. The silence was almost eerie and was broken only by the ringing of a telephone. 'Perth calling for Greg Chappell.'

CATCH OF THE SEASON: Martin Snedden bends low and takes a remarkable outfield catch at the MCG... but Greg Chappell refused to walk and advanced his score from 58 to 90. Cricketer magazine

'No, not here, you've rung the wrong place,' said Trevor Chappell, who was nearest.

Doug Walters grinned and said: 'Just goes to show you,' he said, 'the game's not over until the last ball is bowled!'

'Just wait until the Poison Typewriter Club (the press) gets to you,' said Lillee. For once, someone else was in trouble.

Next door, in the New Zealand rooms, Burgess had hurled his cup and saucer against a wall and Howarth and manager Ian Taylor were hurriedly examining the tour conditions. If that was the way the Australians wanted to play it, they could have some of their own medicine in the next match in Sydney. Senior Australian Cricket Board officials Parish and Ray Steele moved among the New Zealand players, apologising profusely.

High in the Olympic Stand, where Richie Benaud and the Channel Nine commentary team were based, Benaud was typically eloquent and on the money. The doyen of Australian TV cricket commentators believed that Chappell must have miscalculated in the final hour; otherwise his No. 1 bowler Lillee, rather than the youngest Chappell, would have bowled the fateful final over. 'Now, you can have your own opinions about that (the delivery). Let me tell you what mine is. I think it was a gutless performance from the Australian captain.'

Past and present players were also appalled. Channel Nine's Tony Greig called for Chappell's immediate resignation. The *Daily Telegraph's* Keith Miller said one-day cricket had died and Chappell should be buried with it. 'I felt like crawling into a big hole,' he said, 'wishing I'd never played the game.' Writing in the *Sydney Morning Herald*, fellow legend Bill O'Reilly blamed Australia's win-at-all-costs attitude on the increased prizemonies on offer that summer. 'Just how far does the lure of the lolly [money] go to deprive us of basic self-respect? It was an injury to all the great players who have played over the last 100 years.'

McKechnie agreed that the financial rewards exacerbated the pressure. 'Very seldom were discussions held without the mention of how much money could be won,' he said. 'Perhaps this leads people to do things that they might not otherwise do.'

McKechnie was never to play for New Zealand again.

> THE PREVIOUS underarm to be bowled at the MCG occurred in 1922-23. Victoria's Arthur Liddicutt sent one down shortly after the tea interval during a day-long partnership by MCC pair Geoffrey Wilson and Wilfred Hill-Wood. According to historian Ray Webster, the delivery was a one-off and was bowled purely out of frustration at the stonewalling tactics of the two Englishmen. Hill-Wood took more than three hours to make 50 and more than four hours for his 100.

Chappell flew to Sydney that night. He didn't have to listen to the ABC to realise he'd created a monster. The underarm led every news bulletin. He'd told journalists afterwards it was within the laws of the game as they currently stood. What he didn't say was that he was at breaking point and not fit to be captain. That was to come later.

Awoken at midnight at his Wellington home by a reporter from the *Sydney Morning Herald*, Muldoon exploded, calling it 'the most disgusting incident in the history of cricket'. He said canary yellow was a most appropriate central colour of Australia's one-day uniform. 'If the bloody Australians want it, they'll get it fair between the eyes,' he said.

The next morning, at Tullamarine and Kingsford Smith airports, there was an incredible commotion. 'It was as though we had assassinated the president of the United States,' said Allan Border in *An Autobiography*. 'There were camera crews, reporters, photographers, all trying to get somebody to say something.'

At Sydney's Sheraton Hotel, Chappell was also being besieged, his phone having first rung at 6 am. Amid calls for his resignation, he said he had been hunted by all sorts of people. 'I fair dinkum expected somebody to crawl through the window,' he said.

GRUBBY END TO A GREAT GAME, said the Melbourne *Age* in its editorial. 'Australian cricket is in disgrace and the country's reputation severely damaged.' Others were just as damning:

- 'It (was an action) which has since been described as shameless, spineless, disgraceful, churlish and gutless. The Australian sporting image has been tarnished as never before.' — The *Australian*

- 'Greg reached an all-time low in win-at-all-costs gamesmanship.' — The Melbourne *Herald*
- 'One ball dints Australia's image as a sporting nation.' — The *Sydney Morning Herald*
- 'There could not be a lonelier man in the cricket world than Greg Chappell.' — The *London Times*

In Wellington, a flag flew at half-mast over the office of a big Australian insurance firm. Within days Qantas was promoting a special $299 return airfare to New Zealand. The advertisement featured a picture of the underarm delivery along with the caption: 'NZ $299 return. Once again the opposition will accuse us of cheating.'

Chappell was reprimanded by the ACB and formally reminded of his responsibilities as national captain towards the spirit of the game. A telephone link-up of ACB delegates immediately outlawed under-arm bowling. Those who wanted him to stand down accepted his carefully worded statement of regret: 'I have always played cricket within the laws of the game. I took a decision yesterday which, whilst within the laws of cricket, in the cool light of day, I recognise as not being within the spirit of the game. The decision was made whilst I was under pressure and in the heat of the moment. I regret the decision. It's something I'd never do again.'

Even his brother Ian asked: 'Fair dinkum, Greg, how much pride do you sacrifice to win $35,000?' According to biographer McGregor, Jeanne Chappell rang Ian and said that as Greg's brother he should have been more supportive. 'I'd never say anything against you if you did something wrong,' she said. 'I'd always support you even if you were on a murder charge.' Ian said he couldn't make a 'wishy-washy' comment. He told his mother that if that was the only mistake Greg made in his first-class career, he would be blessed.

The Board offices in Jolimont on the fringes of the MCG received more than 1000 letters, 90 per cent of them condemnatory. Within 24 hours, the *Sydney Morning Herald* had received more than 100 letters complaining of Chappell's action. At the *Courier Mail* in his home town of Brisbane, however, some letters defended him.

Chappell was booed walking onto the Sydney Cricket Ground for the fourth final the following day. He was a little apprehensive approaching the wicket until Howarth patted him on the rump and wished him good luck. On reaching 50, Chappell raised his bat defiantly to the Channel Nine commentary box. In a torrent of criticism, none had stung like Benaud's post-match review. Chappell had been captain of Australia on and off since 1975. He believed Richie, more than anyone else, should have realised the increased pressure and demands of the modern game. Chappell finished on 87 to spearhead an Australian win and be named Player of the Finals.

On his retirement three years later, he had led in 48 Tests and 49 one-day internationals, comprising more than 250 days play. Yet for many, his leadership is best remembered for those 60 seconds late on a cricket day that Melburnians still vividly recall as 'Black Sunday'.

On the 15th anniversary of the incident, in an interview with Sydney journalist Mike Koslowski, Chappell admitted: 'I shouldn't have been out there. Mentally I was struggling to get through the season. I wasn't fit on the day ... had I not been out there or had I been in a better frame of mind, it would never have happened.' He said his actions were 'indefensible' but that the captaincy demands were so intense and the schedule so exhausting that he had simply cracked. Soon afterwards, the ACB had appointed a full-time media manager to lessen the load.

'It wasn't something done in isolation,' Chappell said. 'It was the culmination of years of frustration, anger and annoyance at the way we were being treated.' Marsh, who had opposed the under-arm, said 'it was about 48 degrees' in the centre of the MCG and that Chappell 'was simply gone'.

DISTRAUGHT: Martin Snedden challenged Chappell, but neither umpire could confirm the catch had been taken

Asked how he would have reacted in a similar circumstance, English Test umpire Don Oslear said, 'I might have said, "Come on Greg. It has been a tremendous game. Let's bowl it up."'

THE REACTION

'The noise was so tremendous I doubt whether [Trevor] Chappell even heard Marsh. But no one went up to Chappell to point out the consequences,' – New Zealand's LANCE CAIRNS

'Greg Chappell brought a holocaust of criticism down on his head and his prestige as a sportsman was left in the dust,' – NZ Test selector DON NEELY

'Many will remember Greg Chappell from his actions that day – I prefer to remember him for being one of the great batsmen,' –NZ wicketkeeper IAN SMITH

'To this day I have no idea why he did it ... we were all under pressure but it would never cross my mind to do anything so blatantly stupid and unsportsmanlike,' – NZ captain GEOFF HOWARTH

'It was a bloody stupid thing to do and I hope it will never happen again,' – HAROLD LARWOOD

'My main regret was that Trevor probably suffered more than anybody else. That was unfair. He didn't have any say in it,' – GREG CHAPPELL

'Fifty thousand people left the MCG today feeling just like I did when I saw the movie *The Sting*; they were shaking their heads asking: 'What the hell happened there?' – DOUG WALTERS

'Greg should have been praised rather than pilloried for exposing, albeit to his own advantage, a glaring loophole in the laws,' – DENNIS LILLEE

'The chance of my hitting a six must have been one in thousands,' – BRIAN McKECHNIE

'Yes, Greg Chappell, you may be a great man who doesn't sledge, never unnecessarily appeals when bowling and never shows disapproval of the decisions of umpires. But in a game surrounded by fine sportsmen intent only on playing the game, you dared to publicly display that you were prepared to win without actually cheating. You should have been more underhanded,' – journalist HUGH LUNN

Trevor Chappell says his infamous underarm delivery against New Zealand has haunted him ever since — and he fears Australia's 2018 ball-tampering trio Steve Smith, David Warner and Cameron Bancroft may be similarly affected.

Calling the finish to the ODI in Melbourne in 1981 as one of 'Australian cricket's darkest days', he said the moment has lived with him ever since. 'It will be the same for Smith, Warner and Bancroft,' he told Sydney's *Daily Telegraph*. 'They will struggle for the rest of their lives and be known as the ones who brought Australian cricket into disrepute.'

New Zealanders have always treated him kindly and with respect since the underarm incident. 'Mostly the incident is taken in a light-hearted manner,' he says. 'There were certainly plenty of comments from the crowds at the cricket, but nothing more than at games I've been involved in back in Australia.'

He has been regularly invited back to NZ to talk about the underarm — and on the first occasion to play in a double-wicket competition alongside … McKechnie!

Chappell is irked that the incident still is linked with bigger scandals such as the betting and match-fixing allegations which saw international captains Muhammad Azharuddin, Saleem Malik and Hansie Cronje disgraced.

'Cricket is not the gentlemen's game that it has long been made out to be,' he said. 'I have no problem accepting that the underarm was not in the spirit of the game and shouldn't have happened, but it wasn't cheating and it was nothing like the controversies of Bodyline or matchfixing.'

7 Underhanded

EARLIER THAT TUMULTUOUS DAY: NZ captain Geoff Howarth clips Dennis Lillee through midwicket. He made 18

- THERE WAS A comical finale to the Chappell grubber in Sydney in-between ODI finals. Doug Walters said if anyone tried to bowl at him underarm he would hit it for six. Allan Border was immediately sceptical and bet $10, with Rod Marsh acting as referee and stakes-man. After practice the trio went out to the SCG No. 2 and Border bowled an underarm. Walters waltzed out to meet it, flicked the ball up with his foot and hit it high over the boundary and onto nearby Driver Avenue! An incredulous Border appealed for lbw. 'Nar, not out,' said Marsh. 'He was too far down the wicket.'

  NZ's captain Howarth said there was a green lining to the incident with cricket being on every front page. 'All New Zealanders were up in arms,' he said. 'It was a marketing ploy sent from heaven. It was the best thing that ever happened to the game here. Everyone was talking about it.'

RINGLEADER: Dennis Lillee was pivotal in the establishment of the rebel World Series Cricket movement. Cricketer magazine

8 WORLD SERIES CRICKET

Packer's raid

'C'mon… there's a little bit of whore in all of us. How much do you want?' said Kerry Packer to Australian cricket powerbrokers Bob Parish and Ray Steele in the magnificent Victorian Cricket Association mahogany room in the winter of 1976. 'Gentlemen… name your price.'

The pair demurred and Packer left the meeting feeling he'd been treated with contempt. He'd offered them seven times more than their long-time TV partners the ABC. Packer ran second to nobody. Within months the opportunity came to get even…

Still intoxicated by the runaway success of its mega birthday party, the 1977 Centenary Test, Australian cricket foremost authorities were stunned when almost 30 of its finest, including Greg Chappell, Dennis Lillee and Rod Marsh were pirated by TV tycoon Kerry Packer to form a breakaway cricketing troupe.

In a masterstroke of daring, confidential planning, Packer and World Series Cricket smashed an establishment monopoly, introduced exciting, entertaining innovations to captive new global audiences and ushered a fresh prosperity for the game and its elite players.

The world's best secretly signed contracts guaranteeing them the security they had always been denied. Establishment cricket was plunged into a bitter 23-month conflict with Australia's richest man, hell-bent on obtaining exclusive television rights for his Channel Nine Network. For him, cricket was a rating's goldmine…

Ironically Melbourne's epic Centenary Test was also to be the venue for Packer's coup de grace, when the media magnate knew that he had the Australian cricket establishment at his mercy. After the rejection of his $2.5 million five-year offer for exclusive television rights for his Nine Network, Packer embarked on a ruthless revenge mission which changed the game forever.

WORLD SERIES WARRIORS: *Back row, left to right: Dennis Lillee, Martin Kent, Ray Bright, David Hookes, Richie Robinson, Max Walker, Ian Redpath, Kerry O'Keeffe. Middle: Rick McCosker, Graham McKenzie, Wayne Prior, Ashley Mallett, Len Pascoe, Mick Malone, Ian Davis, Gary Gilmour. Sitting: Trevor Chappell, Doug Walters, Greg Chappell, Ian Chappell (captain), Rod Marsh, Bruce Laird, Ross Edwards.* Austin Robertson/Cricket's Outlaws

Believing the ACB to be insular and ultra-conservative, Packer said, 'we'll do all we can to cooperate with the Cricket Board and, if they cooperate with us, there is no reason why Test cricket as it is now will be affected. But if they don't, they'll walk straight into a meat mangler.'

By injecting his considerable reserves of private capital into the game he loved, Packer refined and expanded the embryonic World Series Cricket concept of some weekend one-day exhibitions, into a brilliantly contrived assault on the game and its traditions. So successful was the bombshell raid on the establishment's finest that the original wish to underwrite a series of matches for his prime-time summer television audiences was transformed into a full-blown winner-take-all international triangular tournament involving the champions of the game from almost every country.

As Packer's intermediaries made contact with the very best cricketers worldwide, they unearthed a wall of resentment apathetic administrations had ignored for years.

In the game's biggest controversy since Bodyline, not only did world stars and Test captains such as England's Tony Greig and West Indies' Clive Lloyd turn renegade, so did every notable Australian player — including major box office attractions the Chappell brothers, Lillee, Rod Marsh and, in the second year of the rebel league, Jeff Thomson.

In two seasons Packer's costs ballooned past $30 million but he had also gained 600 hours of television for his network and an arsenal of new advertisers all jockeying for prime-time slots. Cricket and TV was a beautiful mix and Packer was preparing to fund a third season, with a Pakistani visit followed by a tour of India when the ACB, having also accumulated heavy losses throughout the furore, brought an end to the impasse, a hush-hush meeting between Packer and Sir Donald Bradman critical in a compromise.

The Board granted its arch-foe exclusive television rights for 10 years, totally reassessed its scale of player payment and included the provision for bonus prize monies. WSC players were allowed to re-enter official competition without prejudice or penalty, many having originally been stopped from even training with their long-time club teams. From 1977-79, none could play in officially endorsed competitions. In Melbourne, the highest-available standard to rebels Ray Bright and Richie Robinson was suburban club cricket. Max Walker spent the early weeks of the season with Melbourne CC's Club XI.

Many of the players referred to Packer as 'The Godfather', someone who genuinely loved to dote on and mix with the sports stars he so admired. 'He kept every promise and then some,' said frontline Victorian batsman Ian Redpath. 'I snapped my Achilles in my second game and Packer came down by helicopter, landed on Kardinia Park and came up to see me at the Geelong hospital. He even organised a TV for me. Kerry Packer had the resources and the medium of his television network to do the experiments the ACB had never contemplated. In the end both learned from each other.'

Redpath was guaranteed more in two years of WSC than he earned in six years with the ACB — without the heartaches. 'For the first time players had a financial base in which they could plan their lives,' he said. 'And Packer realised just how important cricket's traditions were. The cricket was hard and tough. And we travelled all over the place. But Packer himself was very, very good. I'd come back from playing every Test in the West Indies [in 1973] and didn't even get a game the following summer against New Zealand. I couldn't afford not to play [WSC].'

The South African Barry Richards was offered three times his annual salary playing county cricket with Hampshire. After years of isolation the opportunity to once again mix with and oppose the world's very best was heaven-sent.

Not only did Australian administrators restructure key player conditions and soon implement the first fulltime contracts, it based many of its future financial projections around the day/night formulas which had so flourished under Packer. Even his establishment arch-rival Bob Parish conceded that Packer deserved deep gratitude for the game's facelift, which ushered in fresh riches and followers and dramatically raised its popularity and profile. 'He did the game a good turn,' Parish said. 'With the expense of all the court cases, some we won, some we lost, cricket was losing a lot of money.'

Day/night cricket and now its extensions like Twenty20 cricket have been a veritable money tree for the game. There has also been a considerable flow-on effect, with white-ball fans also following Test match cricket. Until Packer stamped his imprimatur so

> ### FOUR WORLD SERIES HIGHLIGHTS
>
> - Greg Chappell's Caribbean batting brilliance in 1979: he hit three 100s in consecutive Supertests, none better than his 150 in Port-of-Spain when he came to the wicket at 2-0 and left at 9-256, a match-winning contribution in a low-scoring game won by the WSC Australians by 24 runs.
> - Dennis Lillee's seven for 23 to rout the WSC West Indies for 89 in the fourth Supertest at the Sydney Cricket Ground in 1978-79. He dismissed six of the top seven batsmen in one of his finest yet least-recognised moments.
> - Barry Richards' masterly double-century for the WSC World XI in the Supertest at Gloucester Park in Perth in 1977-78. He added a WSC record 369 for the first wicket with Gordon Greenidge. Next in was Viv Richards. He made 177!
> - David Hookes' astonishing 81 from as many balls at the Sydney Showgrounds in 1977-78. He struck Joel Garner for 17 and Michael Holding for 22 from an over in an exhilarating display on the fastest, bounciest strip any of the players ever encountered. Shortly after the tea break he was in a car being driven by Kerry Packer to hospital, his jaw broken by a Andy Roberts' bumper. So lightning-fast was the wicket that earlier in the day Greg Chappell had struck Viv Richards in the face with a bouncer.

boldly on the game, short-version cricket had been little more than an incidental. The ACB's very first one-day international fixture had been fixtured purely as an afterthought.

Before WSC, the only major grounds with lights were football stadiums. Now all Australia's major grounds are floodlit. And at the bastions of traditional cricket — the Melbourne Cricket Ground, Adelaide Oval and elsewhere — the Packer blueprint is increasingly fashionable, with quality turf wickets being prepared in huge concrete bases off-site before cranes lift them into position at the start of each new season. Equally important are other Packer-inspired innovations such as coloured clothing, on-field microphones, white balls with black sightscreen and numerous extra television cameras giving fans the best seat in the house from both ends.

Packer's millions changed the very look of the game and the lives of the world's Test stars of the 1970s — and those who followed. The man may have been brazen and abrupt — the ACB first learned of the rebel matches via the media — but cricket's popularity spiralled incredibly in the '80s thanks to increased marketing, jingles, merchandise and quality TV coverage. Two teams toured each summer, for Tests and/or ODIs, encouraging captive new audiences.

Pre-Packer, Australia's world-champion cricketers, including some of the game's most charismatic stars, were earning peanuts — little more than $66 a day, plus ever-so-modest expenses. While their take home pay had increased by the time of the Centenary Test, the idea of an updated provident fund had floundered. So discontented was the influential elite that most couldn't sign quickly enough. There was certainly no 'partnership' as exists now with players and administrators working towards growing the game.

Not surprisingly, the maverick fast bowler Lillee was the first to commit… and the last to sign. He was one of the instigators so there was no need to chase him too hard. According to his manager and founder and director of WSC Austin Robertson jnr., Lillee, circa 1977, was being paid 'fish and chip money'. With no base contract and ongoing physiotherapy bills to pay for a bad back sustained while representing Australia, what choice did he have? Lillee believed that starting salaries for the game's best cricketers should be $25,000 minimum. Under a rival promoter, he was to receive a guaranteed $35,000 a year for three years (allowing for inflation, this equates to almost $150,000 a year now).

CHAPPELLI: with his I Bat for World Series t-shirt. Bruce Postle/Cricketer magazine

As others joined in the crusade, a bitter wedge was driven between the ACB and its leading players, with the Board too late to recognise the level of discontent. When it did act and agreed to increase match fees, the breakaway plans were already hatching.

In the late-'90s champion cricketers threatened strike action to help their state-level peers win a larger slice of cricket's thriving income streams. The high-profile frontliners of the '70s did the band of young, up-and-coming future stars a financial favour by activating a set of lucrative salaries and contracts that form the basis of the game's new professionalism and rewards with 26 cents in every dollar tracking back to the players. Today's champions can play well into their mid-30s, even at state level, whereas their predecessors would have long retired to re-enter private enterprise and work at reviving their cricket-deprived personal incomes. Bob Cowper, one of the few to score 300 in a Test match, played his last Test for Australia at 27 so he could pursue

STATESMAN: *Bob Parish in 1977 with a young Ken Piesse, then a feature writer with* Cricketer *magazine in Melbourne*

a career in international finance. Fellow Victorian Paul Sheahan was even younger at 26 when he retired to be a schoolteacher.

Even the best players were uncertain of ongoing selection and dismayed by the modest rewards it brought. Graham McKenzie was never the same after his stunning omission as a 26-year-old in mid-series against the 1967-68 Indians, explained by the selectors as allowing them to experiment with pace back-ups approaching an upcoming Ashes tour selection. McKenzie was the world No.1 paceman at the time — one journalist in Perth described him as 'more popular than Vegemite, more famous than the Swan River'. In his previous Test in Melbourne he had taken seven for 66 and three for 85. At midday on the murky opening morning, India was 5-25. They'd been McKenzied. It was the most stunning start to an MCG Test in years.

When Bob Simpson announced that he would be retiring at the end of the series, having just captained Australia in a record 29th Test, he was dropped and like McKenzie missed a match fee. He always regretted sharing his future intentions so early with Don Bradman. McKenzie's non-selection was a public relations disaster for the Board and further widened the gulf between the administration and its players. Soon afterwards, at the conclusion of an arduous six-month tour of Ceylon, India and South Africa in 1969-70, a fifth Test match in Johannesburg was mooted only for the two sets of administrators to argue over the player payments. The Australian Board was only prepared to pay an additional $20 for a total of $200 per player. Vice-captain Ian Chappell wanted $500. He believed after such a long campaign that the Board owed it to the players to give them a decent bonus. 'We were sick of being pushed around,' he said in his book *The Cutting Edge*.

Captain Bill Lawry insisted that the players had to be unanimous in their approval, but with Chappell and McKenzie leading the dissenters, the game was never played.

It was just three years since the death of Kerry Packer's father and media monolith Sir Frank Packer. Kerry's inheritance included Sir Frank's flourishing television and media empire. His eldest brother Clyde had fallen out with his father years earlier.

Packer, 39, was a hard-nosed, domineering, sports-loving businessman dictated to by no-one. His enemies portrayed him as a hammerhead shark. Rarely was he ever beaten in business.

His interest in underwriting a rebel series and providing his network with hours of extra, potentially top-rating sport was fuelled by the game's 1970s boom period when the Australian XI under Ian Chappell revived and rose to world-champion status in front of huge, adoring nationwide television audiences.

Packer was shocked how little they were earning, but he didn't enter cricket to be philanthropic. He wanted top-rating shows and if it was sport, so much the better. Cricket was ideal as advertisements could be shown every four minutes in-between overs.

Just months after his unsatisfactory meeting at Jolimont with Parish and Ray Steele, John Cornell, 'Strop' from the popular Paul Hogan Show, floated the idea of Packer staging some one-day matches involving some of those he was co-marketing like Lillee, Marsh and a swashbuckling youngster from Adelaide by the name of David Hookes.

Packer liked it. But why not do it properly, he said. 'Get the world's best cricketers to play the best Australians. All of them.'

He was well aware of cricket's ballooning, irresistible popularity. In the summer of 1970-71 viewers in the capital cities and most major country areas were for the first time able to watch virtually every ball via the ABC. The six Tests drew more than 600,000 spectators, while the daily television audience by the summer's climactic end were estimated at being around one million. Between 1974-75 and March 1977 and Melbourne's Centenary Test, more than two million fans were to attend 16 Tests, with millions more watching on TV. In 1977 Packer's Channel Nine offered 150,000 pounds — twice the asking price — for exclusive rights to the Ashes series in England.

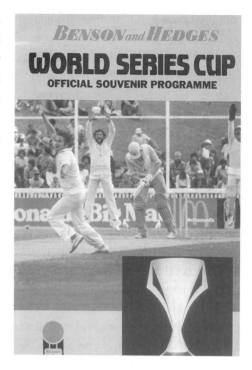

Once Packer started his revolutionary day/night match coverage, his network reported even bigger ratings. The first match under lights, at the Sydney Cricket Ground in late 1978, was a runaway success, with Packer ordering the gates to be opened after the dinner interval. While the cricket itself was mundane, more than 50,000 jammed into the ground.

Richie Benaud, leading the Channel Nine commentary team, said it was one of the most wonderful sights he had witnessed. In *Not just an Autobiography*, he wrote: 'The Hill was packed, the outer was packed. The members' stands were packed… the attraction of the day/night match, the excitement of the lights and the wonderful atmosphere combined to make it an evening I'll never forget.'

Tony Greig had echoed these thoughts on the first night at VFL Park in Waverley 12 months earlier. 'Between innings, we took supper in the underground restaurant and the sight that greeted us as we walked up to pitch level again was one that will live with most of us for the rest of our lives. More than 22,000 were in the stadium and the big-powered lights beaming down onto the green turf created a tingling, expectant atmosphere. There is something about sport at night which touches the nerve ends and this was no exception. We knew at that moment that the battle was being won.'

In other capital cities such as Adelaide, the one-day games also captured the imagination. The very first WSC one-dayer at Football Park, West Lakes, attracted just 1690 fans, but the last, when local hero Hookes hit West Indian Andy Roberts for two 6s in a row, drew almost 20,000.

The WSC Supertests produced a set of tough, unrelenting contests with winner-take-all purses guaranteeing peak effort, every over, every match.

World Series also made money on its tour of the West Indies in 1979. By comparison, the ACB lost heavily in 1978-79, despite the presence of its traditionally biggest drawcard, England, for six Tests.

The television ratings and gate figures favoured establishment cricket, but the standards achieved by the WSC players was on another level to those participating in traditional ranks.

Some of the performances were truly breathtaking from the mega-stars such as Lillee, Viv Richards, Greg Chappell, Barry Richards, Andy Roberts and Hookes.

Tailenders no longer batted without helmets with opposing fast bowlers peppering their counterparts with almost as many bouncers as the recognised batsmen.

Many, like Lillee, performed at a stellar new level. It was unlikely that Lillee would have played much past 1977 in establishment ranks unless payments and conditions dramatically improved.

While he loved cricket and, in particular, bowling as fast as was humanly possible, without the momentum and extra monies created by World Series, he believed he would have finished well before his 30th birthday. For years, even the top-liners received only minimal rewards and as Test selection was by invitation only, if a player preferred not to play there were dozens of others desperate to take his place.

Lillee's enthusiasm and motivation for the game were rekindled by Packer's dollars and the challenge of the Supertests, which were played with an unmatched intensity and hostility. When the plan was being hatched and fine-tuned in New Zealand in early 1977, WSC masterminds Austin Robertson and Cornell conducted an experiment during the Auckland Test. Having gleaned from Lillee how keenly the players would compete for winner-take-all prize money, they offered him $50 for every run he made over 20 and $200 for every wicket he took before their late afternoon connection back to Sydney. He made 23 not out and was savage when Australian No. 11 Max Walker holed out. In the first 40 minutes before Robertson and Cornell left, he took four wickets. He was $950 richer.

So how could a private promoter so boldly usurp the ruling body and secretly sign the cream of its stars, many during their finest hour? Those responsible for the recruiting operation, Robertson and Cornell, still marvel at the ease of the strike.

Lillee was the initial go-between who made most of the Australian introductions in the opening months of 1977. While most meetings were in dressing-room corners and hotels, others were in less salubrious surroundings. In Doug Walters' case, it was a dusty, out-of-the-way cement bunker at the back of Auckland's Eden Park. Waiting for Walters in the room, which had no chairs and a solitary light globe only just hanging from a thread from the roof, Cornell, ever the joker, couldn't help himself. 'Dougie,' he said, looking serious. 'Don't suppose you can lend me a couple of bucks!'

The Centenary Test in March provided the perfect forum to consummate the deals, not only with all the current players but with the recently retired old stars like 36-year-olds Redpath and McKenzie, attending as guests of the Board. Robertson was a regular in the rooms. One night he handed Walters his WSC signing-on cheque with a 'here are those theatre tickets Dougie'. Eleven of the 12 Centenary Test Australians (all except Gary Cosier) had been earmarked by sole selector Ian Chappell. Most signed on the spot. While all of them knew they were risking long-term bans, the prospect was exciting of being part of 'The Best versus The Rest' breakaway matches. The two- and three-year contracts guaranteed money only achievable in traditional ranks over a six- or seven-year period – *if* their form was good enough to keep them in the Test mix.

Tony Greig handled the overseas signings. For the leading West Indians like Viv Richards and Michael Holding, their $25,000-a-year salaries represented almost five times the monies earned touring England with the official West Indian team the previous winter. Unlike the Australians, the WSC matches were unlikely to affect their international schedules. 'We weren't philanthropists. We had a job to do,' said Robertson. 'There was no "Ha-ha, this is behind everyone's back."'

Only a few of the Rest of the World squad rejected the advances, the most notable being England's Geoff Boycott, who initially said he was 'in' before he was disallowed to take the contract away to have it checked by his solicitor. Boycott had even attended the Packer's luxury house to assess his young son James' cricket. Boycott wasn't enamoured, but Packer disagreed. 'Packer thought he knew more about cricket than me,' Boycott said. 'I told him that making money was his job and playing cricket was mine.' He was immediately replaced by Greig as the World XI's skipper.

Some players who went uninvited were shattered, like the just-retired Australian leg-spinner Terry Jenner, who was playing suburban turf competition in Adelaide. He was desperate to be given a contract. Instead the reserve spinner job went to his long-time ally Ashley Mallett.

Until 1977, the Australian Cricket Board's annual sponsorship stream and surpluses centrally revolved around the corporate support of its No. 1 backer, the Benson & Hedges Company. Media rights were insignificant. Never before had an entrepreneur ever offered anything like the money Packer proposed in Melbourne in mid-year 1976. 'I could tell by their looks,' Packer said later in a court hearing. When Parish demurred and suggested it best for Packer to try again in three years, a collision course was inevitable. Prepare to be mangled.

By the following May, 35 of the world's finest players had signed with JP Sport, Robertson and Cornell's sports promotions company, at a cost of more than $2.6 million. Most agreed to terms of two and three years. Some, like steely Englishman John Snow, then 35, committed for only one.

Each player approached kept the details confidential. 'But there were no secrecy clauses or anything like that,' said Robertson. 'They were just asked to keep it to themselves. Their word was good enough for me.'

Nothing was leaked in the press — though in late April there was a single-column item in a South African Sunday paper with an indirect reference to a privately promoted international cricket series likely to involve four of the leading Springboks Richards, Graeme Pollock, Eddie Barlow and Mike Procter.

On the last day of the Centenary Test, with Australia in sight of its epic 45-run win, Marsh, having finally agreed to sign, took up his usual position behind the stumps after the lunch break. Looking across to slip and Greg Chappell, he said: 'Well, pal, looks like this is about the last time we're going to be standing out here for a while.'

With his best poker face, Chappell said, 'Wadda ya mean?'

'You bloody well know what I mean,' said Marsh, smiling.

One of the last to sign, Marsh knew he was forfeiting his chance to captain Australia. But as he said in *Cricket Outlaws*, 'I knew I could never play without my mates. In the end it was a no-brainer. I just had to be a part of it.'

Only a few of cricket's biggest names refused the lures from World Series. Among them was India's little master Sunil Gavaskar. He was committed to come to Australia anyway with the 1977-78 Indians.

Graeme Pollock and fellow South African signee Denys Hobson were late exclusions after members of the West Indian team, including emerging fast bowler Michael Holding from Jamaica, said they were not prepared to play alongside anyone with direct links to Apartheid cricket. Neither Pollock nor Hobson had played professionally outside South Africa. Packer met with Jamaican Prime Minister Michael Manley and a compromise was achieved. WSC agreed to contract only those South Africans who had played at English county level.

Soon afterwards, Packer expanded his operation to include an entire West Indies squad, most of whom had toured England in 1976. He hosted a party for the West Indian players, wives and partners at the luxurious Sandy Lane Hotel in Barbados, using his private jet to help pick up the guests from each of the islands.

Packer had earlier won an injunction and claimed damages in the London High Court in an action against the ICC and the English Test and County Cricket Board, which had decided from October 1 1977 that any WSC-contracted players would face Test bans. In a marathon hearing which went into a seventh week, Justice Slade said such a ban was an unnecessary restraint of trade. He was surprised that a private promoter had not mounted an earlier challenge.

Packer told Ian Chappell that he was to be captain. Told that his brother Greg was captain of Australia, Packer said: 'No, you're captain. What do you think this is? A democracy?'

The 66 players initially contracted to World Series Cricket were:

AUSTRALIA (28): Ian Chappell (captain), Ray Bright, Greg Chappell, Trevor Chappell, Ian Davis, Ross Edwards, Gary Gilmour, David Hookes, Martin Kent, Bruce Laird, Rob Langer, Dennis Lillee, Ashley Mallett, Mick Malone, Rod Marsh, Rick McCosker, Graham McKenzie, Kerry O'Keeffe, Len Pascoe, Wayne Prior, Ian Redpath, Richie Robinson, Jeff Thomson, Max Walker, Doug Walters, Graeme Watson, Kepler Wessels, Denis Yagmich.

WEST INDIES (18): Clive Lloyd (captain), Jim Allen, Richard Austin, Colin Croft, Wayne Daniel, Roy Fredericks, Joel Garner, Gordon Greenidge, Desmond Haynes, Michael Holding, David Holford, Bernard Julien, Collis King, Deryck Murray, Albert Padmore, Vivian Richards, Andy Roberts, Lawrence Rowe.

REST OF THE WORLD (20): Tony Greig (captain), Dennis Amiss, Alan Knott, John Snow, Derek Underwood, Bob Woolmer (England); Eddie Barlow, Garth Le Roux, Mike Procter, Clive Rice, Barry Richards (South Africa); Asif Iqbal, Haroon Rasheed, Imran Khan, Javed Miandad, Majid Khan, Mushtaq Mohammad, Sarfraz Nawaz, Zaheer Abbas (Pakistan); Richard Hadlee (New Zealand).

Alvin Kallicharran (West Indies) withdrew; Intikhab Alam (Pakistan) originally signed but wasn't required. Superstars Jeff Thomson and Graeme Pollock appeared in the second year.

Peter McFarline, cricket writer with the Melbourne *Age*, first found out in March that something big was developing. An influential contact in cricket administration had asked him to find out if there was any substance to a story revolving around some leading players and a series of exhibition games. In association with Alan Shiell, an Adelaide-based journalist, McFarline went delving. A colleague at the *Age*, Mike Sheahan, who was in New Zealand for the short tour which preceded the Centenary Test, had reported back that the television personality John Cornell was spending a lot of time with the team, especially Lillee. When quizzed, he had said it was all about arranging some TV work for Australia's No. 1 fast bowler to help supplement his cricket income. In one of the great sports media careers, it was one of the few times Sheahan didn't get the full story.

McFarline flew to England keen to do some further exploration. The Australians were at Hove, playing an inconsequential county game against Sussex, when the story finally came together. Shiell learned about it over lunch with the manager of Barry Richards, the great South African whose Test career had tragically lasted just four Tests after South Africa was isolated from the world game. McFarline, too, found out much in conversation with the legendary John Arlott, the doyen of English broadcasters.

At last some of the throwaway lines from cricketing acquaintances and friends that they would be seeing him for Christmas started to make sense. 'Sheff [Shiell] and I went for a walk,' said McFarline in the Age, 'and pooled our information… together we went to the Australian dressing room and asked to see Greg Chappell, the captain. After explaining what we knew, Chappell uttered one of sport's great untruths. Leaning casually against the door, he said, "Sounds like a good idea. I'd like to know more about it." With that, he retired to the sanctuary of the dressing room. But Shiell and I had our story. With a lot of guessing we came up with 44 names we believed had signed with Packer. Forty-four out of 52 [who initially signed] wasn't bad.'

When news of the scoop circulated that night at a party at Tony Greig's house in Hove, beginning a wave of headlines which made the Ashes series suddenly insignificant, Chappell wrote to Parish and Bradman outlining his reasons for signing with World Series Cricket and saying that the players hoped they could play in the private matches with Board permission. Deep down he resigned himself to never playing for Australia again. Chappell had committed to Packer for five years. Twelve of the other 16 tourists to England in 1977 had also agreed to cross to Packer-controlled cricket.

Had the ACB had their time again they would have withdrawn the rebels then and there and picked an entirely new squad. The first of the five Ashes Tests was still six weeks away. It seemed they were still basking in the euphoria of the Centenary Test. The team battled on but was ultimately thrashed 3-0 and in fact won only eight of their 31 matches on tour. There was little camaraderie or focus. Their hearts and minds were elsewhere. 'We should have been sent straight home,' said David Hookes, years later.

Chappell's biographer Adrian McGregor said that on Parish's arrival in London in June for an International Cricket Council meeting, Chappell saw him in the foyer of the team's hotel, the Waldorf:

> CHAPPELL: 'Excuse me, Bob. I'd like to have a chat with you at some stage.'
>
> PARISH: 'I don't think we have anything to discuss.'

HOOKSEY: Was the darling of World Series crowds

Given the enormity of their decision to leave the cricket fold, the failure of the 1977 team was understandable. They were facing lengthy bans, which for the younger players, in particular, left them alone and uncertain. Hookes had only just turned 22 and had joined initially believing he could play both World Series and traditional cricket.

Even a meeting with Packer and Cornell in Packer's swank private suite at the Dorchester had left questions unanswered. The itinerary was open-ended and dependent entirely on venues, which were still to be negotiated. It was debatable whether any of the mainstream grounds would be available. There was talk of bans and restraint-of-trade actions. Also weighing heavily was the public backlash against the players, who were perceived as mercenaries unconcerned with centuries of tradition. One newspaper dubbed them 'The Dogs of Cricket'.

Greg Chappell was accused of betraying trust and deceiving the Board. He was part of the player sub-committee established just a year previously to give players a stronger say in the running of the game, including increased pay and improved conditions.

It was a troubled time and merely the prelude to almost two years of a cricket war which cost jobs and sponsorships, affected friendships, slashed dividends and triggered huge financial losses. But long-term, the upside was to be considerable. Packer had done everyone a favour. As Hookes loved to say: 'Every modern cricketer should thank Kerry Packer each and every night before he goes to bed.'

THE REACTION

'They seem to think we're only interested in bleeding the game dry, without worrying about the consequences it would have on future cricketers,' – IAN CHAPPELL

'There are 500,000 cricketers who would love to play for Australia for nothing,' – Australian Cricket Board of Control secretary ALAN BARNES

'We've been accused of betraying the game because we decided to play for the money we think we're worth,' – TONY GREIG

'People think I'm crook on cricket circuses. I'm not. I think there's a place for that kind of cricket – some place like Siberia,' – Australian Cricket Board of Control treasurer RAY STEELE

'He [Ian Chappell] pointed out that if I did not join WSC cricket, there would be something missing from my life,' – India's champion SUNIL GAVASKAR

'I feel privileged to have been personally involved in something which shook the cobwebs out of our game, breathed new life into it and elevated the professional cricketer to a financial status he had never before enjoyed,' – VIV RICHARDS

'World Series Cricket, or some such revolutionary institution, was always going to happen. You cannot suppress highly talented, intelligent men,' – English cricket writer IAN WOOLDRIDGE

'If you want to look at circuses, you'd better look at Australia fielding its third XI,' – KERRY PACKER

'The use of private promotional money to establish top-class cricket outside the existing international framework is undesirable,' – English cricket writer ROBIN MARLAR

He [Kerry Packer] had no intention of screwing the [traditional] game, but the ACB forced his hand,' – DAVID HOOKES

'Forty years on, the impact of the *World Series Cricke*t revolution is still being felt in every facet of the game,' – SHANE WARNE

Meckiff: "I quit it all— dagger blow"

The Sun
NEWS-PICTORIAL
44 FLINDERS ST.
12,855. Melbourne, Tuesday, December 10, 1963. 56 Pages

BUREAU SAYS: CITY: Mild. Humid. Fine with thunderstorms towards evening. Expected top temp... Weather map is on Page 43.

by IAN MECKIFF
exclusive to The Sun

I HAVE retired from all forms of cricket.

I have done this on the advice of Australia's two most senior Test selectors, Sir Donald Bradman and Mr Jack Ryder.

Since Col Egar, the umpire, called me four times for chucking in my only over on Saturday I have had long conferences with both men.

And they have left it indisputably clear that the only course left for me is to quit the game I love so dearly.

Sir Donald talked with me for two hours on Sunday and he was obviously upset and shocked at Saturday's calamity, which hit me like a dagger in the back.

He left no doubt in my mind that my selection for the First Test against South Africa had been with his full approval.

'Premonition'

Although I'm quitting, I am, of course, prepared to play this Test right through.

I am deliberately breaking the player-writer rule to make my story known to the public. I can't be fined anyway.

Sir Donald was not out-voted in my selection by Mr Ryder and Mr Dudley Seddon and he told me he thought my bowling action basically fair this season.

But he said that he had an awful premonition that I might be called for throwing by either Umpire Egar or Umpire Lou Rowan.

"The best thing you can do, Mecky, is retire," he said.

And I acted as ordered.

Mr Ryder, who came to my hotel room on Sunday morning, gave me three choices.

- To retire forthwith.
- To keep on playing for Victoria in Melbourne, but to step down for matches when either Umpire Egar or Umpire Rowan was officiating.
- To take a fortnight away from cricket before making a decision one way or the other.

I knew I'd had my chips — P. 2

GLAMOR was on a pedestal at St. Kilda beach yesterday ... in the form of Norwegian-born Ellen Neydal.

Ellen made her own lifeguard's look-out by piling these beach chairs.

Glamor in the chair

KIDNA SINAT jun. H...

STATELINE, Mon., AAP. — men kidnapped Frank Sinatra's old son, Frank, j... motel on the Nevada border...

As a big police ed, Sinatra, sen., used plane to fly from Palm Reno, and took a car to scene.

Police are hunting fo... men they describe as "dangerous," who they... from a Californian voc... tute and are wanted for b...

Local sheriffs followed th... kidnappers' car into Nevada, obliterated the tracks.

Sinatra, jun., also a sing... at a motel called Harrah's Californian side of the bor...

He was believed to be performing at Harrah's Casino, 50 yards away on the Nevada side of the border.

A companion, John Foss, 24, a trumpeter, said that they were eating dinner in Sinatra's room.

About 9 p.m. someone knocked at the door and said that he had a package for Sinatra.

The man, wearing a ski jacket, rushed into the room with a revolver and ordered Sinatra to go with him.

Another man in a ski jacket was outside. The two drove off with young Sinatra.

Taped w...

Sheriff Ernest Carlson said detectives the gunman ord... Sinatra to lie down, and tap... together.

His partner came in... they took a wallet and one of the men said, "We better take one of them with us."

Mr Dean Evans, of Harrah's Casino, said that Foss told him one of the men also exclaimed: "We've got him. We've got to get him to Sacramento."

Sacramento, the Californian State capital, is about 85 miles due west...

9 1963 BRISBANE

Thrown out

Until the rise of match-fixing in the '90s, throwing was cricket's most heinous crime. The most high-profiled victim was Australian express bowler Ian Meckiff who was brutally no-balled from the game in an undignified public humiliation of the highest order. Was the slim Victorian left-armer really a cheat? Was it a set-up? And what role did Australia's selection chairman, the all-powerful Sir Donald Bradman, play in it all?

Saturday, December 7 1963 is an unforgettable date in Ian Meckiff's life. His joy at his shock recall to the Australian Test XI was short-lived. Outlawed for almost three years for a suspect action caused by his permanently bent left arm, Meckiff was no-balled four times for throwing in his return Test. Stunned by the renewed taints and wondering if it was all a set up, he retired immediately from all grades of the game, even refusing to play social matches in case someone yelled: 'Chucker'.

In just one gut-wrenching over from the Vulture Street end of Brisbane's Woolloongabba ground, Meckiff's world crumbled. His second, third, fifth and ninth deliveries of the opening Test against Trevor Goddard's 1963-64 South Africans were no-balled from square leg by South Australian Colin Egar. As he repeatedly thrust out his right arm, Egar knew the ramifications. As Australia's senior umpire, he believed he had a responsibility to act, even if it meant ending a friend's career. 'Let's face it, somebody had to do something,' he said.

He could have called more, but that would have only magnified Meckiff's humiliation. Only one other Australian had ever been called for throwing in a Test match — Ernie Jones, 70 years previously.

For years, illegal bowling had been an enormously emotional issue. Australian captain-to-be Bobby Simpson called it 'an insidious evil' and recommended all throwers be run out of the game. India's Nari Contractor almost died from a skull fracture after ducking into an express pitch from 'Chuckin' Charlie' Griffith in Bridgetown. South Australia's new-ball pair Alan Hitchcox and Peter Trethewey possessed actions so questionable they were dubbed 'Pitch-cox' and 'Treth-throwy'. In England, the actions of several were also under question but umpires, loath to damage their own careers and those of others, rarely created ripples.

Many thought Meckiff a victim of a conspiracy to cleanse the game of anyone with a less-than-pure action.

'I'd never say that "Meck" was a chucker,' said teammate Ian Redpath, one of three South Melbourne players along with Meckiff and debutant Alan Connolly in Australia's XI on that fateful day. 'He was stiff.'

Even a captain as celebrated as Richie Benaud has been targeted, the inference being that he was 'in' on the dramatic events and that he had deliberately batted higher than usual, at No. 6, so the selectors, chairman Sir Donald Bradman, Jack Ryder and Dudley Seddon, could choose a fifth specialist bowler as 'insurance'. The truth was that Benaud had no say in selection and like everyone else read about it in the newspapers. And when Meckiff was no-balled, Benaud was as upset as anybody. 'His eyes were fairly popping,' said wicketkeeper Wally Grout in *My Country's Keeper*.

Ryder, 74, who had given a lifetime of service to the game on and off the field, was staunchly pro-Meckiff and even after his no-balling in Brisbane, told Meckiff he'd be picking him again for Victoria if he so desired. He had always refused to study slow-motion film. The umpires had to judge on eyesight and so would he.

Redpath said Meckiff was a genuine in-swing bowler who, especially earlier in his career, hit the pitch as hard as anybody he opposed, including all the much-vaunted West Indians. 'It's a very difficult thing to do: throw a ball and swing it at the same time,' said Redpath. 'We were all very surprised.'

Despite his wickets blitz, guaranteed to embarrass even the thickest-skinned selector, Meckiff's against-the-odds recall was the bombshell of the long-awaited Springbok summer which also introduced the hottest teenage talent in the world, 19-year-old left-hander Graeme Pollock from Port Elizabeth.

Meckiff's re-emergence as the most devastating strike bowler in the country had seen him amass 75 wickets in two full seasons — two-thirds being top-order wickets including 20 opening batsmen. He'd taken 11 wickets in Victoria's first two games of the new season. From the time Meckiff had dismissed Western Australia's star West Indian import Rohan Kanhai for 0 and 5 in Victoria's opening match of the 1961-62 Sheffield Shield season in Melbourne, loyal Victorians had been advocating his return. Not only was he genuinely sharp, he could swerve the ball back into the right-handers and jag it away.

The support for his recall reached crescendo levels. At the MCG, Melbourne's sporting shrine, he was almost as popular as wintertime folk hero, Ron Barassi. He'd hold the new ball up to them at the start of a game and they'd roar like they were at a football match. His mates called him 'The Lord Mayor' or 'The Count' and said if he ever stopped cricket, he could take a pick of any job he wanted in politics.

Among his backers were many media men with influence. They were disdainful of the selectors bolstering an ageing pace attack with others who were slower and not as well performed. Tall Victorian Colin Guest played in the third Ashes Test against Ted Dexter's tourists and the much-admired South Australian all-sportsman Neil Hawke in the fifth. Both were purely medium-pacers.

Few could argue with Guest's inclusion, even if it was to be a one-off. He'd taken 31 wickets in five matches and played for the Australian XI against the Englishmen. However, a month later when the athletic Hawke was promoted for the first time, his figures of 17 wickets in eight matches paled against Meckiff's 41 in seven. Hawke relied mainly on seam rather than intimidating speed for his wickets.

When visiting South African captain Trevor Goddard casually mentioned his hunch that Meckiff would make Australia's first Test XI, an Australian Board of Control member immediately offered him 33/1. According to Ray Robinson, Australia's most noted cricket writer, at least two Board delegates, including Queensland's Clem Jones, had objected to Meckiff's return. Even with his so-called 'new' action, they reckoned he was a thrower and should remain in the back-blocks. Wasn't it the International Cricket Conference's desire to eliminate bowlers with suspect actions? The makers of the *ABC Cricket Book* penned a list of potential Australian players likely to play in the 1963-64 Test series and Meckiff didn't even make the top 25.

Bradman and Ryder had watched Meckiff bowl in Victoria's Sheffield Shield game against Western Australia in Melbourne, a game in which he took the first five WA wickets to fall during an inspired opening spell of five for 34 in eight overs. At one point he was into his third over and had three for 0. When John Inverarity took a single to momentarily thwart Meckiff, the crowd booed.

In an extraordinary high-scoring start to the summer — in which Bobby Simpson's first four knocks were 359, 4, 246 and 247 not out — few fast bowlers had any form at all. The great Alan Davidson had retired. So had potential first change, Queensland all-rounder Ken Mackay. Western Australia's strapping young paceman Graham McKenzie was a stand-alone No. 1 replacement despite in the lead ups having taken just five Shield wickets at an average of more than 90 apiece.

But the depth in the back-up ranks fell away dramatically. In the absence of the left-armer Hugh Bevan, chosen for the Australian XI after snaring 13 wickets mainly with angle in two games against the visitors, McKenzie's new-ball partner back at the WACA was an Englishman, Peter Loader. In South Australia, the new ball was shared by another player ineligible for the Test team, visiting West Indian Garry Sobers. New South Welshman Frank Misson hadn't figured in any of Australia's previous eight Test matches, controversial teammate Gordon Rorke with the big drag had played his last interstate match, Hawke was experimenting with his action, while Meckiff's club and Victorian teammate Connolly was then an uncapped tearaway.

When Bevan failed to take a wicket against the Springboks for the Australian XI in the Melbourne 'Test trial' and Misson was only marginally more successful against the tourists in the following match — the same weekend in which Meckiff devastated the WA top-order — Bradman and Co. decided they had no choice but to pick the popular Victorian. Retirements of key players had left Australia vulnerable. The Springboks were shaping as a very powerful unit, Brisbane was a batting paradise and young Pollock a threat, as shown by his century-in-a-session against formidable New South Wales.

Despite the selectors' change-of-heart to recall Meckiff, it seemed it must have been a split vote. Or maybe they sought a once-and-for-all answer into the legality of Meckiff's action, with two neutral umpires making judgement away from Meckiff's home town.

Egar's umpiring partner was Brisbane detective Lou Rowan, who said he was shocked when he heard of Meckiff's recall.

Meckiff himself said you could have knocked him down with a feather. 'I still can't believe it has happened,' he told reporters. 'It was like winning a record dividend in the soccer pools.' Three long, frustrating years in the wilderness were over.

As a fourth-form student at Mordialloc-Chelsea high school 40 minutes south of the Melbourne CBD, Meckiff once roosted a ball over fully-grown pine trees bordering the school and onto the opposite side of the Mordialloc creek, a huge hit, especially for one so slim and in his mid-teens.

In his first four seasons of competitive cricket with the Mentone under 16s in the Frankston-Glenhuntly (later Federal) Cricket Association, he was a sensation, taking almost 200 wickets. Mentone Oval where he began his career on matting-covered concrete is now known as the Hogben-Meckiff Oval.

Season	Wkts	Ave
1947-48	26	11.31
1948-49	51	4.03
1949-50	62	3.20
1950-51	58	3.48

In his final year, aged 15, he played in the under 16s in the mornings and with South Melbourne in the afternoons. In 1951-52, having just turned 17, he opened the bowling in South's first-ever senior premiership. One of his teammates, Jeff Hallebone, was to be stand-by player for Australia's 1956 touring team to England.

After seeing his cricket career end prematurely, Meckiff became a single figures golfer and reduced his handicap to three. He also rose to the rank of captain at the prestigious Victoria Golf Club, in tree-filled Cheltenham, south of Melbourne.

DOUBLE-JOINTED: Ian Meckiff could engender near express speed from just 16 paces

The international outcry against the legality of Meckiff's action had begun in the New Year of 1959 when Peter May's Englishmen were humbled for 87 with Meckiff, in only his sixth Test, taking three for 69 and six for 38. That night in the Melbourne *Herald*, Meckiff, the local hero, was accused of 'throwing England out' by just-retired Test player Johnny Wardle, his rapid-fire demolition sharing front page billing with a Soviet attempt to fire a rocket at the moon. Many in Fleet Street shared Wardle's indignation, one dubbing Meckiff an ogre and a cheat who was bringing the game into disrepute.

In the Melbourne *Age*, cricket writer Percy Beames had a more measured response: 'It is a great pity English pressmen had to wait until Meckiff's success on Saturday to launch their accusations against the fairness of his delivery,' he wrote. 'But it is not surprising. It has its precedent in the first match of the tour with West Australian Keith Slater. No exception was taken to Slater's bowling action until he burst into prominence by taking four for 17 in a devastating burst in the second innings. Immediately he was dubbed a chucker.'

For Meckiff, a softly-spoken father of two, who had never been 'called' at any level, the criticism was stinging, especially with the throwing controversy ballooning throughout the Empire. In the 1960 English season, five county players were called and the South African Geoff Griffin reduced to bowling underarm after being repeatedly no-balled by England's No.1 umpire, Sid Buller.

Australian administrators were so concerned that its potential 1961 Ashes attack could be decimated by similar calls that six months before the tour's scheduled start, it negotiated a truce where throwing would be allowed without penalty, at least for the first six weeks of the tour leading into the first Test. Only from June 7 would English umpires be permitted to call any suspect bowlers. Previously, if they had suspicions, they could object only in writing. It seemed an extraordinary compromise. As it eventuated, none of Australia's most suspect bowling specialists, Meckiff, Rorke or WA's Keith Slater, were chosen.

Meckiff's omission from the Ashes squad was particularly controversial, Victorians believing he'd been made a martyr. Other than the country's premier paceman, Alan Davidson from New South Wales, Meckiff was the most experienced fast bowler in the nation. He was also the fastest, despite being hamstrung in the only two Tests he did play in 1960-61, an Achilles injury re-flaring in the tied Test in Brisbane and a back problem ending his summer in mid-Test in Sydney.

Four fast bowlers were chosen: Davidson, who had played 34 Tests, Misson three, Ron Gaunt one and McKenzie none.

With the Australian Board of Control's 'no comment' contracts applying only to the 17-man squad, Meckiff released a book, *Thrown Out*, proclaiming his innocence. He'd been 'passed' in five major cricket playing countries, Australia, New Zealand, South Africa, Pakistan and India, and was sick of being branded. Ever since the salvo from the English press, he'd been harassed, at practice, in his office and even at his golf club. If his ball happened to land in a bunker, wise-cracking partners told him to chuck it out.

BEST SELLER: Ian Meckiff's breezy autobiography appeared soon after his exclusion from the 1961 Ashes tour party

Meckiff admitted his wristy, front-on action may not have been as pure as some, but any jerkiness was an optical illusion. He'd been born with a permanently bent elbow and was unable to fully extend or straighten his arm. He firmly believed he remained within the laws and spirit of the game. Despite only a languid, 16-pace run-up and shortish follow-through, he could bowl at express pace thanks to being double-jointed in the shoulders, which allowed him extra flexibility.

Meckiff had enjoyed a meteoric rise, making his first Australian touring team, to New Zealand in 1957, after just seven first-class matches. His demolition of England in his hometown debut in 1958-59 was to be his highpoint. And for two years he was among the headlining cricketers in the country, before suffering the ligament damage to his back in the 1960-61 Sydney Test which sidelined him for the rest of the summer.

Casting aside his immediate thoughts to retire after his non-selection for England, Meckiff began training with the South Melbourne footballers, looking to increase his endurance. He also modified his action leading into the popping crease, trying to keep his left arm as straight as possible.

Several at Board level, however, believed his action was still dodgy. By not calling Meckiff and others with suspect actions, administrators believed they were inadvertently encouraging a legion of fresh chuckers.

At the centre of the issue was Sir Donald Bradman, Australia's selection chairman and prominent member of the Australian Cricket Board of Control. He and Board chairman Bill Dowling had been to London where the issue was keenly debated by the International Cricket Conference, the game's ruling body. As part of a clean-up campaign, it was decided that umpires would have full official backing to enforce Law 26 against those they felt were throwers or draggers (bowlers who flouted the no-ball rule by dragging their back foot across the crease). Each State held a forum involving captains, senior players and umpires. In Adelaide, at the old members' dining room, During his address the Don reinforced the need for bowlers with suspect actions to be discouraged.

In the opening months of 1963, Meckiff was twice no-balled for throwing, by Jack Kierse in Adelaide and second-game umpire Bill Priem in Brisbane. And in 1963-64, 11 players in club ranks around Australia were called. Egar, who had stood in nine of the previous 10 Australian Test matches, led by example, targeting two Adelaide club players, West Torrens' Fred Bills and a long-time offender, Prospect's Tom Watt. Two years earlier, at Sheffield Shield level, Egar had caused a stir by standing back from the bowler's end stumps and twice calling South Australian Brian Quigley at the Adelaide Oval. Quigley never represented his State again.

Until January that year, one of Meckiff's biggest allies had been his Victorian captain Bill Lawry. During the Adelaide Test, Bradman held a dinner for the visiting Sheffield Shield captains at his home in suburban Kensington. Lawry, Richie Benaud (NSW), Barry Shepherd (WA) and Ken Mackay (Queensland) were present. He showed frame-by-frame film of Meckiff and others with suspect actions. The case against Meckiff was damning, even with his so-called 'new' action.

Previously Lawry had sided with Jack Ryder. He didn't believe Meckiff was a thrower. 'But that evening ... a camera showed that Meckiff bent his left arm at the point of delivery,' he said.

In what amounted to the first emphatic use of video film technology in Australian cricket, it was clear that when slowed down, Meckiff's action was questionable and contravened the laws and spirit of the game. Benaud's reaction was immediate. He said he wouldn't continue to bowl anyone who had been called for throwing. Furthermore, he'd not bowl anyone in his team he considered suspect. Yet, just 10 months later, here he was being asked to captain a player whose action had been damned and by one of the people who selected him, Bradman.

As Lou Rowan and Col Egar walked onto the 'Gabba for the start of the Test, they already knew their ends. Rowan, being from Brisbane, would take the northern end and Egar, from Adelaide, the south. It was a habit they were to have through all 19 of their Tests together.

WILL HE, OR WON'T HE?, the *Courier Mail* had asked on the morning of the match, pondering Meckiff's fate.

Local umpire Bill Priem was so convinced that something was about to erupt that he'd taken his camera to the game and was fully focused on Egar. Standing outside the square leg boundary filming Meckiff from in front of the scoreboard was South Africa's team manager Ken Viljoen.

After Australia had started with 400-plus and South Africa began its reply right on 2 pm on day two, Richie Benaud opened with McKenzie down-breeze and Meckiff, the quicker of the two, coming back up the slope. Normally at the 'Gabba, the fastest bowler came down the hill from the Stanley Street end.

Egar, at square leg, was suddenly in the position of being the chief executioner. He allowed the first ball, to Springbok captain Trevor Goddard, to pass before making the first of four calls which created worldwide headlines and closed down a career.

'It was the biggest decision I had to make in cricket,' he said years later in the Melbourne *Sun*. 'I thought the first ball Meckiff bowled was suspect. On the next I took the plunge and called him. I think I heard a pin drop in the outer. It was that electric. Then I called him again ... and again — four times in all. Meckiff bowled 12 balls and I would rate eight of them as illegal. But if I had kept calling him, when would he have finished his (8-ball) over?'

Meckiff said his first delivery had been deliberately slow, his normal warm-up delivery. His second (which was called) was faster. 'I felt vastly more relaxed for my second delivery. I wound up more easily on my approach and sent one down much faster. Almost simultaneously with my release of the ball came the most condemning shout I had ever heard. "My God," I thought. "He's called me."'

Meckiff stood in mid-pitch, bewildered. 'I couldn't believe what was happening. My knees were weak and my legs were shaky as I came in again and again a man I had counted a friend called me. This was the most numbing blow of all.'

Watching on from the pavilion, South African fast bowler Peter Pollock said it was as if 'an atomic bomb had hit the place'.

Benaud approached Meckiff in mid-over:

> BENAUD: 'I think we've got a problem here, Dad… just keep your arm as straight as possible.'
>
> MECKIFF: 'That's what I'm doing.'

Meckiff was in a daze as he finished off the over. Benaud told him why not let one go at full throttle and see what happens? Meckiff's mind was so scrambled he hardly

> **CALLED FOR THROWING IN A TEST MATCH**
>
> 1. Ernie Jones (Australia) v England (Melbourne), 1897-98 (by umpire James Phillips)
> 2. Tony Lock (England) v West Indies (Kingston, Jamaica), 1953-54 (Perry Burke)
> 3. Geoff Griffin (South Africa) v England (Lord's), 1960 (Sid Buller)
> 4. Haseeb Ahsan (Pakistan) v India (Bombay), 1960-61 (S. K. Ganguli and A.R. Joshi)
> 5. Ian Meckiff (Australia) v South Africa (Brisbane), 1963-64 (Col Egar)
> 6. Syed Abid Ali (India) v New Zealand (Christchurch), 1967-68 (Fred Goodall)
> 7. David Gower (England) v New Zealand (Nottingham), 1986 (Ken Palmer)
> 8. Henry Olonga (Zimbabwe) v Pakistan (Harare), 1994-95 (Ian Robinson)
> 9. Muthiah Muralidaran (Sri Lanka) v Australia (Melbourne), 1995-96 (Darrell Hair)
> 10. Grant Flower (Zimbabwe) v New Zealand (Bulawayo), 2000-01 (Darrell Hair)
>
> - India's Syed Kirmani's no-ball to end the Fourth Test at Bridgetown in 1982-83 was believed to be for throwing

heard him. After his 10th delivery, he turned to umpire Rowan and asked how many balls were left. 'Two,' he said before grinning: 'if they're legitimate.'

Others too had been no-balled for throwing, but not after being recalled from years in exile, like Meckiff. No cricketer had ever been so publicly humiliated.

Egar said the no-balling of Meckiff was the biggest decision he ever made in cricket. Years later at the height of the controversial reign of Sri Lanka's bent-armed spinner Muthiah Muralidaran, the rules were changed to allow a flex of around 15 per cent at the point of delivery. It kept a champion in the game. Egar told Meckiff: 'The way the rules are today, you'd be 100 per cent pure.'

Meckiff said he and Egar never really discussed the events of that December Saturday in Brisbane. 'Whether he was told by Bradman (I don't know). It was said that Bradman called together a lot of the umpires in Adelaide because he wanted them to clean up a lot of throwing problems because they had a couple of guys there that were a bit suspect.'

Egar had umpired Meckiff five times previously without calling him. 'The season before he'd stood in a Shield game in Adelaide and I bowled something like 30 overs for the game without him calling me,' said Meckiff. 'He was at the bowler's end all the way through.'

Asked if he believed he'd been victim of worldwide action to suppress throwing, Meckiff said: 'It's difficult to know if it was pre-arranged … but the more I hear, the more I believe it was got up to put me out of business.'

Umpire Lou Rowan said if there had been a conspiracy to no-ball Meckiff from cricket, he wasn't told. 'I simply refuse to believe that such was the case,' he said in his autobiography, *The Umpire's Story*.

Egar said if I had not made the calls, he would have been 'less than fair and honest to myself, Ian Meckiff and to the game of cricket'.

Rowan looked across to Egar several times during that fateful over. 'I gave him a little signal as if to say: "Whatever happens, pal, I'm with you."'

Egar said his no-ball calls against Meckiff had not been pre-meditated. 'My only judgement was what I saw at the time,' he said.

Asked why he hadn't no-balled Meckiff previously, Egar said he was either at the

'MECKIE': One of cricket's genuine nice guys

bowler's end or hadn't believed, then, that Meckiff was operating illegally. 'Never did I have pre-meditated thoughts about any of the bowlers I called,' he said. 'At times there were bowlers I believed suspect and I did speak to their captain. Invariably they'd oblige and say, "Let him finish the over" and then take him off. This happened at club and Shield level.

'With "Mecko" the press kept writing things up. You tended then to occasionally have a look. It had been an unwritten law though that only the fella at square leg would call. When I broke it and called a guy for throwing from the bowler's end, the crowd gave me a real shellacking.'

In 1965, Egar was invited to South Africa and stood in three games. He also privately offered his opinion about several bowlers Springbok officials thought may be suspect.

Richie Benaud denied a deliberate example had made of Meckiff. Throwing had been cricket's hottest topic in the late '50s and early '60s. He rated Egar as one of the game's finest umpires. 'His work in the tied Test series with Col Hoy (1960-61) was outstanding and if I had the choice of two umpires to stand in a cricket match it would be Egar and England's Sid Buller,' he said.

Having also umpired Australian Rules football from 1950, Egar said he was used to the abuse. 'I've never regretted anything I've done,' said Egar, 'or things like the criticism, the brick through the window [at work] or the filthy letters which my wife refused to show me.'

Meckiff was just 28 and in his prime. Having bowled the final deliveries at half pace, he trudged in a daze into the off-side ring. While the 'Gabba crowd sheltering from the heat on the old mounds under the ground's huge weeping fig trees clapped and roared encouragement, not a word was said on the field. Everyone was too stunned.

The 'Gabba crowd was so boisterous and Alan McGilvray's ABC description so loud and invasive in the middle that Goddard complained and umpire Rowan approached the pavilion, asking for a message to be relayed to the crowd to turn down their transistors, or at least use their ear-pieces.

During the delay, Benaud consulted with Meckiff. 'I'm afraid this is the finish, Dad. I can't bowl you any more.'

Meckiff: 'Well, if that's it, OK.'

Minutes later, at the start of the fourth over, Benaud introduced Connolly for his first over in Test cricket. Meckiff, capless and standing at the stumps, was a forlorn figure. There were prolonged jeers all around the ground, even from the members, for Benaud for withdrawing Meckiff, and later too, when it was obvious he didn't intend to switch him around to the Stanley Street end.

'I wasn't just the brunt of the booing, I was almost the total booing!' Benaud said. 'There was just over 10,000 in, but they sounded more than that. They wanted to see Ian bowl from CJ's (Egar's) end so that Lou Rowan would have to give a second opinion. I stuck to what I'd said for some years, that I would accept whatever an umpire said and did about any of my bowlers. I can't remember being surprised (at the hostile reception), but Alan Connolly and Tom Veivers were, as they were also booed when I brought them on to bowl. And, they were making their Test debuts, Tom on his home ground!'

The eight-minute over and resultant uproar was the most dramatic scandal in Australian cricket since Sid Barnes took the austere Board of Control to the Supreme Court over his non-selection for reasons other than cricket in 1951-52.

Pro-Meckiff supporters condemned umpire Egar and the timing of his calls. Benaud was also abused for not switching Meckiff to the Stanley Street end.

Chants of 'We want Meckiff' and 'Give 'im a go!' continued all afternoon. At the close, a number of the crowd rushed the field and hoisted an embarrassed Meckiff shoulder-high and carried him to the players' race.

'It was just not possible to bowl him again,' Benaud said at his Saturday night media conference. Explaining he wanted to avoid any more acrimony, Benaud said to have continued with Meckiff would have only added to the fall-out. 'I bowled Meckiff for hundreds of overs before umpires who approved his delivery and I have accepted their decision. Now that an umpire does not accept Meckiff's delivery, I accept that decision, too. I will not bowl him again.'

Former Australian captain Lindsay Hassett was among the critics who believed Benaud had taken the easy way out. Others to support Meckiff included another ex-Test captain Ian Johnson and Invincible tourist Doug Ring.

BRISBANE 1963: South Africa's captain, the left-handed Trevor Goddard is on strike to Meckiff. Richie Benaud has three slips and a gully and a leg slip, a popular catching position now rarely used

Benaud said there had been widespread suggestions pre-match that Meckiff's action would be subject to the closest scrutiny. But the no-ball calls had still come as a tremendous shock. Writing in his Sydney newspaper column several days later, Benaud said: 'It defies description — the feeling that hits players when there is a no-ball called for throwing... one can only assume that the game was carried on by instinct for a while, for the Australian players were not "with it". You could count the number of words spoken on the field on the fingers of both hands... it was an experience no one would wish to go through again.'

Yet no one endured as much as Meckiff, and it seems amazing that he had to be publicly humiliated in a game as important as a Test match. Later on that night, at Lennon's Hotel, Egar was invited to join several of the players, Meckiff included, for dinner. 'I'm sorry this had to happen,' he told Meckiff. 'The second most upset person in the world is me.'

Leading into the infamous Test, the pair had won a lawn bowls competition together. Egar had even brought the trophy to Brisbane to give it to him. They remained good mates right up to Egar's death in 2008.

Days after his explosive exit from Test cricket, Meckiff agreed to a series of ghosted articles in which he said Bradman had spoken with him for two hours the following day advising him to retire.

'He was upset and shocked at Saturday's calamity,' said Meckiff. 'Sir Donald was not outvoted in my selection by Mr Ryder and Mr Dudley Seddon and he told me that he thought my bowling action basically fair this season. But he also said that he had an awful premonition that I might be called for throwing by either Egar or umpire Rowan. He told me: "The best thing you can do is retire Mecky," he said.'

Meckiff claimed he had been 'the fall guy'. Had he not been recalled into Test ranks he would have happily continued with Victoria for years.

Years later he conceded: 'In the cold hard light of everything… I must now concede I was a chucker.'

One night at a cocktail party at the Melbourne Cricket Ground, Meckiff was abused by a cricket official who'd heard Meckiff was considering legal action to clear his name. 'He threatened that if I went ahead with a court action, I'd be very sorry,' Meckiff said in *Cricketer* magazine.

'I was told I wouldn't be able to play first-class cricket anywhere but Victoria. To even play district cricket in Melbourne you could always run into an umpire who wanted to get his name in the paper. I was far better out of it all."

Twenty years after the Brisbane drama, Meckiff did bowl again – and with Egar umpiring. Both were at a gathering of former cricketers, umpires and media at Ayers Rock for a friendly match between celebrity teams captained by Colin Cowdrey and Rod Marsh. Egar was one of the umpires. And he was at the bowler's end for Meckiff's first delivery. 'No-ball,' he yelled, just for old time's sake. Everyone knew it was a set-up.

THE REACTION

'When you get your feet chopped from underneath you, it's pretty hard not to be bitter,' – IAN MECKIFF

'A very decent Australian has been sacrificed from the altar of stupid officialdom and I don't mean by that umpire Egar. I have never liked Meckiff's action but it should never have come to this,' – JACK FINGLETON

'I feel sorry for the wretched Meckiff. There is something pathetic about watching a man's life crumble, especially a man who is a charming character off the field. without a shred of conceit or malice in his make-up,' – GRAEME POLLOCK

'No dog's hind leg could have been straighter than Meckiff's arm as he delivered most balls of the fateful over,' – RAY ROBINSON

'The selection misfired and it must now be recognised as the greatest mistake in cricket administration wished on a nation for many years,' – PERCY BEAMES

'When "Meck" was younger, jeez he was sharp. You'd stand in the slips to him and any edges would really fly. He was one of the quickest blokes into the pitch you'd ever see, easily as quick as the West Indian fellas. I have no hesitation in saying he was forced out of the game,' – IAN REDPATH

'Mecky was one of the nicest guys you could possibly play with. It's a great credit to him that he hasn't been soured by the whole incident. It was a tragic thing to happen,' – ALAN CONNOLLY

MORNING OF HIS LIFE: Frank Tyson's seven for 27 at the MCG castled the Australians. He celebrated by going to the movies with a couple of his teammates

10 1955 MELBOURNE

Time of the Typhoon

The heat was murderous: 104 degrees one day and 107 the next. Even at midnight on the rest day of the New Year's Test, the temperature touched 96. So dry and cracked was the Melbourne Cricket Ground's Merri Creek pitch that first-game curator Jack House broke the rules and watered it when most of Melbourne was still at church. There was a furore. Highly embarrassed by House's renegade act, senior Australian officials even offered to call it a 'no match'.

Frank Tyson was furiously fast; the most menacing Englishman downunder since Harold Larwood and Bodyline. As a 16-year-old representing his village XI Knypesley, he'd crashed through the defences of the champion Australian Cec Pepper first ball in a leagues match.

Eight years later, his debut Ashes Test in Brisbane had been a disaster. Preferred to ageing champion Alec Bedser for the 1954-55 series opener — a virtual world championship showdown — he'd been smashed and England humiliated.

But having been 'sconed' by Ray Lindwall in the preceding Test in Sydney, Tyson responded with a frightening burst of sheer speed which saw the tourists square the rubber.

Suddenly the Melbourne Test had an extra edge. This truly was going to be an Anglo-Aussie showdown to savor.

Famed for its size and massive seating capabilities, the MCG's northern stand had been flattened in preparation for an even bigger three-tiered stand being built for the 1956 Olympic Games. Those in lofty Yarra Park suddenly had a free peek of cricket and football games. On the opposite side, the large gap between the southern stand and the green concrete stand housing the old scoreboard often saw peak-hour traffic in adjacent Brunton Avenue slow to a stand-still, fans enjoying the opportunity of

TERRIFYING: Frank Tyson, 24, was the intimidating difference in England's series win in 1954-55. Twenty-five of his wickets came in three Tests mid-series. Never again was he to bowl so consistently fast

seeing a ball or two bowled. Some of the trains from Flinders Street would stop. Everyone was cricket mad and huge crowds were to attend despite searing heat rising to unprecedented levels.

The game started in heatwave conditions on New Year's Eve, the soaring temperatures continuing unabated for 48 hours, the northerly wind fierce and unrelenting.

So oppressive was it on the Saturday that England bowled just 54 eight-bowl overs in five hours, captain Len Hutton employing deliberate go-slow tactics to conserve the strength of his bowlers and lull the Australian top-order into impatience.

With Australia 8-188 chasing England's 191, the game was delicately poised but seemed unlikely to go beyond four days given a disconcerting ridge at one end of the pitch. Enormous cracks had developed. So wide and deep were they in places that the fattest of fountain pens could easily disappear.

So rock-hard was the wicket by the second morning that expressman Frank Tyson's pace partner, the lionhearted Lancastrian Brian Statham twice skidded and fell in his delivery stride. Batsmen running up the pitch could hear their boot spikes clatter on the surface as if they were wearing tap shoes.

The wicket had been damp early, Keith Miller producing one of his greatest spells: 9-8-5-3 pre-lunch on the first day, less than 24 hours after having his wonky knee rejuvenated by one his racing mate Scobie Breasley's trusted masseurs who normally worked only with jockeys and horses.

Making his debut in front of family and many mates from the inner-west, Len Maddocks was relieved to see off the menacing Tyson and Statham and make it to stumps on the Saturday night unbeaten on 36. Batting for the first time in his career with a thigh-pad, borrowed from England's 12th man Vic Wilson, Maddocks had the major share of an important 37 run unbroken stand for the eighth wicket with captain Ian Johnson. 'Virtually every ball I faced from Tyson, if I'd missed it, it would have drilled me in the throat,' said Maddocks. 'I don't claim him to be the best bowler ever but he could well be the fastest ever. I'd step behind it, hold my bat in front of it and hope that it would hit a bottom edge and go for one. He didn't bowl any half volleys.'

Describing the wicket as like concrete in the final session on Saturday night, Maddocks and his captain were amazed on Monday morning to see the transformation. The cracks had all but closed. It was almost like a first day wicket all over again, only wetter.

'We went out to open the batting on the Monday and it was like walking on cheese,' said Maddocks, 'Your spikes were making a popping sound. The curator had watered it (on the rest day on Sunday) to try and hold it together. It was virtually a sticky (wicket) before falling apart again. Without the extra water the Test would never have lasted five days. It would have been all over in four. By the last day there were cracks going up and down and across the pitch that were literally inches wide. Depending on whether Tyson landed on the off side or the leg side, you'd get a fast, lethal leg or off cutter, or if he landed on the cracks going across, it either hit you on the foot or threatened to take your head off. It was impossible to bat on. Once the cracks re-opened, we fell apart.'

With seven for 27, Tyson tore through the pride of Australia's elite batsmen. The Australians were bowled out in an hour and a quarter on the final morning. Suddenly England had a 2-1 series lead with two Tests to play.

Just weeks before the wicket had also crumbled in the Victoria-MCC game and veteran groundsman Jack House was seconded to assist in preparing the best possible wicket for the Test match, the last at the ground for four years. House, 66, was responsible for the Albert Ground, the MCC's No.2 oval in nearby St Kilda Rd. He had joined the groundstaff just after World War I and had been crafting and repairing pitches and outfields for almost four decades.

With the fierce northerly winds sending the temperature gauge soaring, so cracked was the wicket by the Saturday night that House believed drastic action would have to be taken if the match was to extend past Monday night. Weeks earlier during the Victoria-MCC game, the club's new No.1 groundsman Bill Vanthoff had defied convention and repaired some very deep holes which had developed mid-match. Sir Donald Bradman was prime among many critics saying the quality of the wickets at the MCG were poor and not nearly of the standard reached under the previous care of Bert Luttrell, curator at the ground for 38 years. An out-of-favor Vanthoff was moved sideways and House promoted to oversee and prepare the pitches for the all-impoortant Christmas- New Year holiday matches between Victoria and NSW and the Test, which was due to run an entire week.

THE TOSS: *England's captain Len Hutton (left) and Ian Johnson at the toss on New Year's Eve, day 1 of the dramatic 1954-55 Melbourne Test. Having called correctly and elected to bat, Hutton watched in horror as his team collapsed for just 191 before Frank Tyson and Brian Statham triggered a brave comeback.* Gordon Vidler/Ken Piesse collection

But with 18 wickets falling on the first two days and fully cogniscent of how the mysterious holes had suddenly disappeared during the MCC match, House decided the pitch again needed some mid-match restoration. He dared not discuss his radical plan with secretary Vernon Ransford. Marylebone regulations forbade any watering of the wicket once a game started. House turned on the hose and showered the wicket for three, maybe even four minutes. Amazed at his temerity, his support staff went home to avoid being implicated.

BEST MATES: *Frank Tyson (right) with his pace partner, the lion-hearted Lancastrian Brian Statham*

Percy Beames, a former Victorian captain, covering the match for the Melbourne *Age*, was working from the newspaper's Collins Street office late on Sunday afternoon when he learnt of House's wildcat actions. Vanthoff had played football at Melbourne with Beames and was still steaming at his sudden downgrade.

Beames approached sports editor Harold Austin and told him of the scandal.

'Is it legal?' asked Austin.

'No.'

'Will it be good for cricket?'"

'No.'

'Well, we'll put it aside then, but get all the facts together.'

Alongside Beames' Sunday night copy, Austin included a paragraph, in reverse type, about how it was illegal to water wickets. Come the following morning, it was clear that the story had substance, despite the indignant denials from Ransford's office. Beames made a full exposure in Tuesday morning's paper. It was the scoop of his career.

'The game wouldn't have lasted,' said Beames. 'The curator (House) was overseeing his first Test. It was illegal but he did it with every good intention to save face. He wanted the game to go the full distance. We wrote that it had been watered and they (the Melbourne Cricket Club) threatened to sue us. But you could tell the way the spikes sunk in (that it had happened).'

GROUNDSTAFF: The MCG groundstaff including Jack House, who is second to the left behind the light roller. In his younger years House had been a League footballer with Melbourne. Also pictured are 'Dolly' (left), George Cross, Jack Brown, Ernie Tout, Herb Fry, Charlie Over, Alan Davidson, Ted Morton and the famed curator Bert Luttrell. This picture was taken in 1920.
David Studham/Melbourne Cricket Club

While Vanthoff had provided Beames with the tip-off, so open was the MCG that dozens of passers-up late on the Sunday afternoon must also have seen House with the hose.

The furore saw the Australian Cricket Board of Control go into damage control and consider offering the Englishmen a replay had they been beaten.

The Melbourne Cricket Club collected statutory declarations from staff including House, saying the pitch had not been tampered with. All sorts of theories were forwarded, from the apparent presence of an underground stream to abnormal sweating under the covers triggered by Monday's cool change.

The Australians established a 40 run lead, the courageous Maddocks finishing with 47, before England experienced the best batting conditions of the match and made 279. Reducing his run-up, Bill Johnston took five wickets and extracted sharp turn with his left-arm orthodox slows.

Set 240, Australia tumbled from its overnight 2-75, to be all out for 111, the last eight wickets falling for 34 runs, Tyson taking six for 16 from 51 balls. As stunned spectators took early trains back home, their lunches untouched, Tyson and his English teammates returned to the Windsor, Tyson among three or four to take in a movie matinee. For the second time in consecutive Tests, Australia had failed to chase down modest fourth innings totals.

In his autobiography, *A Typhoon Called Tyson*, Tyson said the abnormally hot conditions had so panicked House that he believed the match would finish in four days, if not earlier. 'If one put oneself in Jack House's shoes on that black Sunday, it must have seemed logical to water the wicket,' he said. 'He had been brought in to

1954-55 AUSTRALIANS (in Sydney, fifth Test): Back row, left to right: Len Maddocks, Ron Archer (12th man), Richie Benaud, Peter Burge, Billy Watson; Front: Les Favell, Neil Harvey, Keith Miller, Ian Johnson (captain), Ray Lindwall, Alan Davidson, Colin McDonald. The umpires are Mel McInnes and RR Wright.

prepare the Test wicket, expressly to prevent the recurrence of the crumbling wicket of the Victorian game (a fortnight previously). Had he not acted there can be little doubt that there would have been hardly any wicket left on the Monday.'

After holding the 'high ground' for much of the match, the much-vaunted Australians had been humbled. The holiday crowds were enormous, more than 300,000 seeing the five days, including 50,483 on the final morning, some of whom scampered onto the ground afterwards and secured a souvenir piece of precious centre wicket turf.

House had brought infamy to the match and Melbourne, but the financial benefits were enormous. The gate receipts totaled almost 50 thousand pounds, despite the loss of reserved seat revenue from the demolished Northern Stand. The tourist's share of the gate was almost 24,000 pounds, the largest cheque ever paid to a visiting team for a single week's cricket. And the Victorian Cricket Association's share of the receipts was 9000 pounds, almost half its total income for the entire 1954-55 summer.

- England was to win the series 3-1, 25 of Tyson's series haul of 28 wickets coming in England's three memorable victories in Sydney, Melbourne and Adelaide. It was the first time England had won the Ashes downunder since 1932-33. 'The 'Typhoon' was rarely again as lethal and always blamed the spin-friendly featherbeds at his home wickets at Northants for his premature exit from big cricket. He came to Melbourne to coach and teach Latin. His son Philip was also a keen cricketer, without ever even hinting at his Dad's furious pace. His mates at Carey called him 'The Breeze'.

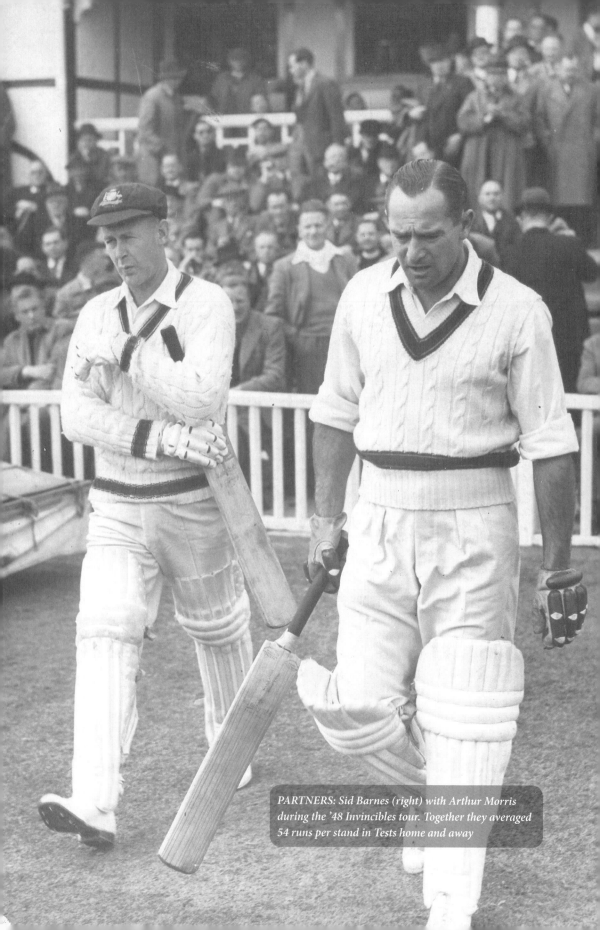

PARTNERS: Sid Barnes (right) with Arthur Morris during the '48 Invincibles tour. Together they averaged 54 runs per stand in Tests home and away

11 SID BARNES

Supreme Court

Sid Barnes had a lifetime habit of colouring opinion and being dismissive of authority. A showman, firebrand and an opportunist, he saw his selection for the most triumphant post-war Ashes campaign of all as an honour — and a chance to swell his tour fee through his wheeling and dealing. He was also the biggest name ever excluded from selection by a dictatorial, aloof and vindictive Australian Board of Control which was plunged into Supreme Court action in 1952 after Barnes was sensationally omitted from a Test XI for reasons other than cricket. Why was a 40-year-old clause used to terminate a career?

Not until 2017 was there to be a more publicised dispute or as stark a gulf between player and administration. The headline-chasing, argumentative war-timer Sid Barnes had a spectacularly-high Test average, matching his number of enemies in high places. Denied some of his best run-scoring years by World War II, Barnes withdrew from the 1949-50 tour of South Africa complaining that the tour fee was miserly and not befitting an Empire sportsman of his celebrity stature.

When Freddie Brown's Englishmen arrived in 1950-51, he again sat out even from club cricket, preferring a lucrative wage as a newspaper columnist rather than taking his chances at the selection table. His 'Like It or Lump It' column in Sydney's *Daily Telegraph* regularly took contemptuous aim at administrators, the majority of whom Barnes reckoned had never played anything but park cricket and were totally out of touch.

Had Australia not been as powerful and Barnes less brash and provocative, there may have been a greater urgency and well of support for his return in an Ashes year. Fast bowler Ray Lindwall claimed Barnes at the time to be the premier batsman in the world, superior even to the record-breaking Yorkshireman Len Hutton.

After three years of virtual inactivity and only two games of Sydney first-grade in four years, Barnes, then 35, committed himself to a comeback for the arrival of John Goddard's 1951-52 West Indians. He'd rise at dawn on the frostiest of Sydney winter mornings and jog around nearby Lindfield Oval. At lunch times, he'd practise his batting skills and arrange gifts for those who came along to bowl to him in the nets. Such was his profile that after only mediocre grade form with Gordon, he was immediately lifted into the New South Wales XI for the traditional season opener against Queensland in Brisbane. Later, he also acted as NSW's stand-in captain when Arthur Morris was absent on Test duty.

VINDICATED: *The front page of next day's* Sydney Daily Mirror

Australian selector EA 'Chappie' Dwyer was impressed by Barnes' form on his return to big cricket at the 'Gabba. While he made only 35, he told co-selector Sir Donald Bradman 'he was never at fault, hitting the ball in the middle and unfortunately the decision of LBW against him was extremely doubtful. While standing upright he was hit several inches above the pad (by Len Johnson)... remembering our difficulties regarding openers last year and having watched Barnes bat in Brisbane, I am of the opinion that he is very fit and his form stamped him as our best opener for the first Test (a somewhat surprising statement given that Morris had made 253 in the same match)

Australia's new opening pair Morris and Queensland's Ken Archer had been only semi-successful and when the old firm Barnes (107) and Morris (210) amassed an enterprising double-century stand for NSW against the old enemy Victoria in Melbourne, there was a clamour for his re-selection. Among those present were Test selectors Dwyer (from NSW) and Jack 'The King' Ryder (Victoria), who warmly congratulated Barnes in the rooms afterwards.

Barnes was confident Bradman would support him. He was also encouraged by a conversation earlier in the summer with Aubrey Oxlade, chairman of the Board of Control, who dismissed speculation that Board officials were disapproving of Barnes and said the sheer weight of runs remained the most important factor in Barnes' bid to regain his Test place. In his autobiography *It Isn't Cricket*, Barnes says Oxlade told him:

'You know what I think of you as a cricketer and as a man. It's just a matter for your own cricket bat. Good luck.'

While he'd averaged only 35 for the season, Barnes was included in a squad of 13 for the third Test, an extra player having been named because of doubts over the fitness of Australia's captain and No.3 batsman Lindsay Hassett.

But the Board referred the list back to the selectors, saying they objected to one of the 13. While they didn't name Barnes, it was clear who they were targeting. A newspaper poster proclaiming BARNES IN, BARNES OUT was the opening salvo in the controversy which was to grip leading politicians and end in the Supreme Court of Australia.

'I felt bitterly resentful,' said Barnes. 'It would not have worried me had the selectors not chosen me, had they considered me not good enough. That would have been their judgment, a judgment deserving every respect because of their deep knowledge of the game, but to have been chosen by the selectors and then tossed aside by the Board was the supreme insult. It made me feel like an unwanted cur.'

The flamboyant Sydney-based cricket writer Jim Mathers, never one to hide his opinions, said the Board had treated the selectors 'like flippant schoolboys'. The NSW Cricket Association had also been insulted, he claimed, as it had made Barnes its captain. An editorial in the *Sydney Morning Herald* said: 'If the Board thinks that its decisions are beyond question, it is due for disillusionment. This secretive and even furtive method of damning a player deserves strong censure.'

Most former Test players backed Barnes unequivocally. Arthur Mailey said if he was a selector he'd resign, Jack Fingleton claimed Board delegates were thin-skinned and snooty, Bill O'Reilly believed the Board deserved nationwide condemnation and Stan McCabe, best man at Barnes' wedding, called the whole affair 'scandalous'.

Days earlier in Melbourne, Hec de Lacy of the *Sporting Globe* had scooped everyone and telegraphed Barnes' sensational omission: 'If Barnes doesn't make the third or fourth Test teams, don't blame lack of ability or the selectors. If the selectors were unanimous in wanting Barnes, I doubt whether their wishes would be granted. When the selectors choose the side they must send it to the Board [for approval]. That might be Barnes' biggest hurdle. Usually approval is automatic. But I know for certain that if Barnes were named by the selectors, opposition by Board members would be strong enough to keep him out.'

The Board had never before exercised its option to veto. Chairman Oxlade, Frank Cush (also from Sydney) and Bradman opposed the motion, but nine other delegates voted against Barnes' inclusion. Recognising the inevitable backlash, given Barnes' popularity with the man-in-the-street, they successfully moved that matters of selection remain confidential and go un-recorded in the minutes. Whether it was coincidental or not, by July several members of the Board in Roger Hartigan and EC 'Son' Yeomans had stood down.

> **Re Barnes.**
>
> My advice is for you to keep quiet as an oyster and under no circumstances say anything. I can't tell you all the moves but I'm sure that is sound. You may be forced to speak later. If so please consult me beforehand. The position is very delicate.
>
> I shall await further news with interest.
>
> Kind regards,
>
> Don

HUSH HUSH: Sir Donald Bradman's advice to fellow selector Chappie Dwyer, March 5, 1952

In a chance meeting at McCabe's Sydney sports store, Oxlade congratulated Barnes on his Melbourne century and in the hearing of others claimed he had 'nothing to do with this nasty business'. Oxlade said what happened was scandalous and vowed at the next meeting to 'ask questions'.

Instead, Barnes had to endure a massive wall of silence. Frustrated by the inactivity, he eventually issued a press release, via prominent QC Jack Shand, saying that the secrecy surrounding the Board action had led to disturbing speculation 'injurious' to the well-being of both himself and his family. He was also angered that the powerful NSWCA continued to back him as state captain, yet did not demand an explanation from the Board as to his banishment from international cricket. It was clear that there were divisions at state headquarters in George Street as well, the third NSW delegate to the Board, Keith Johnson, manager of the '48 tour, inadvertently having been embroiled in affairs of protocol when Barnes filmed the royal family.

At the height of the controversy, it was learnt that hard-nosed Brisbane lawyer Jack Hutcheon — soon to be honoured with a CBE for his services to cricket — had led the pre-Christmas confidentiality motion. A domineering, stubborn and authoritarian figure, Hutcheon was among Barnes' most powerful adversaries, the two having fallen out years before when Barnes threatened to withhold his NSW team from the field in response to the Brisbane outfield being cut on the second morning of a Sheffield Shield game against Queensland. Hutcheon originally told him to mind his own business but backed off when Barnes said: 'Call off your panzer unit (curating staff) or I'll take my team off.'

Barnes further fuelled the controversy with a century against the Queenslanders in Sydney, days after the Australians had been beaten by the West Indies in just three days in Adelaide. In that Test, Hassett's 11th-hour withdrawal and Barnes' non-selection created an imbalance, with fast bowler Lindwall being promoted to No.6.

At the advice of Shand, Barnes wrote letters to each of the Board delegates but received only guarded replies, each word-for-word:

FEBRUARY 1952: Sixteen-year-old NSW debutant Ian Craig with 35-year-old Barnes at the Sydney Cricket Ground in the Sheffield Shield match against South Australia. Gordon Vidler/Ken Piesse collection

'Dear Sir, — I have your letter of the 11th inst., and I have noted the contents. I am unwilling to enter into any correspondence with you on the subject matter set forth in your letter.'

A dispirited Barnes felt defeated and that he had no further option, other than to appear in front of the Board at their next meeting, in spring. 'They were too strong and too silent for me,' he said.

SID BARNES IN SYDNEY GRADE CRICKET

BATTING

	Mts	Inns	NO	HS	Runs	Ave	100	50
PETERSHAM CC								
1934-35	8	8	1	113	249	35.57	1	0
1935-36	13	14	1	84	513	39.46	0	5
1936-37	10	11	1	190	723	72.30	3	2
1937-38	2	3	1	60*	63	31.50	0	1
1938-39	6	6	0	160	223	37.16	1	0
1939-40	9	11	3	187*	611	76.37	2	1
1940-41	7	9	2	228	506	72.28	1	2
1941-42	8	8	0	165	266	33.25	1	0
1942-43	20	21	6	125*	1333	88.86	4	9
WAVERLEY								
1943-44	10	10	1	119	449	49.88	2	1
NORTH SYDNEY								
1944-45	7	7	1	158*	707	117.83	4	2
1945-46	5	5	1	138*	254	63.50	1	0
1946-47	2	2	0	114	217	108.50	2	0
1947-48	did not play							
1948-49	did not play							
1949-50	2	2	0	28	30	15.00	0	0
1950-51	did not play							
GORDON								
1951-52	6	6	1	145	407	81.40	2	2
1952-53	2	3	1	13	31	15.50	0	0
Totals	117	126	20	228	6582	62.09	24	25

• Denotes not out

BARNES THE BOWLER: He also took 145 wickets at an average of 18.51 with a best performance of six for 92. He twice took five wickets in an innings.

He first played at Petersham from 1932-33 in the lower XIs.

Chart: Lyall Gardner

In a letter to Don Bradman in late February, Chappie Dwyer said the Board 'had handled the matter very badly'. He said even his own NSW Board had 'fallen down'.

The issue was unexpectedly reignited in April when a letter from Jacob Raith, a master baker and cricket lover, appeared in the Sydney *Daily Mirror*: 'It must be abundantly clear to all that they (the Board) would not have excluded Mr Barnes from the Australian XI capriciously and only for some matter of a sufficiently serious nature.'

At last Barnes and his supporters, who now included Dr Herbert V. Evatt, Leader of the Opposition and a vice-president of the NSWCA, had some ammunition. Claiming he had been slurred, Barnes went to court, seeking damages from Raith for libel — but more particularly to clear his name.

In essence, the Board of Control was on trial and Shand portrayed the delegates as elitist, cloistered, unaccountable and vindictive. To defend himself, Raith was forced to subpoena Bradman, Oxlade and other key members of the board.

Sir Donald was unable to attend as his son, John, had polio. But over two days, fellow Board men from secretary Bill Jeanes to Johnson and chairman Oxlade were grilled. Jeanes' initial objection to Board documents being made public was overruled by Mr Justice Lloyd.

Oxlade said in his evidence that Barnes was 'a bit childish' but did not consider overly serious any of his so-called misdemeanours which included:

- hurdling a member's turnstile after failing to produce his player's admission ticket during a Test in Melbourne;
- bowing to the crowd;
- filming the Royals;
- & playing tennis during a county match in 1948.

Manager Johnson was forced to expand on his written report after the '48 tour in which he said that the behaviour of the team, both on and off the field, had been exemplary. Indeed, Barnes had received a 150 pound good conduct bonus. As Mr Shand asked, why should he now, three years later, be making an issue of Barnes' behaviour?

Shand inferred that Johnson as a friend was treacherous. In fact, he was popular with most players it seemed, except Barnes.

Asked in detail about the incidents which made Barnes unworthy of selection, Johnson agreed the turnstile incident was prior to the 1948 tour and certainly had not made him unworthy of representing Australia on that tour.

Ernie Toshack and Barnes had played tennis at the back of the pavilion at Northampton in 1948, but it was Barnes' game off and Toshack, as 12th man and over the age of 21, was responsible for his own actions.

HOW SID BARNES COMPARES WITH THE BEST

ALL-TIME BEST TEST BATTING AVERAGES

Average	Name	Tests	Runs	HS	100s
99.95	Don Bradman (Australia)	52	6996	334	29
63.05	Sid Barnes (Australia)	13	1072	234	3
61.87	Adam Voges (Australia)	20	1485	269*	5
61.37	Steve Smith (Australia)	64	6199	239	23
60.97	Graeme Pollock (South Africa)	23	2256	274	7
60.83	George Headley (West Indies)	22	2190	270*	10
60.73	Herbert Sutcliffe (England)	54	4155	194	16

EIGHT OF THE BEST-EVER AUSTRALIAN OPENING PAIRS

Ave	Pair	Runs	100 run stands
71	Matthew Hayden & Phil Jaques	784	2
63	Bill Brown & Jack Fingleton	1020	3
63	Arthur Morris & Colin McDonald	949	3
59	Bill Lawry & Bob Simpson	3596	9
54	Sid Barnes & Arthur Morris	706	3
51	Matthew Hayden & Justin Langer	5655	14
51	Chris Rogers & David Warner	2053	9
51	Mark Taylor & Michael Slater	3898	10

Charts: Ric Finlay

Barnes had also obtained permission from Lord Gowrie, the aide-de-camp to the King, to take film of the Australians being presented to the Royals at Lord's. Permission had also been granted for him to film the Queen Mother at Windsor Castle and he had continued to be selected afterwards.

Johnson was forced to admit at best he was a fourth-grade cricketer. He agreed the worst thing that could happen to a cricketer was to be dismissed from a team on grounds other than cricket ability. The public could rightly speculate that the discarded player was guilty of dishonourable conduct. Quizzed further about the significance of the incidents, Johnson said that none of them, treated in an isolated fashion, justified exclusion from the Australian side; nor did two of the incidents. But he considered all three did. He also believed Barnes temperamentally unsuitable to be NSW captain — but he'd been outvoted.

NATIONAL SELECTORS: EA 'Chappie' Dwyer (left) with Sir Donald Bradman

Asked if he would select Barnes if he became a world beater who could bowl slow and fast, never missed a catch and averaged 200, Johnson initially refused to answer. When pressed by the judge, he said: 'No, I wouldn't.'

SHAND: And you say you have a wide national outlook for the best of the game?

JOHNSON: Yes.

SHAND: Do you still think you are qualified to be a member of the Board?

JOHNSON: Yes.

The Board was painted as an elitist band of autocrats, who had acted in a high-handed and unjustified manner. Raith told Barnes he would have never written his letter had he known all the facts. Raith agreed to pay Barnes' costs, Barnes waiving his damages claim of 1000 pounds, happy to settle for the crushing moral victory over the Board.

Newspapers proclaiming Barnes' victory sold out all over Sydney and beyond. It was as big as a St George premiership. VINDICATED trumpeted the *Daily Mirror's* banner.

THE AMAZING WORLD OF SID BARNES

- He once took 40 runs from a nine-ball over from North Sydney's Ginty Lush (four 6s and four 4s) in a Sydney grade match in 1936-37.

- World War II robbed him and other emerging champions like Keith Miller, Cec Pepper and Arthur Morris of five of their very best years. In the final near full season of first-class cricket in 1940-41, Barnes, 22, made six first innings centuries in consecutive first-class matches, passing 1000 runs and averaging 75.

- There were almost eight years between Barnes' first and second Test appearances. His debut game against the Englishmen at The Oval was memorable for Len Hutton making 364, Test cricket's new all-time batting record.

- Barnes loved to monopolise the strike, even if his batting partner was Don Bradman. In the 1946-47 Sydney Test, Barnes became the first man to bat for 10 hours, he and Bradman adding 405 for the fifth wicket, a Test record which stood until 1990-91. Both were out for 234, Barnes later claiming he had deliberately tossed his innings away so he could be bracketed *with* The Don, rather than ahead of him!

- Playing a season of Lancashire League cricket with Burnley in 1947, Barnes was disappointed at the size of the first 'collection' — bonus monies donated by appreciative spectators to players who'd made a 50 or taken five wickets. On being told that some patrons, seeing his flash Sunbeam Talbot and fine dress, may have felt he didn't need their donations, Barnes parked his motor car a mile from the ground and appeared in an old suit, cloth cap and raincoat. According to historian Rick Smith, his proceeds immediately doubled! His time in the Leagues was fleeting. He punched a teammate and was barred.

- Some benefits arose from Barnes brooking authority. His move, in 1948, to question an antiquated Australian Board of Control rule and have wives at least within visiting distance on tours of England has been welcomed by tourists ever since.

- Tired of the demands of having to sign dozens of autograph sheets on board the *Strathaird* on the voyage to England in 1948, Barnes had a rubber stamp made of his signature and paid a youngster to stamp the sheets. The original sheet is now one of the most eagerly-sought by collectors of Bradman team memorabilia.

- Ever mischievous, Barnes thrust a mongrel dog under the nose of English umpire Alex Skelding one day, saying the dog could go with his white stick.

THE AMAZING WORLD OF SID BARNES continued

This Test Series
COULD KILL
Cricket

The deadly effect of slow scoring and time wasting fast bowling could well sound the death knell of cricket.

By SID BARNES

AUSTRALIAN cricket, for many years sick nigh unto death, this season could quietly pass away. They stand a fair show of seeing Australia regain the ashes, but not in the atmosphere of scintillating cricket they

PROVOCATIVE: Barnes' writings were colorful and occasionally caustic

- After backing himself to make 100 in the 1948 Lord's Test, Barnes celebrated his money-making feat by smashing Jim Laker for 20 runs from five balls. The doyen of Australia's cricket writers Ray Robinson said when Barnes was in such a mood 'the ball beat against his bat as helplessly as a dog's paw against a barn door '.

- Barnes and Arthur Morris were one of the greatest of all opening pairs, averaging more than 50, including back-to-back century stands in their last two Tests as teammates in 1948. 'I'm sorry he didn't stop in cricket longer,' said Morris.

- In Don Bradman's testimonial game in Melbourne in 1948-49, Barnes took guard with a mini bat.

- In his final season, Barnes dropped himself to 12th man in a Sheffield Shield game in Adelaide. Appearing at a drinks break in an expensive double-breasted suit, he brushed players' flannels, gave bowlers iced towels, combed players' hair, sprayed deodorant under their armpits, played a portable radio and even offered around cigars.

- On the day the 1953 Australian touring team to England was announced, the just-selected Alan Davidson answered his door. It was Barnes with his cricket bag. 'Here, son,' he said. 'I won't be needing this anymore.'

- In 1956, when Barnes wrote off the touring Australians as 'a bunch of pie-eaters', the Aussies won at Lord's and Barnes posed for photographs beside a huge tray of pies, pretending he'd eat the lot.

'I have fought my fight and won,' said Barnes, ever the crusader. 'Another fight yet to be won is the saving of cricket from the hands of the autocratic few, drunk with power and self-importance. They have reigned too long.

'I am very happy with the verdict in my favour, and I feel that my name, which was besmirched by the action of the Australian Board of Control, has been completely restored. I will be ready to play for Australia again, if selected, and, of course, approved as a 'good' citizen by the Board of Control.'

In a letter to co-selector Chappie Dwyer in the autumn of 1952, Sir Donald Bradman agreed that the Board personnel was too top heavy towards those with a legal, rather than a cricketing background. 'One of the great troubles of the Board at present is that things are discussed far too much from a legal angle instead of the common sense and practical angle. What we badly need are a few men with practical playing experience so that when we discuss a vital matter as affecting cricket, such as for instance this bumper business (Miller and Lindwall being criticised for their constant short-pitched bowling), the delegates will understand the importance of what they are talking about.'

EGO-CENTRIC: Few loved the limelight like Sid Barnes

Despite his famous court victory, Barnes never played for Australia again, nor recovered from his slighting by the Board. He became bitter and vitriolic, squandering friendships and targeting even loyal mates like Keith Miller — the pair lashing out at each other in a front-page war which triggered soaring sales for their respective newspapers and Barnes' colourful 1953 autobiography *It Isn't Cricket*.

Barnes blamed the loss of the Coronation year series in England to the excesses of the team, especially vice-captain Miller who he believed had acted imprudently, quarrelling openly with umpires, being absent from the team when English race meetings were on and 'conveniently' developing a sore back at the same time as the running of the Epsom Derby.

In an extraordinary tirade, Barnes wrote: 'Miller repeatedly transgressed in a way which affected adversely Australia's cricket prestige and repeatedly offended against the code of sportsmanship and ethics.'

Barnes further claimed the Australians only drew the second Test at Lord's because players were in a London night club until early morning before the last day of play. They were more anxious to attend Wimbledon than being concerned with the outcome of the match. Barnes further accused them of neglecting practice for personal gain and of rudeness to the Nottinghamshire CCC which made arrangements and paid for the tourists to go to the Coronation.

Even Australia's universally-admired captain Lindsay Hassett was targeted, Barnes alleging Hassett wielded a 'fatal lack of control on the team'. Furthermore, social junkets and slovenly demeanour on the field characterised the team's five months in England.

Miller said Barnes was bitter and jealous, a former great cricketer and clown who missed the crowd's applause. He defended his attendance at horse racing meetings by saying players took it in turns to miss a game. How they relaxed was their own business. He denied ever arguing with umpires and added dryly, 'And when it comes to sportsmanship I know as much about it as Sid Barnes.'

His defence filled the front pages of newspapers in Australia and England. 'Barnes is known as the Master Gimme man of Australian cricket. Gimme this — gimme that!' said Miller.

'He's shrewd. He has made sure his book will be a best-seller by attacking me and the Australian XI. But he will be remembered as the only Australian squealer after we lost the 1953 Ashes tour. Actually, this was the quietest tour I've been on. The youngsters looked up to Lindsay Hassett as an idol, much the same way as members looked up to Don Bradman in 1948. Lindsay was the ideal touring captain. For me, it was the happiest tour of all.'

After his broadsides against the 1953 tourists, Barnes' book *Eyes On the Ashes* soon went into reprint — but the rifts with many old mates were irreparable.

Those he was closest to regarded him as warm-hearted and loyal. 'He did a lot of charity work and cricketers down on their luck always found him a soft touch,' said fellow 1948 tourist Toshack. 'But somehow the warm, human side of him never got through to the newspapers.'

Barnes played his last game of both state and club cricket, at 36, before pursuing his business interests. He believed there was no point to playing if he was considered too old for his country. Even an opportunist recognises when he's beaten.

- Sid Barnes struggled with his increasing anonymity and his business suffered. He hated growing old and in his later years suffered badly from depression. In 1973 he was found dead, with a bottle of sleeping tablets next to him. He was just 57.

1945 EASTBOURNE: Cec Pepper and Leigh Baker at The Saffrons, the initial base of the Australian Services' XI leading into the Victory Tests and nine months of non-stop cricket in 1945-46. Jeanette Bond/Pepper family archives

12 1945 ADELAIDE

Don't cross Don Bradman

The announcement that Don Bradman was launching a comeback in the summer of '45 was greeted joyously throughout Australia and the Empire. His wife Jessie had sown the seed. 'You know Don,' she said. 'It would be a shame if young John never got to see you play.' Bradman, 37, had played only once in five years. Having been invalided out of the Army after just six weeks, so debilitated was he during parts of the War that he often couldn't even raise his arm to shave. So gaunt was he that Keith Miller hardly recognised him when the Australian Services arrived in Adelaide to oppose a South Australian XI, which included Australia's folk hero...

No one commanded a crowd like Don Bradman. More than 10,000 cricket-starved fans were at the Adelaide Oval as Bradman skipped down the narrow walkway from the rooms past the members onto the ground. It was just before noon on New Year's Eve 1945. The reception was rapturous. Even the writers in the open-air press box to the side of the rooms were standing and applauding. Other than a match, also in Adelaide, the previous week, Bradman had hardly held a bat in five years. He'd confided to friends that he may mount a full-on comeback, but only if his health improved and he felt he could play to a standard he considered satisfactory. Known as the eighth wonder of the world, his wondrous achievements included an Australian-first six consecutive centuries in 1938-39. His record-equaling sixth 100 came in his old hometown of Sydney against New South Wales. At 96, there was a muffled, half-hearted appeal from fledgling allrounder Cecil Pepper at short-leg when the Don appeared to touch a leg-side ball from paceman Albert Cheetham. No one else supported Pepper, so he shook his head and withdrew his appeal. Officiating umpires George Borwick and Fred Lyons told Cheetham later there actually *had* been a touch and Bradman would have been given out had Pepper not back peddled. Later Pepper was asked by a writer from Sydney's *Truth* newspaper if Bradman had hit it. 'Too right he did,' he said.

SUMMER OF 1945-46: Cec Pepper with his Services XI captain Lindsay Hassett in Sydney.
Gordon Vidler/Ken Piesse collection

Minutes later when the Don reached his coveted century, all the NSW players including those fielding on the boundaries, converged mid-pitch to congratulate him. Cricket after all was a gentleman's game, always played in the right spirit…

Almost seven years on, Bradman was marking his guard again and eyeing the gaps in the field. Opposing him was Pepper, by now a combative, extroverted, tempestuous wrist spinner of variety and adventure. He'd been away to the War, serving in the Middle East and New Guinea. Bradman hadn't. His war had lasted just six weeks. Pepper was the Services' No.1 bowler, his fizzing flipper his signature. It zeroed into the stumps at pace, like a fast in-dipper. Weeks earlier he'd muddled even some of the India's greatest players… and no one played spin as well as the champions from the sub-continent.

THE WARTIME DON: Don Bradman was invalidated out of the Army after just six weeks

Few had a memory like Bradman. He went into automatic pilot. He'd opposed Pepper before the war. Play forward, no matter what. Straight bat. Hit it to mid off and mid on. No cross-bat shots. No risks. Not against this fella. Not early.

Pepper and the Services XI had been playing virtually non-stop since April. Included were five Victory Tests in England and three more Tests in India, all unofficial. Pepper was a bigger menace than even Keith Miller, who was yet to convince even himself that he was anything more than a change bowler. The team had initially rebelled against the prospect of more cricket back home. They were stale, tired, dejected and weary. They wanted to be with their loved ones. But Australia's wartime commander-in-chief, General Thomas Blamey had insisted. He backed his cricket mates who had suggested a set of matches in each city to help reactivate the game downunder; the ideal entre to an English visit mooted for the following year. The war had finished but team members had little idea when demobilisation was to occur. They were still serving King and Country. Orders were orders.

Like the Don, Pepper was a country boy. He hailed from Parkes via Forbes in the New South Wales central west and in his mid-teens was also just as renowned for his ability at tennis. Before coming to the Big Smoke as a teenager in 1936, he'd made 2834 runs and taken 116 wickets. It was an extraordinary season, still unequalled at bush level. He'd arrive at games with a smile and a swagger: 'It's a great day for a six boys!' he'd say. One of his sixes at Woodward Park soared over the boundary, over the cars, over the tennis courts and landed at the foot of the entry gates at the local showgrounds. Stepped out later that week, the hit was measured at 160 yards. It was simply gigantic. No one in Australian cricket hit the ball harder. On the eve of the war in Brisbane, he'd smashed a ground record seven 6s. He and the legendary Bill O'Reilly were a formidable twin-spin combination with NSW. Pepper was also agile in the field and an outstanding slipsman. As allrounders go, his bosum buddy Miller reckoned there was no one superior anywhere in the world.

THE BEST NEVER TO PLAY: The cover of Pep, the Cec Pepper story, by Ken Piesse

In-between his wartime duties, while on leave Pepper married his Wollongong sweetheart, vivacious blonde Maurine Ford at her father's hotel in Wagga Wagga – married men received an extra shilling in their allowances each week. He'd worked since he was 14 and always liked to have some extra silver in his pocket.

With both wars, in Europe and the Pacific officially over, he was now keen to once again showcase his cricket credentials, not just as a Test fringer but as one of the best players in the country.

Months earlier in England he'd been a revelation in the keenly contested Victory Tests. In May he made the winning hit with just two balls to go in the first international at Lord's. And in June he received two standing ovations from the Yorkshire crowd for his outstanding bowling against Walter Hammond and Co. in the second at Bramall Lane. So enamored were several in charge of Lancashire League clubs that late in the '45 summer one made him a guest pro for a day and he responded with a whirlwind 84. Later he received a sizeable collection from the appreciative crowd. He and the even more charismatic Miller were riding a rare wave of popularity, with rich offers to return to England and play professionally.

Like Miller, Pepper had a rare ability to attract women, lots of them. From his mid-teens in Parkes, his brother Keith reckoned Pep had a different girl for every day of the week. He'd stay out late and clamber through a bedroom window invariably waking his younger brother.

With his new wife back home in Wollongong, he'd had a fling with a bus conductress at High Wycombe where the cricketers were based late in 1944. Nine months later, with Pepper and the 1945 Services team in London, she'd rung the regiment to say she'd had his baby. She tried once, twice, three times, only to be told by the adjutant to stop pestering him, otherwise he'd say that she had slept with the entire unit. Pep kept his dalliances strictly to himself. These were different times. At the height of the war, no one made long-term plans. There was a unbreakable bond and brotherhood between those who had served.

AN AUSTRALIAN XI *NOT* TO PLAY TEST CRICKET

1. Bill Alley
2. Jimmy Maher
3. 'Sunny' Jim Mackay
4. Jamie Siddons
5. David Hussey
6. Cec Pepper
7. Frank Tarrant
8. Darren Berry
9. Ashley Noffke
10. Wayne Holdsworth
11. Andrew Zesers

EASTBOURNE 1945: Cec Pepper with American tennis legend Margaret Osborne DuPont. Pepper had three sons with three different women, two out of wedlock. Jeanette Bond/Pepper family archives

Before General Blamey's edict for the Services' XI to stay together and play in each of the major Australian cities, including Hobart, Pep was preparing to go straight to Wollongong to be with Maurine. Instead, with his homecoming delayed, she came to Adelaide. It was the first time they'd seen each other since their honeymoon. It was to be a fateful week…

Bradman was slow to settle and his footwork leaden. The crowd was uneasy. They were willing him to succeed. Before he'd reached even 10, Pepper struck him twice on the pads with his deadly flipper and appealed as only Pepper could: full-throated and demanding. Every eye went to umpire Jack Scott, bending low over the stumps. 'Not out', he said. Twice. He didn't want to spoil the Bradman comeback. If the first was close, the second was plumb, so Pepper believed. Quoting from *Pep, the Cec Pepper Story*: 'Pepper flew into a paroxysm of rage. Not only was Scott accused of cheating, Pepper reckoned he was working to a separate set of rules to Bradman, the almighty hometown hero. Pepper's torrent of abuse could be heard all over the field. Bradman approached Scott and told him he shouldn't have to put up with such a tirade. It was unsportsmanlike and totally against the spirit of cricket. These matches were supposed to be friendlies. An official complaint was laid against Pepper for his "continued filthy language" and his card marked, especially when a promised apology was never received.'

FLIPPERMAN: Cec Pepper's deadly flipper swung late and zipped through. It was his signature delivery

Bradman, NSW's EA 'Chappie' Dwyer and the Victorian Jack Ryder were the national selectors deliberating over the composition of the 13-man autumn-time squad to New Zealand. Dwyer was adamant that Pepper should not be considered. He may or may not have sent an apology. Bradman was an even more powerful enemy. He was the most influential personality in the game, a stickler for its ethics and spirit. For reasons other than cricket, three other leg-spinners made the squad. Pepper didn't. He was devastated. Within 48 hours of discharge in early March, he and Maurine sailed for England and a new life in the professional leagues of Lancashire. Pepper was never to play big cricket in Australia again.

12 Don't cross Don Bradman

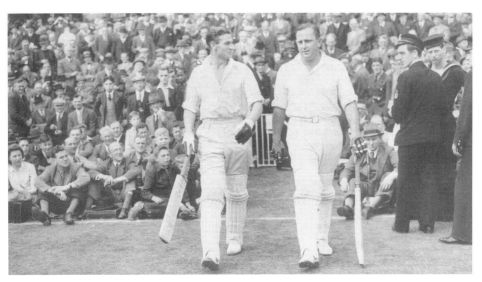

VICTORY TESTS 1945: *Pepper (right) with Keith Miller*

Years later, the wild colonial boy talked about the frustration of being excluded from teams and tours he had every right to be on. Had he remained he would almost certainly have made the famous 'Invincibles' tour of 1948. 'At the height of my enthusiasm at being back on the famous Australian cricket grounds and playing in the top rank, I was harshly treated because I was honest,' he said.

Asked about the Don's role in his premature exit, he said: 'I always got on well with Bradman. But I got the little bugger out twice in one innings and the umpire wouldn't give him out. When I told the umpire what I thought of his decisions I was expected to apologise. I wouldn't. And I came to England.'

In the foreword to *Pep*, the legendary Arthur Morris said had he been less voluble and more diplomatic, he would have been assured of the Test cap he so desperately desired. But his own competitive juices had road-blocked his options. He was his own worst enemy.

- For a decade from 1946, Pepper was the highest paid cricketer in the world. He three times achieved the League double of 1000 runs and 100 wickets. Charitable and generous, he could also be mercurial, temperamental and aggressive. He fathered three sons, by three different women. For 30 years he lived in a ménage a trois with his lover and her husband. He died in 1993, splitting his fortune with his youngest son and a woman who he'd only just met.

Don Bradman's influence on Australian cricket affairs was all-embracing even into his 70s when Kerry Packer came to his Adelaide home and negotiated an end to his rebel World Series Cricket movement. Allrounder extraordinaire Pepper was just one of Bradman's many 'victims'. Among others who believed themselves unfairly treated by the Don were Jack Fingleton, Clarrie Grimmett and even the iconic Keith Miller.

LARWOOD's MCG APPROACH: The Notts Express 'pinged' Australian batsmen five times a Test in 1932-33. Local authorities threatened to abandon the program after the provocative Adelaide Test

13 1932-33 BODYLINE SUMMER

Endangering an Empire

Bodyline bowling exposed MCC captain Douglas Jardine as a cricketing tyrant, threatened the fibre of the game and endangered Empire relations. Designed to stifle the batting genius of batting virtuoso Don Bradman, so unstoppable in England in 1930, it triggered extraordinary feeling. Australian batsmen were hit 25 times in five ill-tempered Tests by the Nottinghamshire Express, Harold Larwood, in the most violent and volatile summer of all.

Only five men were present in the Australian dressing rooms at the Adelaide Oval when Bill Woodfull, still ashen grey after been struck a tremendous blow under the heart by Harold Larwood, delivered the most stinging rebuke in Anglo-Australian cricket history: 'Mr Warner, there are two sides out there. One is playing cricket. The other is not. The game is too good to be spoilt. It is time some people got out of it.'

PF 'Plum' Warner, England's genteel 'Mr Cricket' and his assistant manager, Richard Palairet, had come to extend their sympathies. Instead they'd been hit with a sledgehammer.

Within 24 hours, Woodfull's reprimand was headline news, all around Australia and in London. The Australian captain was the gentleman's gentleman, scholarly, erudite and caring. For him to be so provoked and accuse the English of playing outside the spirit of the game showed just how raw emotions were in the face of Bodyline.

As well as the Australian team masseur, who was deaf, Australian 12th man Leo O'Brien was present. Just before Warner and Palairet's arrival, Woodfull emerged from a shower and told O'Brien: 'There are some terrible things happening out there, "Mo" (O'Brien).' O'Brien re-joined his teammates and said: 'Woody's in a bad way', before relating his captain's steamy tirade.

As the only professional journalist present, Jack Fingleton was blamed as the one who went public with the story. However, he always denied his involvement and said there were others, too, who had media links — Alan Kippax, for example, who wasn't playing, and Vic Richardson, Stan McCabe and Don Bradman, who were.

The furore became an international incident when popular wicketkeeper Bert Oldfield reeled from the wicket, his skull fractured, after edging an attempted hook shot onto his temple on the third day. While Oldfield was to tell a concerned Larwood that it wasn't his fault, the view from around the boundary was stark. Oldfield had slumped to the ground, motionless. Seeing their hero seriously hurt, there was an immediate hush, before an angry swell of shouting. Had one person jumped the fence, thousands more would have followed.

To the mob, it mattered little that Larwood wasn't bowling Bodyline either when Oldfield was sconed or when Woodfull had been struck under the heart late the previous afternoon. The Australians had been intimidated all summer, the pitches had become battlefields and the ballooning resentment had reached a cresendo.

As Oldfield was being treated, the noisiest elements on the northern banks of the 30,000 strong crowd began to count Larwood out. The Englishmen gathered in the centre, looking anxiously back over their shoulders. Umpires George Hele and George Borwick were so sure of an invasion that they'd resolved to arm themselves with a stump each for protection.

Oldfield said later that he had 'lost' the ball in the background, Larwood's arm at the point of delivery being higher than the oval's sightscreen. Seeing Oldfield crumpled on the ground seriously hurt, Larwood had raced up to him saying 'I'm sorry, Bertie.'

'It's not your fault, Harold.'

As 'Gubby' Allen tended to Oldfield's cut with a towel and a jug of water, Woodfull, dressed in civilian clothes, came onto the field, helped Oldfield up and supported him as they walked off.

Next-man-in Bill O'Reilly said it was a task in itself even getting down the steps from the George Giffen Stand onto the Adelaide Oval amid the pandemonium, members standing on their seats and in the aisles remonstrating. A platoon of mounted horse troopers stood at the ready.

'It was a toss-up for several minutes whether someone would jump the fence,' said Richardson. 'If one man had, it is almost certain that thousands would have followed him. What could a few policemen have done had the field been invaded by angry spectators?'

Larwood was booed and hooted and sat down waiting for the noise to subside. Play re-started to the extraordinary spectacle of police ringing the boundary. Throughout it all, English captain Douglas Jardine remained composed, his face set. He even went down to deep fine leg, contemptuous and defiant in the face of danger. Later, when England batted again, he wore his elitist, multi-coloured Harlequin cap.

13 Endangering an Empire

BODYLINE FIELD: *Larwood normally started with an orthodox field for his opening two overs before switching to a Bodyline field featuring five and sometimes six short legs. Only Stan McCabe and Vic Richardson played the short-pitched deliveries with any authority*

After unsuccessfully asking managers Warner and Palairet to intervene and stop leg-theory bowling, within days the Australian Board of Control, through its chairman Dr Allen Robertson in Melbourne, had penned the first of the famous set of telegrams which almost ended the tour and endangered friendly relations between the two countries:

> 'Bodyline bowling has assumed such proportions as to menace the best interests of the game, making protection of the body by batsmen the main consideration, causing intensely bitter feelings between players as well as injury. In our opinion it is unsportsmanlike. Unless stopped at once it is likely to upset friendly relations existing between Australia and England.'

Marylebone Cricket Club, responsible for the English team, sent a dignified, strongly worded reply:

> 'We, the Marylebone club, deplore your cable and depreciate the opinion that there has been unsportsmanlike play. We have the fullest confidence in the

JARDINE'S MEN: the 1932-33 MCC tourists, back row, left to right: George Duckworth, Harold Larwood, Tommy Mitchell, Bill Voce, The Nawab of Pataudi snr., Eddie Paynter, Bill Ferguson (scorer/baggageman). Middle: Plum Warner (manager), Les Ames, Hedley Verity, Bill Bowes, Freddie Brown, Richard Palairet (assistant-manager). Sitting: Maurice Leyland, Herbert Sutcliffe, Bob Wyatt (vice-captain), Douglas Jardine (captain), Gubby Allen, Walter Hammond. Absent: Maurice Tate

captain and team managers. We are convinced that they would do nothing that would infringe the laws of cricket or the spirit of the game and we have no evidence that our confidence is misplaced. Much as we regret the injuries to Woodfull and Oldfield, we understand that in neither case was the bowler [Larwood] to blame. If the Board wishes to propose a new law, or rule, it should receive our careful consideration in due course. We hope the situation is not now as serious as your cable appears to indicate, but if it is such to jeopardise the good relations between England and Australian cricketers, and you consider it desirable to cancel the remainder of the program, we would consent with great reluctance.'

Jardine, too, felt suitably insulted by the Australian cable and vowed not to lead England into the fourth Test unless the charge of unsportsmanlike conduct was withdrawn. In his book *In Quest of the Ashes*, he said: 'I had long since ceased to care what the Australian press said about me, nor did I pay any heed to what individuals frequently said behind my back. I had, however, made up my mind that no Australian body, however august, should, as far as I was concerned, be at liberty to stigmatize the MCC team as "unsportsmanlike" and be allowed to escape from retracting that amazing charge.'

Iron-willed, exacting and determined to win no matter what, Jardine would brook no interference from Warner, a former English captain, who had pleaded with him to reduce his number of leg-side fieldsmen. Often Jardine would have eight on the on-side, except when Larwood was operating against the fleet-of-foot Bradman, whose cross-bat swishes demanded a third man, as well as a cover point.

Warner told Richardson, Australia's vice-captain, that he was powerless to act: 'The skipper is adamant,' he said. 'I can do nothing with him on this subject.' They had argued on the Orontes on the voyage out and Jardine showed him scant courtesy for the rest of the campaign.

SAVAGE: *The normally diplomatic Bill Woodfull said England's tactics were dastardly*

Even before the Tests started, Richardson had known this would be a tour with a twist. 'If we don't beat you,' old foe Bill Voce told him soon after arrival, 'We'll knock your bloody heads off.'

EVER SINCE THE opening weeks of the tour Larwood and his sidekicks Voce and Bill Bowes directly attacked the batsmen, with the leg-side stacked with fieldsmen — as many as five and six in the inner ring and two protecting the fine leg boundary. Puzzled by the gathering of English fielders on the leg side, Leo O'Brien, playing for the first time in the Australian XI side, motioned, 'But I'm a left-hander!'

By mid-series Vic Richardson was taking block 18 inches outside his leg stump and the ball was still coming directly at him. The Australian batsmen expected to be hit. There were 34 instances in the Tests, Larwood responsible for 25.

On the slower English wickets, the 1930 Australians had mainly been untroubled, but on the harder, faster wickets of Australia, even the most agile and quick-footed players like Bradman were pinged, Larwood being at least two yards faster than previously. Captain Bill Woodfull was struck seven times in four Tests and his opening partner Bill Ponsford, six in three.

By the tour end even the English fielders had stopped trying to sympathise. There was little or no camaraderie between the sides, the Australians reciprocating Jardine's cold disdain. When he wanted to see Woodfull, he was made to wait in the corridor, with the door shut.

When Jardine was struck on the thigh in the fifth Test by the thickset Victorian Harry 'Bull' Alexander, thousands stood and cheered. No English cricketer had ever been more detested — or had so openly shown his contempt for the colonials. He genuinely considered himself superior, especially to the Australian public.

Indian-born and English-educated, Jardine was a zealot, a complex and aloof man with a liking for Chaucer, Asian philosophy and mysticism. Even a few of his teammates had reservations, Herbert Sutcliffe (or his ghost writer) referring to him as 'a queer devil' during their first trip together in 1928-29, before making a complete about-face in 1932-33 when he described him as one of the greatest men he'd met!

How Jardine could lead a plan so abhorrent to the very spirit of the game showed just how paranoid all England was about another humiliation at the hands of Australia's batting maestro, Bradman. The thrashings he had handed Percy Chapman's conventional attacks had forced Jardine to formulate something completely different. He believed the Ashes could not possibly be retrieved unless the maulings stopped. He adopted a policy of hate, maybe as a payback for some of the abuse he'd received during his maiden tour.

Jardine's plans hinged almost entirely around his fastest bowler, the 173 cm (5 ft. 8 in) Larwood, who had been in Test cricket since 1926. A strong and willing man who bowled at a thunderous pace and swung it early, Larwood was the outstanding strike bowler in all-England. His 141 county wickets (and 106 from the left-armed Voce) had lifted Notts into fourth place in the 1932 English championship. While he'd previously been expensive at Test level (31 wickets at 41), Larwood's skidding speed had been estimated at around 90 mph (144 km/h) and his accuracy and stamina had improved too. With the opening overs with the new ball he could take the ball 'away', but like Voce, his natural swerve was 'in' to the right-handers.

Two English summers previously, in 1930, 25-year-old Larwood had unsettled Bradman, albeit momentarily, in the final Test at The Oval. On a wettened wicket, Larwood struck his arch foe under the heart. Play was held up for five minutes while the champion regained his composure. He was 175 at the time and went on to make 232.

At a meeting with Larwood, Voce and their county captain Arthur Carr at a hotel in Piccadilly after the touring team had been announced, Jardine spoke of leg-theory and his desire to curb Bradman. He talked of The Oval Test, in which Larwood had been threatening, albeit for a short time.

'I told Jardine I thought Bradman had flinched and he said he knew that,' said Larwood in his book *The Larwood Story*.

Bowled accurately and with enough speed, Jardine felt even Bradman may be vulnerable to a sustained leg stump attack. Others such as feted openers Bill Woodfull and Bill Ponsford and the veteran Alan Kippax could also be discomforted.

Larwood had bowled leg-theory against Bradman and Archie Jackson out of desperation on his maiden trip to Australia in Adelaide in 1928-29. But with only five and six fieldsmen on the leg side and on the flattest of wickets he'd been heavily punished and returned match figures of 1/152. 'They both seemed to play it well enough,' said Larwood, who didn't try it again.

13 Endangering an Empire

OSTRACISED: *The great Harold Larwood didn't play Test cricket again after the infamous Bodyline series in which he took 33 wickets*

Jardine's brutal intentions were well and truly telegraphed with the 11th-hour inclusion of 193 cm (6 ft. 4 in) Yorkshire giant Bowes, the 17th man and a fifth fast bowler to the squad. Touring sides of the era generally included only three pacemen, plus three specialist spinners. In one game late in the 1932 English summer at The Oval, Bowes had bowled persistently short at Jack Hobbs. The old master was so angered he walked down the wicket and remonstrated with Bowes saying he was flaunting the spirit of the game.

Having experimented with his leg-theory tactics during the lead-up games, Jardine was still unsure if the tactic would work in the Tests. He'd discussed field placings with Frank Foster, the great Warwickshire left-arm bowler and part-destroyer of the 1911-12 Australians, and was hopeful, rather than being convinced, that leg-theory bowling with a clustered field, similar to Foster's 'death trap' (where he employed four short legs), may at least halt Bradman's run avalanches.

For the opening Test in Sydney, Jardine played his frontline spinner, Hedley Verity, as his fourth specialist bowler. He used the medium pace of Wally Hammond as a back-up to the pace of Larwood, Voce and the amateur GOB 'Gubby' Allen — the only paceman in the Tests who refused to bowl Bodyline. Stan McCabe's epic 187, maybe the greatest and certainly the bravest Ashes innings ever, almost ended Bodyline there and then. Had Bradman played and also succeeded against the bouncer barrage, Jardine may have withdrawn, or at least modified the attack. Along with Richardson, McCabe was one of the strongest of the Australians through the leg side. It was no coincidence that Bodyline tactics were to be used only sparingly against those two.

THE TERM 'Bodyline' was first used by famous Melbourne sporting identity and ex-Australian Test cricketer Jack Worrall of the *Australasian*, who talked about 'half-pitched slingers on the body-line'. A sub-editor used it in a headline, giving birth to cricket's most infamous term.

Former Australian captain Clem Hill said: 'We call it body-line bowling but it is really bowling at the man. If the members of the MCC [Marylebone Cricket Club] had seen this attack in operation in Australia there would be no doubt about their [disapproving] attitude.'

Despite the shock effect and immediate success of his tactics against all bar McCabe, Jardine was so nervous about the outcome of the opening game that, for long periods when England batted, he sat behind a pillar, able to bear to watch only the occasional delivery.

Jardine intensified his attack when Bradman returned for the Melbourne match, his health improved and a Board stand-off resolved. Amidst a protracted argument at the selection table, Bowes came into the XI for Verity. Jardine's vice-captain Bob Wyatt thought it a major error in judgment. If he couldn't bowl Australia out twice with three fast bowlers, he wouldn't do it with four.

But Bowes played, and in an extraordinary moment, dismissed Bradman first ball with a quick long hop that the young Don tried to pull but only succeeded in bottom-edging onto his stumps. 'The crowd was stupefied,' said Bowes in his autobiography *Express Deliveries*. 'Bradman walked off the field amid a silence that would have been a theatrical producer's triumph. The spell was broken by a solitary woman's clapping. The feeble sound rippled above the hushed throng and then an excited chatter broke out from all parts of the ground. And it was then that I noticed Jardine. Jardine, the sphinx, had forgotten himself for the one and only time in his cricket life. In his sheer delight at this unexpected stroke of luck, he had clasped both his hands above his head and was jigging around like an Indian doing a war dance.'

Wyatt, fielding on the fence at fine leg, said Bradman had simply got too far over and hooked the ball down onto his leg stump. Later he impishly baited the fans, asking, 'when is Don Bradman coming out?'

The Australians had included three spinners in their XI against England's none and were to win on an unusually sluggish wicket by 111 runs, Bradman's second innings century crucial in the series-squaring win.

However, the quality of Larwood's bowling had delighted Jardine and, despite the loss, justified in his own mind his leg-theory tactics. He told journalists in Launceston: 'I can assure you there is nothing new in the leg-theory attack and nothing dangerous in it. The only difference we have made is in evolving a new field. We hope it will go on being successful.'

Larwood had taken 10 wickets in Sydney and four on a wicket affected by lead-up rain in Melbourne. He'd bowled lengthy spells at hostile pace and was revelling in his work. So accurate was he, that his battery of short legs were rarely endangered.

In Adelaide, the most sensational Test of the series, the one in which Woodfull and Oldfield were struck, the fury against Bodyline so intensified that every available police reinforcement was sent to the oval in case of a riot.

Jardine had relented and returned Verity to the XI, ahead of Bowes, who'd had his 15 minutes of fame in Melbourne. Curator Bert Wright's wicket, normally unsympathetic to the faster bowlers, had excellent pace and bounce, and according to Jardine was the equal of any wicket the tourists encountered all tour.

After England had made 341, Australia was immediately under fire with Jack Fingleton falling in Allen's first over and Bradman soon afterwards to Larwood. Larwood's very first delivery with the leg-side packed was so fast it knocked the bat out of Woodfull's hands, incensing many in the crowd. When Woodfull, on five, was struck a crushing blow by Larwood, bowling to an orthodox field, the crowd erupted. In *R. E. S. Wyatt: Fighting Cricketer*, England's vice-captain described it as 'an instant and violent explosion of rage from all over the ground'. 'As the storm broke Jardine signalled for a change to leg-theory bowling. It was an incredibly tactless move and not surprisingly it produced absolute pandemonium. We were all more or less inured to uproar from Australian crowds but this was different from anything we had experienced. We heard that 200 armed police were massed behind the pavilion and ready to intervene if the crowd invaded the field. Douglas intensely resented the agitation. He argued that he was fully within his rights in attacking the leg side, adding, "These Australians are yellow."'

Walter Hammond, one of the team's senior professionals, argued Jardine was merely following his practice of allowing Larwood to bowl conventionally for his two opening overs before reverting to leg-theory while the ball still had its hardness. However, his 'Well bowled, Harold', in Bradman's hearing, while Woodfull was being attended to, defies explanation. The spirit and the game's sporting ideals had never before been so betrayed. Had the incident occurred in Melbourne at Woodfull's home ground, rather than in conservative, law-abiding Adelaide, there would have been hell to pay.

Shortly before stumps, Warner and Palairet made their way along the landing to the Australian dressing room to see Woodfull, who'd been dismissed for 22. They wanted to sympathise with him — but also, as is not widely known, to find out who had called Larwood a bastard out on the field. Richardson answered the door and on being told of Warner's charge said: 'Which one of you blokes mistook Larwood for that bastard Jardine?'

Warner insisted on seeing Woodfull and received his stern rebuff, the most remembered and reported in cricket history, confirming the irrevocable split between the teams. Woodfull hadn't intended it to become public. Nor had O'Brien, Australia's 12th man. But within hours it was being reported around the world, Jardine and his team accused of bringing the game into disrepute.

Jardine locked the door to the English dressing room and spoke with the team, saying there had been 'an unfortunate' conversation between Woodfull and Warner. He offered to stand down, but according to author Gerald Pawle, the team pledged their total support. Most considered that the Australians were making an unnecessary fuss.

FOLLOWING ORDERS: Harold Larwood

At a drinks break during the final Test in Sydney, Jardine was handed a glass of cordial. 'Don't give him a drink,' said one barracker. 'Let the bastard die of thirst.' On another occasion when he went to swish some flies away from his face, a barracker yelled: 'Don't swat the flies, Jardine. They're the only friends you've got!'

After the first exchange of telegrams, in which the MCC said they'd reluctantly agree to the remainder of the tour being cancelled, the Australian Board backed down. The cricket might have been controversial, but the interest was unprecedented with record crowds and near-record gate-takings at every match. In Sydney, the daily attendances were almost 40,000 per day, in Melbourne 50,000 and in Adelaide, where the ground record was broken twice in the opening two days, almost 30,000 attended on each of the six days. More than 50,000 were present on the Saturday, an extraordinarily large crowd given Adelaide's small population.

The Englishmen won the Ashes in the next Test, in Brisbane and the last Test as well, in Sydney again, to take the rubber 4-1, replicating the result of Chapman's side four years earlier.

Englishmen back home rejoiced. They had been served only portions of the true story. Few believed it was a victory without honour. They tended to believe the writings of such notables as ex-Australian captain Warwick Armstrong, who in London's *Evening News* had accused Bradman's back-away tactics as tantamount to being frightened. Armstrong called The Don 'a cricket cocktail', accusing him of playing for himself rather than the team. Even Jack Hobbs in the *Star* had said Bradman 'seemed to jib a bit'.

Interviewed immediately after the tour end, Larwood said Woodfull was too slow to counter his bowling and Bradman too frightened. 'I knew it, as everybody did. Time and time again, he drew away from the ball,' he said.

However, he later withdrew his allegation saying that Bradman was quick-footed and there'd never be another like him. At the Centenary Test in 1977, he told one interviewer: 'I still have no regrets about the tactic though. Bradman had given me a hammering two years earlier. Attacking the leg stump was the only way to combat him.'

Had Bodyline been allowed to survive, Bradman believed cricket would have died, as few batsmen would have been prepared to tolerate it.

Larwood was to be outlawed from the game. He migrated to Australia, where he died in 1995. Jardine's career was all but over, although he did captain England again, including the 1933 home series. At Old Trafford he made 127 against a form of Bodyline from high-speed West Indians Learie Constantine and EA 'Manny' Martindale.

The MCC, highly embarrassed as they learnt more of the tyrannical doings of Jardine, incorporated a new law forbidding more than two men to field behind square leg.

'When Voce bumped the ball at the 1934 Australians, he was stood down in mid-match and county captain, Arthur Carr sacked. Larwood didn't play and soon afterwards claimed administrators were trying to 'hound' him out of cricket. 'I was fit for the last Test,' he said, 'They feared I would burst the Empire.'

The fallout from Bodyline was all-embracing. After the first MCC-New South Wales game in Sydney, in which Voce took six wickets bowling leg-theory and the Englishmen won by an innings, the Bodyline tactics were mimicked in park competitions around the country.

In *Anti Body-Line*, NSW captain Kippax said that the Bodyline tactics caused injury, fist fights and resulted in games being abandoned: 'On Moore Park, Sydney, a batsman walked down the pitch and threatened to hit the bowler over the head with the bat. On the Domain, a match lasted 15 minutes, ending in a free-fight between the opposing teams. In Adelaide junior cricket, a match was abandoned for a similar brawl after 10 minutes of play.

'The ambulance officer on duty at Centennial Park, Sydney reported that his casualty list on that day was four times its usual length, the vast majority of the additions being head injuries.'

BODYLINE OPINION

'We have seen sufficient of body-line bowling this season to realise that it does more to kill cricket than any other force ever brought into play ... it's premeditated brutality... With a speed merchant like Larwood, the element of physical danger is so great that in the interests of cricket he should not use it,' – Former Australian captain MA 'MONTY' NOBLE

'I doubt if England could have won the rubber without body-line bowling. If it had not been used, Bradman, for one, would have made "buckets" of runs. He is a better batsman than ever... If this sort of attack is persisted in, somebody will be killed sooner or later. If I had to play this type of bowling, I would get out of cricket... the Australian batsmen had my sympathy,' – JACK HOBBS

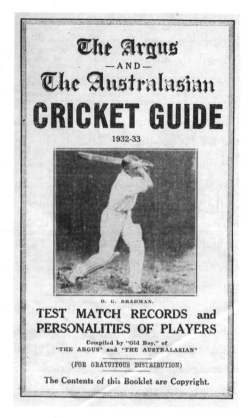

'The determination to win at any price was deplorable,' – DR REG BETTINGTON, former NSW player and ex-captain of Oxford University

'Bodyline is dangerous. I believe that only good luck is responsible for the fact that no one was killed by Bodyline,' – WALTER HAMMOND

'If Jardine's team won the Ashes fairly and squarely by certain methods in Australia (and the M.C.C. maintained that the methods were fair and square) why were we not allowed to try and keep the Ashes by similar methods in this country [England, in 1934]?' – ARTHUR CARR

'It may be our last Test if the squealing goes on ... It is about time that the Test cricket farce was ended. Throughout the world the Australians are branded as squealers and bad sportsmen,' – Queensland fast bowler HUGH 'Pud' THURLOW

'Jardine planned for us, he cared for us, he fought for us on that tour and he was so faithful in everything he did that we were prepared on our part to do anything we could for him,' – HERBERT SUTCLIFFE

'There were occasions when any normal captain would have been ruffled by the unprecedented incidents, due solely to England's bowling methods, but to the credit of Woodfull it must be said that no captain could have led his side in a more restrained *and exemplary manner,'* – WA 'BERT' OLDFIELD

'Jardine bore much harsh treatment and barracking in Australia with dignity and courage. He considered that this type of bowling was within the law, but I fancy that he would admit that it was a stern policy,' – PF 'PLUM' WARNER

Bodyline was not dead and buried after the 1932-33 Australian season. It was used in the 1933 home series by the West Indies and again in England's wintertime tour of India, under Jardine's captaincy in 1933-34.

The bowler most responsible was the highly strung and volatile Northants speedster EW 'Nobby' Clark, who took 10 wickets in three Tests before further controversy in Ceylon (Sri Lanka) when he was accused of deliberately scuffing up the wicket. Operating with three short legs at Chepauk, he caused Indian opener Naoomal Jeoomal to retire hurt after he snicked a bouncer onto his forehead dangerously close to his temple. He also bowled at a body line to the 200 cm (6 ft 7 in) Yuvraj of Patiala, on his debut, the future Maharaja only just avoiding being struck. 'If the young Prince had been hit, I believe the crowd would have rushed the ground,' said Australian Frank Tarrant who umpired two of the three Tests. 'Jardine realised this and took Clark off. To me this was an admission that Clark was bowling with intent to intimidate the batsman.'

In the Australian *Cricketer*, Tarrant said if Clark killed a batsman and had to answer a manslaughter charge, he would give evidence against him.

TARGETED: *Indian Royal the Yuvraj of Patiala was almost struck as Douglas Jardine and the MCC unleashed Bodyline at a shocked Indian XI the following winter*

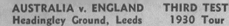
AUSTRALIA v. ENGLAND THIRD TEST
Headingley Ground, Leeds 1930 Tour

CRICKET CATALOGUE
SEASON 1931-3

Bradman going out to bat when he made 334, the World's Record Score for Test Cricket.

A fine view show tion of the and the Hea Ground, Leeds. batting.

MICK SIMMONS LTD

HEADQUARTERS: HAYMARKET, SYDNEY

And at Newcastle and Brisbane

"The Premier Sports House of Australia"

Bradman caught Duckworth, bowle

14 DON BRADMAN

Bradman v the Board

Don Bradman on strike! It seems inconceivable, but Australia's sporting icon was not making any idle threats. His stand-off with the Australian Cricket Board of Control over their refusal to allow him to write about the Tests almost saw him miss the 1932-33 Ashes summer.

Don Bradman's life changed irrevocably from the time he made a double century in his fairy-tale maiden appearance in England, at Worcester in 1930. Bursting like a meteor onto the world cricketing stage, his triumphant solo through England totally overshadowed Australia's Ashes winning feats and made him the ultimate sports hero for thousands struggling through the Depression.

In amassing a record-breaking 974 runs in five Tests, including double centuries at Lord's and The Oval and a triple at Headingley, Bradman scored virtually when he pleased at a run every 1.62 balls, an astonishingly fast rate. He was immediately flooded by a string of lucrative offers which were particularly enticing given the depressed economic climate.

He didn't have a full-time job and was riled when part of his 'good conduct' bonus of 50 pounds – almost 10 per cent of his total tour fee — was withheld when extracts from his life story, *Don Bradman's Book*, appeared in August between the fourth and fifth Test matches. Bradman was further irritated when the Board effectively blocked his move to play the first of two seasons with Lancashire League club Accrington in 1932.

The 600 pounds a year professional contract, supplemented by newspaper work and other endorsements, was truly head-turning and the most ever offered by a northern club. However, it contravened Bradman's 1930s tour contract which stated he could not return to England to play for a period of two years. If the clause was broken, the Board could exercise its right to block Bradman's selection for Australia. At a time when work opportunities were strictly limited, it made Accrington's advances even

UNSTOPPABLE: *The young Don Bradman in England in 1930. He made two double-centuries and a triple, at Leeds*

more attractive. His job at Mick Simmons' in Sydney was only part-time and entirely dependent on him continuing to perform.

The opportunity for Bradman to remain and work in Australia came via a three-tiered contract with the Sydney *Sun* and Associated newspapers, radio station 2UE and sporting retailers FJ Palmer & Son. The terms were a lucrative 1500 pounds a year for two years. It avoided an immediate showdown with officialdom. Bradman was well aware, however, that Board members frowned on players contributing to newspapers.

At the peak of his form and fitness, he'd married Jessie Menzies and they'd enjoyed an extended honeymoon to North America as part of Arthur Mailey's private touring side. In 10 weeks he played 51 innings for 3782 runs with 18 centuries. The opposition was only moderate but it was still an amazing set of scores. On return, on the eve of the arrival of the 1932-33 Englishmen, Bradman's articles in the *Sun* became a more serious issue. Seeking official permission from the Board to continue his involvement with the paper — a request he thought was a formality — he was stunned to learn of Board chairman Aubrey Oxlade's refusal, on the flimsy grounds that journalism was not his *sole* occupation. The regulations allowed latitude only to those, like Jack Fingleton, who were full-time writers.

IN DEMAND: The first of many Bradman's life stories was published in August 1930

'I must earn my living,' Bradman told pressmen, 'and if cricket interferes with my living then I must give up cricket. If the Board has said its last word, I shall not be available for the Test matches.' BRADMAN BOMBSHELL exploded the newspaper headlines, throughout Australia and in London. The game's newest, most-glittering star was at war with his own Board and threatening to stand out of the game for up to two years. The editor of the *Australian Cricketer* magazine, H. Drysdale Bett, rated Bradman one of the greatest personalities of his time, 'ranking with Lindrum, Mussolini, Gandhi, Hitler, Lindbergh, Kingsford Smith and the Prince of Wales'. The game could ill-afford to lose a player of his stature, especially as he gave fresh hope and inspiration to all affected by the Depression.

Bradman was adamant that he would not back down. The dispute scarred him. 'You can imagine my mental state,' he said in *Farewell to Cricket*. 'I promptly did what any man of integrity would do and announced that I would honour my contract and therefore, if the Board was adamant, I would not be available for the Test matches. Not only did it foreshadow the prospect of no Tests for me in 1932-33, but there was the 1934 tour of England in the background.'

Complicating the issue were lucrative offers to cover the Ashes series for newspapers in London.

Given his playing exertions in America, Bradman may have been wiser to bypass an opportunity for an early look at the touring English. However, he, Fingleton and Stan

PRELUDE TO BODYLINE: Mailey's Australians in America 1932. Back row, left to right: Edgar Rofe, Bill Ives, Keith Tolhurst, 'Chuck' Fleetwood-Smith, Dick Nutt, Phil Carney. Seated: Stan McCabe, Don Bradman, Arthur Mailey (manager), Vic Richardson, Alan Kippax, 'Sammy' Carter

McCabe accepted an offer to play in Perth for a combined Australian XI. Bradman scored a century, not with the bat, but with the ball: two for 106 from 19 overs of leg spin. So exhausted was he by the 10-day return train trip across the continent and distracted by the Board's implacability that he missed the opening Test in Sydney on health reasons. He attended the game and completed his daily commentaries, but abided by the Board's edict not to write.

Bradman's withdrawal from the opening Test of the long-awaited Ashes summer was greeted with disbelief. His health issues had been kept from the public until the day before the game. One writer reckoned Australia's champion batsman had had a nervous breakdown. Another ventured that his absence was diplomatic, so frightened was he of England's express bowler Harold Larwood, who had unveiled deliberate leg-theory for the first time in the previous weeks.

'Here was a pretty 'how d'ya do', said Fingleton. 'An Australian XI without Bradman! It was unthinkable and the public and the newspapers lost no time in saying so.'

The impasse with the Board wasn't settled until the day before the second Test in Melbourne, when a motion urging that the player-writer rule be altered was defeated. Associated Newspapers, owners of the *Sun*, its managing director Sir Hugh Denison and its editorial director 'RC' Packer (Kerry Packer's grandfather) immediately released Bradman from his contract, avoiding any backlash from the Sydney public and clearing Bradman's way to play again.

THE DON was not the only frontline Test player to fall into dispute with the Board over playing and writing. Leg-spinner Arthur Mailey, a cartoonist by profession, retired from Tests on the eve of the 1928-29 Ashes series when the Board objected to him pursuing his profession in journalism and commentating on matches in which he appeared. Although he was 42, he had appeared in Australia's previous 14 Tests and in his final game at The Oval in 1926, famous for Wilfred Rhodes' comeback at the age of 48, he had claimed nine wickets.

Relieved, but still far from happy with Board bureaucracy, Bradman vented his anger and frustrations via a press release:

'Through the generosity of the Associated Newspapers of Australia, who requested me to play for Australia instead of occupying a seat in the press box, I have been enabled to play in the second Test. To the great cricket-loving public of Australia, may I express my extreme pleasure at being thus able to represent my country once more.

'Even though the Board of Control continues to prevent me from earning an honourable and permanent living from journalism, it allows other members of the Australian XI to broadcast comments freely, despite the fact that broadcasting to them is only a temporary occupation.

'Again the difference between journalism and radio work is so small as to make the distinction appear ridiculous.

'The Board have all the facts before them at their meeting and their legislation means that they are able to dictate to players the means by which they shall earn their living . . .

'I must emphatically protest against the Board of Control being allowed to interfere with the permanent occupation of any player. To my mind the Board was never meant to have powers directing the business activities of players. It is certainly no encouragement to any player to remain in Australia when such restrictions are brought in.'

Bradman's return to cricket in Melbourne was bitter-sweet. He followed a first-ball duck with one of his most glorious centuries which helped Australia win its only match of the infamous summer, soon to become known for one word: Bodyline.

CAREER-BEST: Clem Hill's 365 not out for South Australia against New South Wales in Adelaide in 1900-01 remained a world record for a left-hander for 50 years until 1952-53

15 1912 SYDNEY

Boardroom brawling

It was the most explosive 15 minutes in Australian cricket history. Having had his captaincy abilities questioned and derided during the 1911-12 Ashes season, Clem Hill responded by punching a co-selector on the nose. It triggered a brawl which all but saw the selector, fiery-eyed Victorian Peter McAlister pushed out of a window in the upstairs boardroom of the NSW Cricket Association in Martin Place, all part of a bitter power-play between rebellious players and administrators for control of the game.

Australia's first great left-hander, Clem Hill, was charming and popular, his geniality matched only by his considerable acumen and cricketing ability. One of just 40-or-so to captain Australia, Hill was normally also among the most sunny-natured. Australia's most famous No. 3 before Charlie Macartney and Don Bradman, Hill was a formidable, focused and influential South Australian, good enough as a teenager to make 360 in Adelaide's famous inter-collegiate between St Peter's and Prince Alfred College and as a Test-man the first Australian to 3000 Test runs at an average superior even to the much-loved Victor Trumper.

As Australia's captain from 1910 to 1912, his record was mixed — five wins and five losses — but he led at a time when England possessed Sydney Barnes and Frank Foster, the most successful new-ball pace pairing of the Golden Age.

One of the most ambitious of Hill's teammates was the stern Victorian Peter McAlister who, once crossed, was a formidable enemy. For years their relationship was rarely anything but tepid, Hill disdainful of McAlister's playing abilities and McAlister resentful of Hill's record, prominence and appeal. McAlister believed Hill favoured others ahead of him, especially all-rounder Frank Laver, his long-time teammate at East Melbourne.

Despite only mediocre lead-up seasons, McAlister's inner rage at his omission from the 1902 and especially the 1905 tours to England spilled publicly during Hill's tenure

1907-08 AUSTRALIANS IN SYDNEY: Back row, left to right: Bob Crockett (umpire), Reg Duff (12th man), Gerry Hazlitt, Warwick Armstrong, Jack Saunders, Vernon Ransford, J. Hannah (umpire). Seated: Victor Trumper, Clem Hill, 'Monty' Noble (captain), Peter McAlister, 'Tibby' Cotter. Front: Charlie Macartney, 'Sammy' Carter. Ken Piesse collection

as Australia's captain. Enjoying fresh power as chairman of the very first selection panels established by the embryonic Australian Board of Control, McAlister, then 39, not only voted himself into the 1909 touring squad to England, he made himself vice-captain and treasurer!

In a preview of the internal trouble which was to irrevocably split the game in Australia less than three years later, Hill immediately withdrew, his dislike of the power-hungry McAlister surpassed only by his objections to 'the high taxation' imposed by the Board.

According to Adelaide-based historian Bernard Whimpress, it was the first flare-up in a long-running battle for power between the Board and the leading players unused to having their healthy on-tour monies challenged.

Hill was also reluctant to spend another 10 months away from home. In 1905, he'd been accompanied throughout the tour by his wife, Florrie, who he'd married only weeks before the boat left for Britain.

Fellow players outside the clique were becoming increasingly frustrated, having recognised that their chances of touring overseas was dependent on the whims of the very best players, who, until then, had been responsible for selection. Some, like McAlister, regarded the establishment of a more active and powerful Board as the only way to break the monopoly.

It was said McAlister had talked himself into the Test team and stayed there for four matches of five in 1907-08, despite rarely distinguishing himself. His reappointment as Victoria's Australian selector ahead of Hugh Trumble in December 1908 was very unpopular among the leading players, confirming their opinion that he was a Board watchdog.

Hill and he had openly disagreed at an acrimonious selection meeting before the release of the 1909 side. McAlister felt he should be in the side; Hill claimed him to be past his best and his style unsuitable to English conditions. Hill wanted fellow South Australian Alby Gehrs, who had toured in 1905, only to be outvoted.

Financially, Hill and the elite players were on the back foot. In January 1909, Laver was sent to Sydney to renegotiate the financial terms for the tour, but found the Board dictatorial and unbending. Under no circumstances were any players, even the best ones, to be given special consideration. While the Board agreed that Laver could manage, they insisted that a Board nominee, McAlister, also tour, as treasurer. Insulted, Hill immediately telegrammed his withdrawal.

If Hill was nettled enough by the off-field events to stay at home, he sorely missed the challenge and glamor of Test cricket, if not the politics. However, the retirement of MA 'Monty' Noble, one of Australia's finest captains at the conclusion of the tour, was to provide an imposing impetus for his career. Named Australia's new captain against Percy Sherwell's visiting South Africans, Hill, for the only time in Test cricket, made two centuries in the same series. His average of 53 was his highest for eight years.

The Board of Control's thorny relationship with Hill and the other leading players was, however, becoming pricklier. They wanted to be the ultimate policy makers and as the controllers of the game, have the ultimate say in team and tour selection, including the choice of captain and manager. Even more importantly they wanted a substantial slice of the profits. Private clubs such as the Melbourne Cricket Club, which had previously backed the tours, were never again to be as influential.

While Hill and others could see merit in a central, controlling authority, they were angered by what they saw as Board greediness in the new financial arrangements — the Board having set the terms in 1909 at six per cent of profits up to the first 6000 pounds and 12.5 per cent of every extra pound earned. Previously profits had been divided basically on equal terms — and purely among the players.

Open warfare developed with a sudden change in rules denying the players their long-standing privilege of selecting their own manager. The Board's decision, in a split-vote, saw six elite players threaten to withdraw their services from the soon-to-start triangular Test tour to England. The rebels were Hill, his vice-captain Victor Trumper, Vernon Ransford, Warwick Armstrong, A 'Tibby' Cotter and H 'Sammy' Carter. 'The Big Six' wanted Laver as manager, but he had been outlawed by senior Board-men after he had initially withheld his accounts from the 1909 tour —saying it was part of

McAlister's touring duties to keep official accounts.

There was a tremendous public backlash, lifelong friendships stalling amid a series of swipes and allegations which sent newspaper circulations soaring. 'What are we to do?' asked one of the key dissenters Trumper. 'Go down on our knees and ask the Board to let us go to England on any terms they like?'

It was in this angry, unsettled climate that PF 'Plum' Warner's 1911-12 Englishmen arrived and the early Ashes battles were played, England taking a 2-1 lead thanks to Barnes and the left-armer Foster, who claimed 40 wickets between them in the first three Tests.

On the eve of the third Test in his home town of Adelaide, Hill telegrammed McAlister in Melbourne:

> Macartney all right. Think must have a left-arm bowler. Suggest Macartney and Matthews in place of Whitty and Minnett. Minnett 12th.

McAlister's response was extraordinary and deliberately provocative:

> My team as forwarded yesterday. Still opposed (to) Macartney's selection. If (co-selector Frank) Iredale agrees with you, favour yourself standing down and not Minnett.

It was the most Machiavellian of replies and Hill was enraged. The first to score 3000 runs in Test cricket and holder of the world record score of 365 not out, Hill's average was even higher than that of Trumper, Australia's most-loved cricketer. Twelve months earlier, in his very first Test as Australian captain, Hill had made 191 against the South Africans in Sydney, Australia scoring almost 500 runs on the record-breaking opening day.

While he'd fallen cheaply to Barnes twice in the previous Test in Melbourne, so had the entire Australian top-order, bar feisty Victorian Armstrong, at his best in a scrap. Barnes, with eight wickets for the game, was the matchwinner, his dynamic opening spell of five for 6 from 11 overs the best ever on the first day of a Melbourne Test.

Charles Macartney from NSW, 12th man in each of the first two Tests, was a genuine all-rounder and deserved a place. So did improved spinner Jimmy Matthews, who'd taken 14 wickets in four preceding games, champion-on-the-rise Jack Hobbs one of his three victims in Victoria's match against the MCC.

Hill's anger magnified when the text of McAlister's telegram leaked to the newspapers. He wrote to the Board of Control complaining of McAlister's wire but received no satisfaction.

Australia lost the Test, despite a game late-match fightback, led by Hill who top-scored with 98 before falling to Barnes.

Approaching the pivotal fourth Test, Hill met with co-selectors McAlister and Iredale (from NSW) on the second floor at Bull's Chambers in Martin Place, the NSW Cricket Association's Sydney offices. Their task was to pick Australia's next XII and discuss the squad to England later in the year. Just-appointed Board of Control secretary Syd Smith jnr. was also present to take minutes.

Soon into the meeting, an argument developed over Hill's leadership skills, McAlister scathing of Hill's batting order (Victor Trumper batted at No. 6 and Hill at No. 7) when the Australians were bowled out for just 133 in Adelaide, having won the toss in perfect conditions. He also felt Hill's bowling changes had misfired, especially his use of leg-spinner HV 'Ranji' Hordern as Tibby Cotter's opening partner.

Still bristling over McAlister's inflammatory telegram, Hill, who'd already been named captain of the team to England, said no Australian side would have toured England under McAlister's leadership, McAlister replying that he was a better captain than Hill and Victor Trumper combined.

McAlister and Hill continued to trade barbs:

> McALISTER: 'You're the worst captain that I've seen.'
>
> HILL: 'If you keep on insulting me I'll pull your nose.'
>
> McALISTER: 'You are the worst captain I've *ever* seen.'

According to the *Australasian* account, Hill leant across the table and struck McAlister, he said, with an open slap. Others claimed later it must have been with a fist, judging by the deep bruising under McAlister's eye. According to eyewitness reports, McAlister ran at Hill 'like an enraged bull', tables and chairs being upended and at one stage McAlister almost tumbling out of the open window.

'They were both game and determined,' Iredale told the *Australasian*. 'And they went at it hammer and tongs. Very few blows were struck; it was more like a wrestling match. Smith and I did our best to separate them, but they were all over the place and when the big table was upset, I was pinned in the corner.'

After 10 minutes, maybe more, McAlister lay on his back with Hill over him, both men panting from the exertion. According to historian and author AG 'Johnnie' Moyes, Smith tugged hard enough on Hill's coat tails to momentarily split the pair. Iredale then held back McAlister, who yelled 'coward' as Hill left the room.

Hill told Smith he could no longer continue on the same selection panel as McAlister. Later that day at Hill's hotel, Smith accepted his written resignation. Iredale and McAlister then chose the fourth Test side, the South Australian Harry Blinman co-opted in case of any deadlocks.

'I would not have minded so much if he had invited me outside,' a bruised and battered McAlister told newspaper reporters on his arrival back at Spencer Street railway station in Melbourne. 'Then I would have known what to expect.'

The *Sydney Morning Herald* ran the three-deck headline: BLOOD FLOWS, VIOLENT BLOWS, HILL RESIGNS and also published pictures of the pair under a large caption: THE ADVERSARIES.

Cricket: A Weekly Record of the Game commented: 'Perhaps it was asking too much to expect Messrs Hill and McAlister to work in harmony together ... there is an old case of friction between them.'

According to historian Rick Smith, Hill was cheered to the wicket in all his remaining innings that summer. However, he failed to make even 25 in four knocks, England winning each of the last two Tests to take the series 4-1.

Hill was never again to play for Australia. Nor would he ever again talk to McAlister.

Hill's invitation to tour England was withdrawn, along with the five other champion players, when it was clear that they would tour only under the management of Laver.

Five players new to Test cricket were blooded, Syd Gregory recalled as captain and Queensland's GS Crouch made manager. 'The Board of Control has acted unjustly and dishonestly and has violated its own constitution,' said the just-retired Noble.

While the inexperienced Australians easily accounted for South Africa, England won the deciding match at The Oval by 244 runs in the first timeless Test to be played in England. Barnes, in typically irresistible form, led the charge, taking five wickets in the Australian first innings to give England the edge.

Hill was selected for one more tour, to South Africa in 1914-15 — by a panel not including McAlister — but declined, along with many others including Trumper, who, tragically, was soon to die from nephritis, a disease of the kidneys. Come August the tour was abandoned, after the outbreak of the Great War.

Hill retired, but in an ironic twist, later served on the Board of Control, as South Australia's delegate. He played his last game, a testimonial match for former teammate Bill Howell, at the age of 47 in 1924-25, a season in which he also became Australian cricket's first expert comments broadcaster during the two Sydney Tests on radio 2BL.

Despite sterling service to East Melbourne CC and consistent efforts at the head of the order for Victoria, including a double century on debut, Peter McAlister's hopes for English tour selection prior to 1909 were soured by poor home seasons immediately preceding selection.

In 1901-02 he averaged only 27 and in 1904-05, 19.

KEITH MILLER HAS THE HALL MARK OF A CHAMPION

By CLEM HILL
Former Test Captain

TODAY was to have been a Bradman day at the Melbourne Cricket Ground. However, the Victorians, batting well into the afternoon, very nearly stole the show.

It is a long time since I have seen a better all-round display of enterprising batting than that given by the Victorians in their first innings which totalled 475—not a bad total, but not a winning score on the plumb wicket provided.

And nobody seemed more like a coming star than young Keith Miller.

FOR the moment I want to forget placing, and the manner in which he about Bradman, and talk about used his feet, showed me that he has

batsman who will wear the green and gold of Australia in young Miller. To me he is a shandy between two great Australian batsmen in Alan Kippax and Bill Brown. Add something of Miller's own personality and genius and you'll have a real star.

I can't think of too much to say about him. I felt privileged at having seen this young fellow knocking at the door of the hall of great batsmen and succeeding in opening it.

Reading back over what I have written I feel that I have not paid sufficient tribute to Percy Beames for the magnificent innings he played today.

A Bradman Knock

COLUMNIST: Clem Hill maintained his association with cricket as a Board of Control delegate and as a feature writer with the twice-a-week Sporting Globe *newspaper in Melbourne*

In 1905, only two Victorians were chosen, Warwick Armstrong and Charlie McLeod, plus McAlister's East Melbourne teammate Frank Laver as manager.

In McAlister's last match before the '05 team was named, he was out for eight and a first-ball duck against powerful New South Wales. He finished ninth in Victoria's averages with a highest score of 59 in eight innings.

No early Australian cricketer made more 90s at Test level than Clem Hill. He succumbed six times in the 90s, in 1901-02 scoring 99, 98 and 97 in consecutive innings against Archie MacLaren's touring Englishmen. He made eight more 90s, too, in other first-class matches.

Johnnie Moyes said he'd never seen a batsman who could hit a fast bowler with greater fury than Hill. 'Ranji' Hordern rated Hill 'the most charming and sporting personality' he ever met in cricket.

Discussing the withdrawal of the Big Six, Arthur Mailey said: ' If these men were rebels, they were also gentlemen. And if there was a fault, I doubted that it was on their side.'

When Hill was controversially run out in Sydney in 1903-04, he stood his ground in an obvious show of dissent against umpire Bob Crockett, who was targeted by the crowd for the rest of the day. So angry were they that many remained behind after play waiting for Crockett to emerge. According to author Phil Derriman, Hill took it upon himself to escort Crockett through the crowd to the tram stop.

Hill also played Australian Rules football for South Adelaide and represented his state. Racing was another of his passions, and after World War 1 he became handicapper at the Victorian Amateur Turf Club.

His nickname was 'Kruger' after the Boer War leader.

EXCLUDED PURELY FOR HIS COLOR: Jack Marsh

16 JACK MARSH

Outcast

Full-blood Aboriginal Jack Marsh was so fast the 1901-02 Englishmen refused to play against him. Ranked among the leading express bowlers of the Golden Age, Marsh so delighted in his blue New South Wales state cap he'd wear it around the streets. A victim of prejudiced selections he was labelled a thrower by MA Noble and never was to be awarded a baggy green Australia cap, his name even scratched from the list of players who could practise with the NSW squad at the Sydney Cricket Ground by officials blinded by the racial customs of the day.

Had Jack Marsh been born white, he would have walked into the Australian XI. For three years he was the outstanding strike bowler in Sydney, the power base of Australian cricket, his exploits simply phenomenal.

Strong and athletic, he was a professional runner and hurdler of note and competed professionally in three states before being 'discovered' by an official of the South Sydney CC while throwing a boomerang for holiday makers at La Perouse.

His double-jointed, wristy bowling action was dubious and resulted in early no-ball calls against him at grade and state trial level. But when he bowled just as fast with his arm encased in splints, it was clear that prejudices outside cricket were clouding his advancement.

Marsh was the find of the 1900-01 Australian season, in which he claimed 24 wickets in four matches. But he was also no-balled for throwing 19 times in two matches by the Victorian umpire Bob Crockett.

His debut game, in Adelaide, was memorable for Clem Hill amassing 365 not out, the world record first-class score. But Marsh took five for 181 and followed with six wickets against Victoria, a game in which he was first called by Crockett, the umpire saying later he was concerned at the twist in his wrist, rather than his elbow.

Australian Cricket Scandals

NEW SOUTH WALES, JANUARY 1901: Back row, left to right: Richard Callaway (umpire), Victor Trumper, Andy McBeath, Bert Hopkins, Syd Redgrave (12th man) W. Green (manager). Seated: Frank Iredale, Les Poidevin, Syd Gregory, 'Monty' Noble, Reg Duff, Jack Marsh. Front: Jim Kelly, Tom Howard. South Australia was thrashed in this match by an innings and 605 runs, Marsh taking 10 wickets, including SA's champion Clem Hill in both innings

A campaign against throwers had been waged in England and Crockett was the first Australian umpire, at representative level, to make a stand. He no-balled Marsh both in Melbourne and Sydney and Marsh became so frustrated that he deliberately threw three balls.

Noted cricket writer JC Davis (under the nom de plume 'Not Out' in The Sydney Referee) admitted that 'there was an undoubted and definable difference between the manner in which those balls were thrown and the usual delivery. The difference was so plain that many who had previously held the opinion that Crockett was right, now began to doubt it'.

Author and historian Bernard Whimpress said Crockett, on the verge of his first international selections, may have deliberately set out on a personal crusade to outlaw Marsh and increase his chances of highest honours, after 10 years spent in officiating purely at intercolonial level. Umpires who had stood up to throwers had been applauded in England.

The controversy so affected Marsh's standing within the NSW XI that it was 15 months before he was selected again and only when MA 'Monty' Noble, NSW's just-appointed sole-selector, was England-bound with the 1902 Australians and didn't have a say. Noble, one of the ultimate power-brokers in Australian cricket, had blocked Marsh's initial selection only to be overruled by then co-selectors Tom Garrett and Ted Briscoe.

Despite his boom first year, Marsh was bypassed for further big matches until February 1902 when named by the Western Cricket Union to play against Archie MacLaren's English team in Bathurst, only for MacLaren to so object that he threatened to call off the game.

Several citizens' meetings were called at which the pro-Marsh lobby was strong. They firmly believed there were reasons of colour behind MacLaren's stand and his objections that his batsmen risked being injured by Marsh in a second-class game was merely a blind. Many felt Marsh unfairly condemned and that his suspect action was no more than a diversion for a darker conspiracy against him to take the heat off others. Noble, for example, had been labelled a thrower himself, by Sammy Woods, a notable all-round sportsman who represented both Australia and England in Tests.

UPSET: MCC touring captain 'Plum' Warner was bowled by Jack Marsh before launching a complaint against the legitimacy of the loose-limbed Aboriginal's action

England was trailing 1-2 in mid-series and Marsh supporters felt MacLaren fearful of Marsh's inclusion as it would highlight Australia's superiority and depth of quality reserves. Though Marsh didn't play, England lost the last two Tests anyway and Marsh drifted into oblivion, playing only sporadically at the highest level, notably when Noble was absent.

Marsh led the Sydney grade averages for three years in a row and may have again in 1904-05 but for missing a portion of the season and touring with the Hippodrome circus, giving bowling exhibitions throughout country NSW and Queensland.

In his solitary 'international' for a Bathurst XV against the 1903-04 Englishmen, he took five for 55 and bowled with such variation, curve and break-back that many of the tourists considered him the finest bowler they had faced on tour, superior even to the great Victorian Hugh Trumble. Warner lost his middle stump to Marsh and claimed later, however, that Marsh threw as many as three balls a over. 'I've never seen anyone throw so deliberately,' said teammate Reg Foster. 'It was a good wicket and he was turning the ball up to a yard at times.'

Marsh dropped pace and experimented with seam and spin changes rather than blasting opponents out and running the risk of being targeted by ambitious umpires. He was rapidly losing heart with prejudiced selections and exasperated by the influential

FILL-IN: Sam Morris played his one-and-only Test for Australia after Billy Murdoch and his XI refused to play over the distribution of the gate receipts in Melbourne

Noble, who not only thought him a chucker, but believed he lacked sufficient 'class' to mix in cricketing circles.

Warner made it known that he would strongly resist any moves by the Australians to play Marsh in the remaining two Tests that summer.

According to author Anthony Meredith: 'Warner, not to be trifled with in negotiations at any times, was always in belligerent mood when playing second-class matches.'

Crockett's presence as umpire in all five of the summer's Tests was a further deterrent against Marsh's inclusion.

Whimpress says Marsh was 'undoubtedly the victim of racism over selection matters' as well as accusations against the validity of his action. Fellow historian Ray Webster says one of the stamps of the Aboriginal race has been their loose-limbed flexibility and this has led to unorthodoxy, particularly as Aborigines were denied the formal early coaching of their white counterparts.

When it was suggested that Marsh should be considered for the 1905 Australian tour of England, prominent doctor and NSW cricketer Les Poidevin said it was a long shot, 'probably because the absurd White Australia policy has touched or tainted the hearts of the rulers of cricket, as it has the political rulers'.

BATHURST SCANDAL: *The Sydney Bulletin's comment on the Marsh-MacLaren controversy.*
Bernard Whimpress/Passport to Nowhere

Years after Marsh's brutal death, aged 42, in a street fight in the New South Wales country town of Orange, former Australian batsman and Test selector Warren Bardsley said Marsh was the best bowler he ever faced, ahead even of the famed Englishman Sydney Barnes. 'The reason they kept him out of big [Test] cricket was his colour,' he said.

Author Phil Derriman found an old cutting from *The Bulletin* calling Marsh 'the greatest bowler NSW ever sheltered'. On his death, it said: 'But he was a darky troubled with manners which white brothers found it impossible to put up with.'

- The first black man to play for Australia was Samuel Morris, born in Hobart of West Indian parents, who played one Test in Melbourne in 1884-85 after the Australian team had withdrawn its services over the split of gate monies.

FURIOUS: Lord Harris (Robert George Canning) was attacked with a stick during the Sydney cricket riot in 1879

17 1879 SYDNEY

Cricket's first riot

The decision to rule local hero Billy Murdoch run out invoked extraordinary scenes at the Association Ground on this Sydney Saturday. When the NSW captain Dave Gregory refused to send out another batsman in protest, gambling interests triggered a wild riot, English captain Lord Harris, 28, being attacked with a stick and one of his team punched as cricket showed its wild side So incensed was his Lordship, cricket's ultimate ambassador, that he used all of his influence to make a mockery of Australia's 1880 return tour, the all-star team even forced to advertise for matches.

Warnings against the detrimental effect gambling was having on important cricket matches freely circulated 140 years ago. Newspapers such as the Sydney *Echo* said that betting 'threatened to eat the heart out of many of our sports'.

Gambling was such an integral part of early Australian cricket that 19th Century cricket annuals regularly including rules for betting. Advertisements were also included from leading city hotels, which boasted 'direct telephone facilities to the Melbourne Cricket Ground and Victoria Racing Club'.

The arrival of teams from the mother country intensified the public interest and large wagers at club and representative level were common. When the gentleman amateur, the fourth Lord Harris (Robert George Canning) led a semi-representative side on tour in 1878-79, there were joyous celebrations after the Australian XI defeated his Gentlemen of England in Melbourne in a game later recognised as cricket's third Test match. Even then, cricket was a national pastime.

Soon afterwards a New South Wales XI team also defeated the tourists and come the return fixture in February 1879 at the Association Ground (now the Sydney Cricket Ground), a myriad of bookmakers appeared looking for more spoils. Despite

EARLY BETS IN AUSTRALIAN CRICKET

BETS.

I.

No bet upon any match is payable unless it be played out or given up.

II.

If the runs of one player be betted against those of another, the bet depends upon the first innings, unless otherwise specified.

III.

If the bet be made on both innings, and one party beat the other in one innings, the runs of the first innings shall determine it.

IV.

If the other party go in a second time, then the bet must be determined by the number on the score.

	Page
Batsmen's Averages	11
Bets on the Game	55
Bowling Analyses	18

BETTING GUIDE: A cut out from the 1857-58 Fairfax Cricketer's Guide for Australasia.
Trove/David Studham/MCC Library

BETTING HAD been a common practice in England from the earliest times. Wagers on matches in Kent occurred as early as 1646. In the 1730s, the Prince of Wales had played cricket for large bets.

In 1817, England's leading professional player, William Lambert, was said to have sold the match between England and XXII of Nottingham, at Forest Ground. A rough diamond, he was forbidden from ever again playing at the home of cricket, Lord's.

Leading into the first intercolonial between New South Wales and Victoria in Melbourne in 1856, the Victorians wanted to have a side stake of 500 pounds, but NSW preferred to play for honour.

Early newspapers often carried the odds. The 1857-58 Fairfax Cricketer's Guide for Australasia includes a guide to betting, with four key points. An article: *Bets on the Game* was even included high-up in the annual's contents.

In 1881 allegations were made that three of Alfred Shaw's touring English team were paid to perform badly in the game against Victoria. Captain Shaw said the rumours were 'not without foundation' after he'd witnessed several simple fielding errors from the accused three: George Ulyett, William Scotton and John Selby. In six innings for the match, none of the trio made even 30.

the earlier English loss, money was again plentiful for England at better odds, despite the return after injury for NSW of 'the Demon' Fred Spofforth.

By late on the second day, the local XI had followed on 90 runs in arrears and were sliding to certain defeat. A crowd of 10,000 was in attendance. Bookmakers in and around the pavilion stood to lose the fortune they'd made earlier in the summer, as loyal English supporters outnumbered those who had backed NSW. There'd been several big bets on England on the very eve of the game.

The bookmakers' agitation was heightened when first-innings star Billy Murdoch was ruled run out by the tourists' nominated umpire, the 22-year-old Victorian George Coulthard. In a tremendous furore, 2000 invaded the ground and surged to the centre. Most were from the terrace area, later to become the ground's famous Hill, where several bookmakers were fixed. Many alleged that Coulthard was incompetent. He was set upon, several accusing him of being a cheat. In the commotion, Lord Harris was hit across the body by a stick. Popular Lancastrian AN 'Monkey' Hornby was punched and his shirt torn after he'd grabbed one of the agitators he thought was Lord Harris' assailant. Only later, at a much-publicised court case, did the authorities discover that Hornby had collared the wrong man.

UNFAIRLY RUN OUT?: Billy Murdoch

'It was a scene of confusion and blows were received and returned,' said the writer from the Sydney *Echo*. 'As a general melee was now imminent a number of gentlemen from the pavilion and grandstand hurried to the assistance of the English team who otherwise might have been seriously maltreated. The small body of police who were present were too late to get to the centre of the ground when the rush occurred and subsequently found it difficult to make their way through the crowd.'

The crowd refused to vacate the oval until a new umpire was appointed. 'Let an Englishman stand umpire,' they said, 'We won't have a Victorian!'

The melee lasted for 30 minutes and made even bigger headlines than the bank hold-up that very same day by notorious bushranger Ned Kelly and his gang on the NSW country town of Jerilderie.

Throughout the riot, a grim and determined Lord Harris kept his players on the field, not wanting the New South Welshmen to claim the game. The NSW captain

THE ASSOCIATION GROUND: Later known as the Sydney Cricket Ground

Dave Gregory told Harris he wanted Coulthard replaced and when Harris refused, Gregory claimed the match over and was only persuaded to continue after discussions with the other umpire, Edmund Barton, whose skills of diplomacy were central in him later becoming Australia's first Prime Minister.

Gregory had initially stood at the gate and told Murdoch to go back and bat, according to historian Richard Cashman.

Harris understood the emotional reaction to Murdoch's run-out. He was the master batsman of the colony and had carried his bat in NSW's first innings for 82. But he fairly bristled at suggestions that his team's sudden improvement in form coincided with the generous odds on offer that February weekend. A great cricket enthusiast and a stickler for the game's ideals, rules and regulations, the playing hours were never long enough for his Lordship.

He said such a demonstration wasn't warranted. It demeaned the game and after all, wasn't cricket a game for gentlemen?

As to the so-called controversial nature of Murdoch's run-out, two of his fielders square on to the wicket said Coulthard's decision was correct.

Play was abandoned for the day when it became obvious that Harris would not back down and allow a replacement for Coulthard. He admitted Coulthard had made mistakes but they had balanced out. A proposed 5 pm restart was aborted.

The *Sydney Morning Herald* described the riot as 'a national humiliation'. And it blamed Gregory for 'aiding and abetting' the disturbance.

In a letter to the London *Daily Telegraph*, Harris maintained his rage, accusing the Australians of being 'poor losers'. A lengthy reply from the NSW Cricket Association's secretary IM Gibson was also published, in which it was claimed Harris had deliberately suppressed some important facts.

Harris again scoffed at suggestions that Coulthard had backed England to win, or that two of his leading professionals, Yorkshiremen George Ulyett and Thomas Emmett, had sullied the game by deliberately performing below their normal standards in earlier matches to make a killing later in the tour.

However, there was no doubt that the bookmaking fraternity was threatened with large losses if England won. 'One well-known betting man acted as a fugleman (ringleader),' said the SMH. 'The crowd, encouraged by his bad example, worked themselves into a state of violent excitement. A large number of larrikins sitting within the boundary fence made a rush for the centre of the ground and were quickly followed by hundreds of roughs who took possession of the wickets.'

The two men who had assaulted Lord Harris and Hornby, William Rigney and John Richards, were each fined 2 pounds. They also were made to pay 25 shillings in costs. A Victorian bookmaker had his 1879 membership fees returned and was barred for life. However, other bookmakers continued to gain admittance and freely operated at the ground, despite signs forbidding their presence.

Insulted by what he described as 'a howling mob', Lord Harris withdrew his team from the scheduled second match against all-Australia in Sydney and, on return to London, angrily defended his team of accusations that they'd been 'strolling actors rather than a party of gentlemen'. He refused to meet the 1880 Australians on their arrival in England, the team having to advertise for matches.

FOR THE GOOD OF THE GAME: The persuasive Surrey CCC secretary Charles Alcock convinced Lord Harris to soften his hardline attitude and lead a full strength English XI against the touring Australians at The Oval in September 1880

It wasn't until the influential WG Grace, the persuasive and diplomatic Surrey administrator Charles Alcock and Victorian and Australian all-rounder George Alexander became involved that a full international was arranged, in London. WG made the first Test century by an Englishman, Harris was captain and the politics which had dogged the early weeks of the tour were momentarily forgotten amid the euphoria of a magnificent English victory.

- Lord Harris later became president of the MCC in 1895 and later its treasurer from 1916-32.

ACCUSATIONS: The all-powerful WG Grace called the Australians 'sneaks' and bustled Billy Midwinter into a London cab…

18 WE MIDWINTER

Kidnapped

Mercenary, mercurial Billy Midwinter was padded up and practising with the 1878 Australians ready to open the innings against Middlesex at Lord's when the omnipotent Dr WG Grace arrived, claiming 'Middy' was needed elsewhere and promptly bundled him into a London cab. Before leaving he called the Australians 'a damn lot of sneaks'. Fancy the visitors trying to pirate his *player!*

William Evans 'Billy' Midwinter was just nine when he joined his family on the *Red Jacket* to Australia, along with hundreds of other struggling Brits excited by the lure of gold fever and the prospect of making their fortunes in the Australian Gold Rushes. His father, William snr, was first a goldminer before working as a butcher in Bendigo and Eaglehawk where William jnr. was soon noted as a cricketer of uncommon promise, playing at 'A' grade level with the men from his early teens.

The scorer, aged 18, of the first recorded double century in Australian cricket, 256 for Bendigo United against Sandhurst in 1869-70, Midwinter's friendship with Harry Boyle, Bendigo's most famous cricketer, saw new opportunities open in Melbourne.

At 191 cm (6 ft 3 in) and 89 kg (14 st), Midwinter was a giant of a man, who became a headliner virtually overnight when, representing XVIII of Victoria against the touring Englishmen in Melbourne, he bowled WG Grace and his brother, GF Grace — the then holder of the world record first-class score of 154.

A member of the inaugural All-Australia XI which played All-England in March 1877, a game later recognised as the first Test match, Midwinter was one of seven of the Australian team born outside the colonies. Handy in the middle order, he particularly impressed with his medium pacers, taking five for 78 and one for 23 from 73 economic (four-ball) overs. Almost immediately he was offered terms by his county-of-birth, Gloucestershire, captained by the legendary WG Grace.

Not as self-confident as some — he once almost withdrew from an important match because he felt he was not in sufficiently good form — Midwinter was also prone to temper, as shown earlier that inaugural Test season when he was reported for threatening to strike a North Bendigo opponent during a club match.

The first in a line of cricket mercenaries to play professionally, six months in England and six in Australia, Midwinter represented Gloucester from 1877-82 and became the first to play Test cricket both for and against Australia.

Enticed by the 700 pounds for each player on offer, with Dave Gregory's 1878 Australians, Midwinter looked to alter his cross commitments, the prospect of benefit matches in Melbourne and Sydney more appealing and far more lucrative than the eight pounds, plus expenses, he was pocketing a game at Gloucester. According to Tom Horan ('Felix') in the *Australasian*, Midwinter 'didn't seem to know his own mind for two minutes together'.

BUSH CRICKET: *Flat land cuttings like this were commonplace in the bush where a young Billy Midwinter first learnt the rudiments of the game*

He'd boated back from Australia with James Lillywhite's 1876-77 tourists and played an inaugural season with Grace's Gloucestershire in 1877. When the 1878 Australians arrived in Liverpool in mid-May, 1878, he played with them.

Having already helped the colonials to their first-ever victory at Lord's, 'The Bendigo Giant' was preparing to open the batting with Alick Bannerman against the men from Middlesex when a pumped-up WG arrived with his closest friend, Gloucestershire county wicketkeeper and rugby international Arthur Bush, on a 'piratical raid' — as described by one of Grace's biographers, Simon Rae.

After 15 minutes of argument, persuasive to the extreme, back into the cab the two Englishmen stepped — with Midwinter beside them! The sweet-talking Doctor had convinced Midwinter of the importance of Gloucester's match with Surrey, just 30 minutes away across London at The Oval.

Several years earlier, Grace had agreed to come to Australia only after his demands of a 1500 pound fee and honeymoon expenses were met.

In an extraordinary week of scoring, in August 1876, Grace had amassed 839 runs for only twice out, including an unbeaten 318 against Yorkshire. He was the all-powerful giant of the game.

AN EARLY PICTURE OF THE 1878 AUSTRALIANS (including Billy Midwinter before his desertion): Standing, left to right: Jack Blackham, Tom Horan, George Bailey, Jack Conway (manager), Alick Bannerman, Charles Bannerman, Billy Murdoch. Seated: Dave Gregory (captain). Front: Fred Spofforth, Frank Allan, Midwinter (hands on his knee), Tom Garrett, Harry Boyle.
London Stereoscopic Co./Gerard Conlan collection

When told earlier that fateful June 20 morning of Midwinter's decision to remain with the Australians, Grace lost his temper and abused Australian manager John Conway and fast bowler Boyle, saying they were 'a damn lot of sneaks'.

With Bush in support, Grace made his infamous dash across town, picked up Midwinter and within an hour of the start of Gloucestershire's game, had re-entered the field, with Midwinter, and, hardly pausing to find out the score, come on at first change. It had been quite a morning. 'Midwinter is a Gloucester man who had promised Mr Grace to play in all county matches,' said one source.

The Australians and particularly Conway were appalled and considered boycotting the fixture against Gloucestershire later in the season. With Midwinter safely back on full-time county duty, Grace admitted to 'unparliamentary language' towards Conway, an old adversary, and hoped that the Australians would reconsider as they'd 'meet a hearty welcome and a good ground at Clifton'. The game was duly played, a thumb injury conveniently sidelining Midwinter and the match being easily won by the Australians without incident.

In the early 1880s, Midwinter was one of the outstanding all-rounders in the world and named for Alfred Shaw's English team to Australia in 1881-82, he played in all four

AUSTRALIAN PLAYERS WHO ALSO PLAYED TEST CRICKET ELSEWHERE				
Player	Country/Span	Place of birth	Aust mts	Total
Jack Ferris	England (1), 1891-92	Sydney (NSW)	8	9
Billy Midwinter	England (4), 1881-82	St Briavels (Eng.)	8	12
Billy Murdoch	England (1), 1891-92	Sandhurst (Vic)	18	19
Albert Trott	England (2), 1898-99	Abbotsford (Vic.)	3	5
Kepler Wessels	South Africa (16), 1991-94	Bloemfontein (RSA)	24	40
Sammy Woods	England (3), 1895-96	Glenfield (NSW)	3	6

Tests against his old teammates. He also shared in a partnership of 454 in five-and-a-half hours with champion all-rounder William Barnes, for MCC versus Leicester — and counted every run as he went. Once when he was accorded a collection at Scarborough, he carried the money away in a carpet bag. The total proceeds totalled 30 pounds, mostly in coppers and it took him two hours to count it all. Asked if he would have preferred a cheque, he said: 'Not a bit of it. I would have to take a cheque to the bank. But the stuff is here and I can do what I like with it.'

According to historian Jack Pollard, when Midwinter arrived back in Australia after the 1882 English season, he said he objected to being called 'Anglo-Australian'. He considered himself Australian to the core. 'Are we to submit to another season of vagueness from this very slippery cricketer?' asked 'Censor' in the Sydney *Mail*. 'One day he is Australian and the next day an English player.'

After his eyesight began to fail, Midwinter quit the game, passing up the opportunity to tour England one last time in 1888 and became the owner of the Victoria Hotel in inner Melbourne. He died at 39 in a mental asylum, after the tragic early death of his wife Elizabeth and two young children, Elsie and Albert and the collapse of his family's stockbroking firm. He'd become paralysed from the waist down and lapsed in and out of consciousness. His pauper's grave at the Melbourne General Cemetery in Carlton for years was marked only 'L286' before being found and restored by the Australian Cricket Society in 1982.

A plaque was unveiled as part of a brief service:

WILLIAM EVANS MIDWINTER
In Memory of William Evans Midwinter
19th June 1851 – 3rd December 1890
International Cricketer.
Husband of Elizabeth,
Father of Elsie, Albert and William jnr.
All deceased.

The only cricketer to play for Australia v England (eight Tests) and England v Australia (four Tests)

The Australian Cricket Society in association with the Victorian Cricket Association, February 1982.

Whilst revered, WG Grace was not immune to scandal. He was accused of sharp practice during the 1882 Ashes Test at The Oval when he claimed a run-out against Australian No. 8 Sammy Jones who, after completing a run, had left his crease to do some 'gardening'. One version has Jones looking at Grace and nodding, implying a tacit agreement between them that he was clear to leave his crease. Another was that the ball was unmistakably still in play. Jones and the Australians were astonished when Grace lifted the bails and appealed.

Initially Robert Thoms, one of England's most highly rated umpires, made no move, seeming to be as stunned as the Australian. He asked Grace if he wanted a decision and on Grace saying 'yes' replied: 'It's not cricket, but I must give the batsman out.'

So infuriated was Australia's 'demon' bowler Fred Spofforth by what he considered poor sportsmanship that he bowled like a man possessed, taking seven for 44, to go with his seven for 46 in the first innings.

England lost by seven runs, prompting the celebrated mock obituary notice in the London *Times* saying the body of English cricket would be cremated and taken back to Australia.

Further reading

BOOKS

Arlott, J., *Basingstoke Boy* (Guild, 1990)

Bailey, P., P. Thorn & P. Wynne-Thomas, *Who's Who of Cricketers* (Newnes, 1984)

Beecher, E., *The Cricket Revolution* (Newspress, 1978)

Botham, I., *My Autobiography* (CollinsWillow, 1994)

Bowen, R., *Cricket: A History of Its Growth and Development Throughout the World* (Eyre & Spottiswoode, 1970)

Bowes, W., *Express Deliveries* (Stanley Paul, 1949)

Brearley, M., *Phoenix from the Ashes:* The Story of the England-Australia Series 1981 (Hodder & Stoughton, 1982)

Cairns, L., *Give It a Heave* (Moa, 1984)

Campbell, RH, *Cricket Casualties* (ABC, 1933)

Cashman, R., *The 'Demon' Spofforth* (University of New South Wales Press/Walla Walla Press, 1990 & 2014)

Chappell, I., *Chappelli: The Cutting Edge* (Swan, 1992)

Chappell, I. with P. McFarline & E. Beecher, *Chappelli:* Ian Chappell's Life Story (Hutchinson, 1976)

Compton, D., *Testing Time for England* (Stanley Paul, 1947)

Crowe, M., *Out on a Limb* (Reed, 1995)

Derriman, P., *The Grand Old Ground:* A History of the Sydney Cricket Ground (Cassell, 1981)

Derriman, P., The Top 100 and the 1st XI (Fairfax Library, 1987)

D'Oliveira, B., *The D'Oliveira Affair* (Collins, 1969)

Down, M., *Archie:* A Biography of A. C. MacLaren (Allen & Unwin, 1981)

Eason, A., *The A-Z of Bradman* (self-published 2002)

Fiddian, M., *A Miscellany of Left-Handers* (South East Newspapers, 1998)

Frindall, B., *The Wisden Book of Test Cricket*, Vols 1 and 2 (Headline, 1995)

Frindall, B., *Limited-Overs International Cricket: The Complete Record* (Headline, 1997)

Gatting, M., *Leading from the Front* (Queen Anne Press, 1988)

Gavaskar, S., *Idols* (Allen & Unwin, 1984)

Gooch, G. & F. Keating, *Gooch: My Autobiography* (CollinsWillow, 1995)

Further reading

Gooch, G. & A. Lee, *Out of the Wilderness* (Guild, 1985)

Griffiths, E., *Kepler: The Biography* (Pelham, 1994)

Griffiths, E., *Jonty: Fruits of the Spirit* (CAB, 1998)

Haigh, G. & D. Frith, *Inside Story*, Unlocking Australian Cricket's Archives (Cricket Australia, 2007

Haigh, G., *The Cricket War* (Text, 1993)

Harris, J. & K. Wust, *Bendigo District Cricket 1853-1990* (Crown Castleton, 1991)

Harte, C., *Two Tours and Pollock* (Sports Marketing, Adelaide, 1988)

Hartman, R., *Hansie and the Boys* (Zebra Press, 1997)

Henry, O. with K. Graham, *The Man in the Middle* (Queen Anne Press, 1994)

Hobbs, J.B., *Recovering the Ashes:* An Account of the Cricket Tour in Australia, 1911-12 (Sir Isaac Pitman & Sons, 1912)

Hookes, D. with A. Shiell, *Hookesy* (ABC, 1993)

Hordern, HV, *Googlies* (Angus & Robertson, 1932)

Howarth, G. as told to I. Hepenstall, *Stirred but not Shaken* (Hodder Moa Beckett, 1998)

Imran Khan, *All Round View* (Chatto & Windus, 1988)

Jaggard, E., *Garth:* The Story of Graham McKenzie (Fremantle Arts Centre Press, 1993)

Kippax, A., *Anti Body-Line* (Sydney & Melbourne Publishing Company, 1933)

Knight, James, *Mark Waugh the Biography* (HarperSports, 2003)

Larwood, H., *Bodyline* (Elkin, Mathews & Marriot, 1933)

Larwood, H. with K. Perkins, *The Larwood Story:* A Cricketer's Autobiography (W.H. Allen, 1965)

Lillee, D., *Lillee: My Life in Cricket* (Methuen Australia, 1982)

Mahony, P., *Mary Ann's Australians* (Cricket Lore, 1996)

Mailey, AA, *And Then Came Larwood* (John Lane/ The Bodley Head, 1933)

Marsh, R., *The Gloves of Irony* (Lansdowne, 1982)

Marsh, R., *Gloves, Sweat and Tears* (Penguin, 1984)

Marlar, R., *The Story of Cricket* (Marshall Cavendish, 1979)

Martin-Jenkins, C., *Ball by Ball:* The Story of Cricket Broadcasting (Grafton, 1990)

McGilvray, A., with N. Tasker, *Back Page of Cricket* (Lester Townsend, 1989)

McGregor, A., *Greg Chappell: Cricket's Incomparable Artist* (William Collins, 1985)

McHarg, J., *Bill O'Reilly: A Cricketing Life* (Millennium, 1990)

Meher-Homji, K., *Cricket's Greatest Families* (Rupa & Co., 1981)

Morrison, D., *Mad as I Wanna Be* (Hodder Moa Beckett, 1997)

Mosey, D., *Laker: Portrait of a Legend* (Queen Anne Press, 1989)

Moyes, A.G. 'Johnnie', *A Century of Cricketers* (Angus & Robertson, 1950)

Moyes, A.G. 'Johnnie', *Australian Cricket: A History* (Angus & Robertson, 1959)

Norrie, D., Athers: *The Authorised Biography of Michael Atherton* (Hodder Headline, 1997)

Oldfield, WA, *Behind the Wickets* (Hutchinson & Co., 1938)

Oslear, D. & J. Bannister, *Tampering with Cricket* (CollinsWillow, 1996)

Patherya, M. & B. O'Brien, *The Penguin Book of Cricket Lists* (Penguin, 1987)

Pawle, G., R.E.S. *Wyatt: Fighting Cricketer* (Allen & Unwin, 1985)

Peebles, I., *Straight from the Shoulder* (Hutchinson & Co/The Cricketer, 1968)

Piesse, K., *Brad Hodge, The Little Master* (cricketbooks.com.au, 2010)

Piesse, K., *Cricket's Greatest Scandals*, match-fixing, corrupt captains, selection scams and more (Penguin, 2000 & 2001)

Piesse, K., *One Day Magic* (Australian, 1996)

Piesse, K., *Pep*, the story of Cec Pepper, the best cricketer *never* to play for Australia (cricketbooks.com.au, 2018)

Piesse, K., *The Pictorial History of Australian Test Cricket* (Echo, 2017)

Piesse, K., *Warne: Sultan of Spin* (Marcus Leonard/Modern Publishing, 1995)

Piesse, K. & B. Hansen, *Wildmen of Cricket* (Brian Hansen Publications, 1997)

Pollard, J., *Australian Cricket: The Game and the Players* (Hodder & Stoughton, 1982)

Pollard, J., *Bumpers, Bosies and Brickbats* (Murray, 1966)

Pollard, J., *Australian Cricket 1893-1917: The Turbulent Years* (Book Company, 1996)

Pollard, J. (ed.), *The Primary Club's Middle and Leg* (Macmillan, 1988)

Pollock, P., *The Thirty Tests* (Don Nelson, 1978)

Procter, M. & P. Murphy, *South Africa: The Years of Isolation* (Queen Anne Press, 1994)

Rae, S., *WG Grace: A Life* (Faber, 1998)

Redpath, I., with N. Phillipson, *Always Reddy* (Garry Sparke, 1976)

Richardson, V. with RS Whitington, *The Vic Richardson Story* (Rigby, 1967)

Robertson, Austin, *Cricket's Outlaws*, inside Kerry Packer's Revolution (Pan MacMillan Australia, 2017)

Robinson, R., *From the Boundary* (Collins, 1950)

Robinson, R., *The Wildest Tests* (Pelham, 1972)

Robinson, R., *After Stumps are Drawn*: The Best of Ray Robinson's Cricket Writings, as selected by Jack Pollard (Collins, 1985)

Rutherford, K., *A Hell of a Way to Make a Living* (Hodder Moa Beckett, 1995)

Scott, J., *Caught in Court* (Andre Deutsch, 1989)

Sharpham, P., *Trumper: The Definitive Biography* (Hodder & Stoughton, 1985)

Simpson, R., *Captain's Story* (Stanley Paul, 1966)

Smith, I. as told to R. Brittenden, *Smithy: Just a Drummer in the Band* (Moa, 1991)

Smith, R., *Cricket Brawl:* The 1912 Dispute (Apple, 1995)

Stone, G, *Compulsive Viewing*, the inside story of Packer's Nine Network (Viking, 2000)

Sutcliffe, H., *For England and Yorkshire* (Edward Arnold, 1935)

Swanton, EW 'Jim', *Gubby Allen: Man of Cricket* (Hutchinson, 1985)

Synge, A., *Sins of Omission* (Pelham, 1990)

Tatz, C., *Aborigines in Sport* (Australian Society for Sports History, 1987)

Tatz, C. & R. Tatz, *Black Diamonds* (Allen & Unwin, 1996)

Tyson, F., *The Century-Makers:* The Men Behind the Ashes 1877-1977 (Hutchinson, 1980)

Wardle, J. as told to AA Thomson, *Happy Go Johnny* (Robert Hale, 1957)

Warner, P.F., *Long Innings* (Harrap, 1950)

Webber, J.R., *The Chronicle of WG* (Association of Cricket Statisticians, 1998)

Webster, R., *First Class Cricket in Australia* Vol. 1 1850-51 to 1941-42 (R. Webster, 1991)

Webster, R., *First Class Cricket in Australia* Vol. 2 1945-46 to 1976-77 (R. Webster, 1997)

Whimpress, B., *Passport to Nowhere:* Aborigines in Australian Cricket 1850-1939 (Walla Walla Press, 1999)

Whitington, R.S. & G. Hele, *Bodyline Umpire* (Rigby, 1974)

Wynne-Thomas, P. & Arnold, P., *Cricket in Conflict* (Newnes, 1984)

INTERNET

cricketarchive.com

cricketbooks.com.au

sportshounds.com.au

MAGAZINES & ANNUALS

Australian Cricket magazine

Australian Cricketer, The

Cricket: A Weekly Record of the Game

Cricketer magazine

Cricketer International, The

David Lord's World of Cricket

Indian Cricket

Pakistani Cricketer, The

Past & Present (John Wisden & Co.)

Protea Cricket Annual of South Africa, The

South African Cricketer, The

Wisden Cricket Monthly

Wisden Cricketers' Almanack

About the author

Ken Piesse is Australian cricket's master storyteller and the author of more than 50 cricket books including *Cricket's Colosseum* (2003), the first 125 years of Test cricket at the Melbourne Cricket Ground and most recently *Pep*, the story of Cec Pepper the best cricketer *never* to represent Australia (2018).

Among his previous sports books for Wilkinson Books was *TJ Over the Top* (1999), the bestselling autobiography of Terry Jenner, Shane Warne's coach.

Born in the year the MCG Test wicket was illegally watered, ever since Ken was given a brand-new copy of the 1965 *Wisden* and memorised most of its 1066 pages, cricket has been his cornerstone and the MCG his second home.

CAULFIELD PARK 1987: Port Melbourne v St Kilda, a twilight Twenty20. Author Ken Piesse opposes Gary Cosier. Darren 'JB' Walker is at gully

A Saturday afternoon club leg-spinner he counts Keith Stackpole, David Hookes and Prime Minister Bob Hawke among his wickets. 'First time I've been caught out by a journalist in 25 years,' quipped the PM as he marched off the MCG.

The president of the Australian Cricket Society since 2006, Ken was shocked and disappointed by the shameful happenings of Cape Town in autumn and was the first to predict 12-month suspensions for the offending Steve Smith and co. via his daily cricket reports for sportshounds.com.au

Ken Piesse website: www.cricketbooks.com.au

Author's acknowledgements

I would like to sincerely thank everyone involved with *Australian Cricket Scandals*, particularly publisher Michael Wilkinson and Wilkinson Books, his executive assistant Jess Lomas and my long-time designer Bruce Godden.

Australian Cricket Scandals is based on a previous book *Cricket's Greatest Scandals* I published with Penguin in 2000 and 2001. My thanks to Jordan Meek at Penguin-Random House in fast-tracking the copyright reversion rights and to Geoff Poulter for his invaluable editorial suggestions.

This book has been completely updated with many new chapters and dozens of illustrations and fresh storylines.

Many at the Australian Cricket Society have been very generous in loaning photographs for this book, the 55th on cricket I have written, edited or published. My particular thanks to ACS tourists David Beames and Wayne Ross who were with Susan and I on our 2018 Adventure in Paradise tour, which included the Cape Town Test, so pivotal in the re-making of this book.

Greg Shipperd lent me his introduction to Brad Hodge, the little Master which he so expertly delivered at our 51st ACS annual dinner in June.

Also my thanks to the Pepper family and in particular Jeanette Bond for sharing some treasured family photos of her uncle Cec Pepper and to Cec's brother, Keith, for sharing some memories from long ago.

I'd also like to particularly thank Jon Anderson, Dr Ali Bacher, Pieter Barnard, the Benaud family, Andy Bichel, Ray Bright, Mark Browning, Greg Chappell, Ian Chappell, Trevor Chappell, Colin Clowes, Malcolm Conn, Alan Connolly, Robert Craddock, Ross Dundas, Col Egar, Ric Finlay, Koketso Gaofetoge, Edward Griffiths, Ian Harvey, the Hookes family, Merv Hughes, Bob Massie, Tim May, Harriet Monkhouse, Ian Meckiff, Bob Parish, Mick Pope, Brian Quinn, A. Aziz Rehmatullah, Ian Redpath, Ron Reiffel, Austin Robertson jnr., Geoff Sando, Bob Simpson, Rick Smith, Michael Storey, David Studham, Mick Taylor, the Tyson family, Ray Webster, Don Weser & Bernard Whimpress.

And also to the many photographers who have kindly allowed their work to be reproduced in these pages.

As always my wife Susan was very supportive of my latest project.

Index

Adcock, Neil 69
Alcock, Charles 181
Alderman, Terry 51, 54, 56
Alexander. George 181
Alexander, Harry 'Bull' 147
Allen, GOB 'Gubby' 144, 149, 151
Allen, Jim 94
Allen, Megan 19
Ambrose, Curtly 25-26, 28
Amiss, Dennis 94
Angel, Jo 37
Archer, Ken 122
Armstrong, Warwick 23, 26, 165, 166, 169
   Accuses Bradman of being
      frightened 152-153
Arnold, Geoff 69
Asif Iqbal 94
Atherton, Mike 6
Austin, Harold 117
Austin, Richard 94
Azharuddin, Mohammad 80

Bacher, Dr Ali 8-9, **47-57**
Bailhache, Robin 67
Baker, Susie 18
Bancroft, Cameron 'Bangers' viii, ix, **1-13**, 80
Bannerman, Alick 184
Barassi, Ron 100
Bardsley, Warren 175
Barlow, Eddie 93, 94
Barnes, Alan 97
Barnes, Sid 109, **121-133**
   Barred from the Lancashire
      League 130
   Criticises Hassett & Miller 132-133
   Forty runs off an over 130
   How he compares with the best 128
   Sydney grade record 126
Barnes, Sydney 163, 166, 167, 175
Barnes, William 186
Barton, Edmund 179
Beames, Percy 103, 111
   Watered wicket 'scoop' 117-118

Bedser, Alec 113
Benaud, John 29
Benaud, Richie 38, 43, 76, 78, 90, 100, 105, 106, 109, 110
Bennett, Murray 53
Berry, Darren 'Chuck' 20, 29, 30
Bett, H. Drysdale 159
Bettington, Dr Reg 152
Bevan, Hugh 101
Bevan, Michael 28
Bills, Fred 105
Blamey, General Thomas 137, 140
Boon, David 26, 31
Border, Allan 'AB' 18, 22, 25, 27, 28, 29, 31, 77, 81
Borwick, George 135, 144
Bosisto, Glyn 74
Botham, Ian 25, 62, 63, 67
Boucher, Mark 15-16
Bowes, Bill 147, 149, 150, 151
Boycott, Geoff 64, 92
Boyle, Harry 184-185
Bradman, Don ix, 5, 44, 88, 95, 100, 102, 123, 125, 127, 130, 131, 132, 141, 148, 154, 163
   Accrington offer 157
   Accused of being frightened 153
   Advises Meckiff to retire 110
   Bodyline summer 143-155
   Concedes a century, as a bowler 160
   Criticises state of MCG wicket 116
   Goes on strike **157-161**
   Meets with Kerry Packer 85
   Opinion of the Board 129
   Out first ball to Bill Bowes 150
   Part of his good conduct
      bonus withheld 157
   Post-war comeback 135-137, 140-141
   Reaction to the Chappell
      underarm 74
   Role in the Barnes affair 122-127
   Role in the calling of Meckiff 99-101, 105-107
Bradman, Jessie 135, 159

Index

Brearley, Mike	62, 67	Croft, Colin	94
Breasley, Scobie	114	Croft, Graham	18
Bright, Ray	61, 63, 85, 94	Cronin, Peter	72, 73
Briscoe, Ted	172	Cronje, Hansie	30, 40, 43, 80
Brown, Freddie	121	Crouch, GS	168
Buller, Sid	103, 108	Cummins, Pat	viii, ix, 5
Burgess, Mark	72, 76	Cush, Frank	123
Bush, Arthur	184, 185		
		Dakin, Geoff	53
Cairns, Lance	72, 79	Daniel, Wayne	71-72, 94
Carr, Arthur	148, 152, 153	Davidson, Alan 'Davo'	101, 131
Carter, H 'Sammy'	165	Davies, Gareth	43
Cashman, Richard	179	Davis, Ian	94
Chapman, Percy	148, 152	Davis, JC 'Not Out'	172
Chappell, Greg	65, 67, 68, **71-81**, 83, 84, 91, 93, 94, 96	de Kock, Quinton	7
		de Lacy, Hec	123
		de Villiers, AB	viii, 1, 5
Commits to Packer for five years	95	Accuses Australia of cheating	2
Damned by Richie Benaud	76	Denison, Sir Hugh	160
Feels sorry for brother Trevor	80	Denness, Mike	68
Not fit to captain Australia	74	Derriman, Phil	169, 175
Strikes Viv Richards in the face	86	Dexter, Ted	63, 101
Ticks off Lillee	66	Dowling, Bill	105
World Series highlights	86	Du Plessis, Faf	6, 9, 19
Chappell, Ian 'Chappelli'	26, 64, 78, 84, 94, 96, 97	Likens Australia to 'a pack of dogs'	2
		Dujon, Jeff	27
'Sick of being pushed around'	89	Dwyer, E. A. 'Chappie'	122-125, 129, 140
Chappell, Jeanne	74, 78		
Chappell, Martin	74	Edgar, Bruce	74
Chappell, Trevor	**71-81**, 94	Edinburgh, The Duke of	68
Cheetham, Albert	135	Edrich, John	69
Clark, EA 'Nobby'	155	Edwards, Ross	94
Clarke, Michael	20, 23	Egar, Col 'CJ'	41, 111
Cole, Des & Fred	18	Calling of Ian Meckiff	99-110
Conn, Malcolm	42	Elgar, Dean	ix, 5
Connolly, Alan 'Al Pal'	100, 102, 109, 111	Elliott, Matty	19, 23
		Elton John	26
Constantine, Learie	153	Emmett, Thomas	180
Contractor, Nari	100	Evatt, Dr Herbert V	127
Conway, John	184-185		
Cook, Jimmy	57	Faulkner, Peter	55
Cornell, John 'Strop'	89, 91, 92, 96	Fingleton, Jack	111, 123, 141, 143-144, 151, 160
Cosier, Gary	94		
Cotter, A 'Tibby'	165, 167	Ford, Maurine	138, 139, 140
Coulthard, George	178-180	Foster, Frank	147, 163
Cowdrey, Colin	68-69, 111	Foster, Reg	173
Cowper, Bob	87-88	Fotheringham, Henry	57
Cox, Jamie	20	Francis, Bruce	50, 51
Crafter, Tony	65	Fredericks, Roy	94
Craig, Ian	57		
Craig, Shawn	30		
Crockett, Bob	169, 171, 175		

195

Gallop, Ted	43	Haysman, Michael	55
Garner, Joel	86, 94	Hazlewood, Josh	ix, 5, 7
Garrett, Tom	172	Healy, Ian	27, 40, 42
Gaunt, Ron 'Pappy'	104	Heine, Peter	69
Gavaskar, Sunil	93, 97	Hele, George	144
Gehrs, Alby	165	Henry, Omar	56
Gibson, IM	180	Hewett, Ian	18
Gilchrist, Adam	21	Hewlett, Andy	51
Gillespie, Jason	19	Higgs, Jim	27
Gilmour, Gary	94	Hill, Clem	150, **163-169**
Glaister, Philip	43	Hill, Florrie	164
Goddard, John	122	Hill-Wood, Wilfred	77
Goddard, Trevor	99, 101, 109	Hitchcox, Alan	100
Gooch, Graham	48	Hobbs, Jack	153, 154, 167
Gowrie, Lord	127	Remonstrates with Bill Bowes	149
Grace, GF	183	Hobson, Denys	93
Grace, Dr WG	181, **183-187**	Hodge, Brad	**15-23**
Graf, Shaun	38	'One of the great mysteries'	15
Grant, Trevor	54	Test cap presentation	20
Gray, Malcolm	43	Hodge, John	18
Greenidge, Gordon	27, 86, 94	Hodge, Val	17, 18
Gregory, Dave	177, 179-180, 184	Hogan, Bruce	43
'Aided and abetted' the riot	180	Hogg, Rodney	48, 57, 66, 67
Gregory, Syd	22, 168	Hohns, Trevor	55, 56
Greig, Tony	57, 76, 84, 90, 94, 95, 97	Hogben, Stan	102
Griffin, Geoff	103	Holding, Michael 'Whispering Death'	86, 93, 94
Griffith, Charlie	69, 100	Holford, David	94
Grimmett, Clarrie 'Grum'	141	Holland, Jon	3
Guest, Colin	101	Hookes, David	42, 89, 90, 91, 94, 96, 97, 192
Gupta, Mukesh ('John' the bookmaker)	35-41	Offered Rebel XI captaincy	50
		World Series highlights	86
Hadlee, Richard	72, 94	Hordern, HV 'Ranji'	167, 169
Hadlee, Walter	57	Hornby, AN 'Monkey'	179, 181
Halbish, Graham	43	House, Jack	**113-119**
Hall, Wes	69	Howard, John	43
Hallebone, Jeff	102	Howarth, Geoff	71, 74, 76, 79, 81
Hammond, Walter	138, 149, 151, 152	Sportsmanship towards Greg Chappell	78
Handscomb, Peter	ix, 10	Howell, Bill	168
Harbourd, Noel	38	Hoy, Colin	108
Haroon Rashid	94	Hughes, Kim	26, 51, 57
Harris, Lord	**177-181**	Hughes, Merv	29-30
Hartigan, Roger	123	Spat with Dean Jones	33
Harvey, Ian	33	Hurford, Chris	53
Harvey, Neil	26, 43, 57, 63	Hussey, Mike	23
Hassett, Lindsay	57, 109, 123, 124, 132	Hutcheon, Jack	124
Hawke, Bob	47-48, 53, 192	Hutchison, Geoff	30
Hawke, Neil 'Hawkeye'	101, 102	Hutton, Len	114, 122, 130
Hayden, Bill	53		
Hayden, Matthew	21, 30		
Haynes, Desmond	94		

Index

Illingworth, Ray	33
Illingworth, Richard	viii, 20
Imran Khan	94
Intikhab Alam	94
Inverarity, John	101
Inzamam-ul-Haq	40
Iredale, Frank	166-168
Jackson, Archie	148
Jackson, Liz	43
Jardine, Douglas	**143-155**
Eight on the on-side	147
'Let the bastard die of thirst'	152
Uses Bodyline in India	155
Javed Miandad	65, 94
Jeanes, Bill	127
Jenner, Terry 'TJ'	92
Jeoomal, Naoomal	155
Johnson, Ian	57, 109, 115
Johnson, Keith	124, 128-129
'Treacherous'	127
Johnson, Len	122
Johnston, Bill	118
Jones, Clem	101
Jones, Dean 'Deano'	20, 22, 23, **25-33**, 41, 54
Dubs the Waughs 'the Koalas'	26
Sledges Mark Taylor	32
Test record ground by ground	31
Jones, Ernie	99
Jones, Sammy	187
Julien, Bernard	94
Kallicharran, Alvin	94
Kanhai, Rohan	100
Katich, Simon	20
Kent, Martin	64
Kelly, Ned	179
Khawaja, Usman	9
Kierse, Jack	105
King, Collis	67, 94
King George V	127
Kippax, Alan	144, 148, 153
Knott, Alan	94
Koslowski, Mike	79
Laird, Bruce	94
Lake, Min	139
Laker, Jim	130
Lalor, Peter	11
Lambert, William	178
Langer, Justin	12, 13, 28
Langer, Rob	94
Larwood, Harold	80, 160
Accuses Bradman of 'flinching'	148
Bodyline summer	143-155
Fells Bertie Oldfield	144
'Hounded' out of cricket	153
Strikes 25 Australians	147
Laver, Frank	163, 165, 168
Lawry, Bill	3, 23, 26, 74, 89, 105
Le Roux, Garth	55, 94
Lehmann, Darren	viii, ix, 3, 9, 10, 12, 13, 20, 30
Liddicutt, Arthur	77
Lillee, Dennis	17, 18, 25, **59-69**, 74, 76, 83, 84
'Dump Deano' column	28
'Good luck with the sales Dennis'	68
Opinions of	66
'Sickening' antics	64
Uses an aluminum bat in a Test	67-68
World Series highlights	86
World Series instigator	87-91
Lillywhite, James	184
Lindwall, Ray	69, 121, 124, 129
Llong, Nigel	viii, 10
Lloyd, Clive	84, 94
Lloyd, Mr Justice	127
Loader, Peter	101
Loxton, Sam	75
Lunn, Hugh	80
Lush, Ginty	130
Luttrell, Bert	116
Lyon, Nathan	1, 5, 7
Lyons, Fred	135
Macartney, Charlie	163, 166
MacGill, Stewie	21
Mackay, Ken 'Slasher'	101, 105
Maclaren, Archie	173
Maddocks, Len	115, 118
Maharaj, Keshav	3
Mailey, Arthur	123, 161, 169
Majid Khan	94
Malcolm, Devon	33
Malik, Saleem 'The Rat'	37-41
Mallett, Ashley	92, 94
Malone, Mick	72, 94
Mandella, Nelson	49
Manley, Michael	93
Marlar, Robin	97

Marsh, Geoff	28
Marsh, Jack	**171-175**
Marsh, Rod	17, 18, 25, **59-69**, 79, 81, 83, 84, 89, 93, 94, 111
'No mate, don't do it'	74
Marshall, Malcolm	28
Martindale, EA 'Manny'	153
Martram, Aiden	viii, 1, 5
Sledged 'every second ball'	9
Martyn, Damien	23, 27, 28
Massie, Bob 'Ferg'	59-60
Mathers, Jim	123
Matthews, TJ 'Jimmy'	166-167
Maxwell, Jim	52
May, Peter	103
May, Tim	30, 38, 39
McAlister, Peter	**163-169**
McCabe, Stan	123, 144, 160
Bravest Ashes innings of all	149
McCosker, Rick	94
McCurdy, Donna & Ryan	48-49
McCurdy, Rod 'Puppy'	48-49, 54, 55
McDonald, Ian	41
McFarline, Peter	95, 96
McGilvray, Alan	109
McGregor, Adrian	75, 78, 96
McIntyre, Peter	30
McKechnie, Brian	72-74, 77, 80
McKenzie, Graham 'Garth'	9, 89, 94, 101, 104, 106
'More popular than Vegemite'	88
McLeod, Charlie	169
Meckiff, Don	102
Meckiff, Ian	**99-111**
Hits a ball into Mordialloc Creek	102
'My God, he's called me'	106
Releases autobiography	104
Meredith, Anthony	174
Midwinter, Elizabeth, Elsie & Albert	186
Midwinter, William snr	183
Midwinter, WE jnr 'Billy'/'The Bendigo Giant'/'Middy'	**183-187**
Melbourne gravestone	186-187
Miller, Andrew 'Dusty'	3
Miller, Keith 'Nugget'	69, 76-77, 114, 129, 130, 135, 137, 138, 141
Minnett, Roy	166
Misson, Frank	101, 104
Moody, Tom	27, 28
Morkel, Morne	7, 13
Morris, Arthur	122, 130, 131, 141
Morris, Samuel	175
Moyes, AG 'Johnnie'	167, 169
Muldoon, Robert	74-75, 77
Muralidaran, Muthiah	27, 107
Murdoch, William	177, 179
Murray, Deryck	94
Mushtaq Ahmed 'Mushie'	40
Mushtaq Mohammad	94
Neely, Don	79
Nielsen, Tim	30
Noble, MA 'Monty'	154, 165
Outlaws Jack Marsh	171-174
Norman, Greg	26
Ntini, Makhaya	8
O'Brien, Leo 'Mo'	143-144, 147, 152
O'Connell, Max	67
O'Keeffe, Kerry	94
Oldfield, WA 'Bert'	144, 151, 154
O'Reilly, Bill 'Tiger'	77, 123, 138, 144
Oslear, Don	79
Oxlade, Aubrey	122-124, 127, 159
Packer, Clyde	89
Packer, Sir Frank	89
Packer, James	94
Packer, Kerry	51, 52, 54, 71, **83-97**, 141, 160
Innovations	86
Picks his own captain	94
Threatens the Board	84
Packer, RC	160
Padmore, Albert	94
Palairet, Richard	143
Paine, Tim	3, 7, 10, 11
Palairet, Richard	143, 145, 151
Pamensky, Joe	53, 57,
Parish, Bob	74, 76, 83, 85, 95, 96
Pascoe, Len	94
Patterson, Patrick	28
Pawle, Gerald	152
Pepper, Cec	113, 130, **135-143**
A different girl for every day of the week	138
Menage a trois	141
Pepper, Keith	138
Philander, Vernon	12
Phillips, Wayne	41, 53
Piesse, Ken	57, 61, 192

Index

Piesse, Susan	57
Poidevin, Les	175
Pollard, Jack	186
Pollock, Graeme	55, 93, 94, 100, 102, 111
Pollock, Peter	9, 106
Pollock, Shaun	15
Ponsford, Bill	23, 26, 148
Struck 6 times in three Tests	147
Ponting, Ricky	12, 13, 15, 17, 21, 22, 23, 26
Exchange with Brad Hodge	16-17
Facing the bowling machine at 100mph	17
Priem, Bill	105, 106
Prior, Wayne	94
Procter, Mike 'Prockie'	9, 93, 94
Queen Elizabeth	68
Quigley, Brian	105
Rabada, Kagiso 'King KG'	2, 7, 8
Rackemann, Carl 'Big Mocca'	48, 50, 54, 55, 56
Rae, Simon	184
Raith, Jacob	127, 129
Ransford, Vernon	116, 117, 165
Ray, Mark	41
Redpath, Ian 'Red'	85, 94
'Meckiff never a chucker'	100, 111
Reed, Ron	31
Reid, John	41, 57
Reiffel, Paul	20, 29
Rhodes, Wilfred	161
Rice, Clive	55, 94
Richards, Barry	3, 11-12, 85, 91, 93, 94
World Series highlights	86
Richards, David	44
Richards, John	181
Richards, Viv 'The Master Blaster'	27, 86, 91, 94, 97
Richardson, Vic	144, 147, 149
Irreverent swipe at Jardine	151
Rigney, William	181
Ring, Doug	109
Roberts, Andy	90, 91, 94
Robertson, Dr Allen	145
Robertson, Austin jnr.	87, 91-94
Robins, Derrick	50
Robinson, Ray	101, 111, 130
Robinson, Richie	85, 94
Rorke, Gordon	101, 104
Rowan, Lou	102, 105-110
No conspiracy against Meckiff	108
Rowe, Lawrence	50, 94
Roy, Iain	12
Ryder, Jack 'The King'	100, 101, 105, 110, 122, 140
Saeed Anwar	38
Saleem Malik 'The Rat'	37-41, 80
Sarfraz Nawaz	94
Sawle, Lawrie	27
Scott, Jack	140
Scholes, John	30
Scotton, William	178
Seddon, Dudley	100, 110
Selby, John	178
Shahid Afridi	6
Shand, Jack	124, 127-129
Shaw, Alfred	178, 185
Sheahan, Mike	95
Sheahan, Paul	88
Shepherd, Barry	105
Sherwell, Percy	165
Shiell, Alan 'Sheff'	95
Shipperd, Greg	15, 54, 55
Dubs Brad Hodge 'The Little Master'	23
Simpson, Bob	22, 27, 29, 41, 88, 101
Throwing 'an insidious evil'	99-100
Skelding, Alex	130
Slade, Mr Justice	94
Slater, Keith	103, 104
Slater, Michael	28
Smith, Donna	45
Smith, Ian	72, 79
Smith, Patrick	43
Smith, Rick	168
Smith, Steve	viii, ix, **1-13**, 80
Smith, Syd jnr.	166, 167
Snedden, Martin	72
Snow, John 'Snowy'	93, 94
Sobers, Garry	101
Spofforth, Fred 'The Demon'	179, 18
Stackpole, Keith	192
Starc, Mitchell	ix, 2,
Statham, Brian	114, 115
Steele, Ray	76, 83, 89, 97
Stillman, Les	33
Sutcliffe, Herbert	147-148, 154
Sutherland, James	ix, 12, 13
Symonds, Andrew	23

Tarrant, Frank	155	Webster, Ray	175
Taylor, Bob	67-68	Wellham, Dirk	53, 54
Taylor, Ian	76	Weser, Don	67, 72, 73, 75
Taylor, Mark	32, 37, 40, 44	Wessels, Kepler	94
Taylor, Mick	55	Whatmore, Dav	55
Thoms, Robert	187	Whimpress, Bernard	164, 172, 175
Thomson, Jeff	51, 64, 66, 84, 94	White, Cameron	13
Combination with Lillee	68	Whitty, Bill	166
Thurlow, Hugh 'Pud'	154	Wilkins, Phil	41
Toshack, Ernie	127, 133	Williams, Bill	2
Trethewey, Peter	100	Willis, Bob	63
Tribe, Peter	61-63	Wilson, Geoffrey	77
Trumble, Hugh	165, 173	Wilson, Vic	115
Trumper, Vic	165, 166, 168	Wood, Graeme	53
Turnbull, Malcolm	12	Woodcock, John	64
Tyson, Frank 'Typhoon'	**113-119**	Woodfull, Bill 'Woody'	144, 148, 151-154
'Sconed' by Ray Lindwall	113	Famous rebuke to Plum Warner	143
Takes 6-16 in 51 balls	118	Struck 7 times in four Tests	147
Tyson, Philip 'The Breeze'	119	Woods, Sammy	173
		Wooldridge, Ian	97
Ulyett, George	178	Woolmer, Bob	94
Underwood, Derek	94	Worrall, Jack	150
		Wright, Bert	151
Vanthoff, Bill	116-118	Wyatt, Bob	57, 150, 151
Veivers, Tom	109		
Verity, Hedley	149, 151	Yagmich, Denis	94
Viljeon, Ken	106	Yallop, Graham	48
Voce, Bill	147, 148, 149, 153,	Yeomans, EC 'Son'	123
		Yuvraj of Patiala, The	155
Walcott, Clyde	41, 43, 44		
Walker, Max 'Tangles'	85, 91, 94	Zaheer Abbas	94

LISTS & TABLES

Walsh, Courtney	28
Walters, Doug	76, 80, 94
Hits an underarm for six	81
Signs with World Series	91-92
Wardle, Johnny	103
Warne, Shane 'Warnie'	viii, 20, 21, 27, 28, 31, **35-45**, 97
Accused of harassment	45
Life in a goldfish bowl	45
Warne, Simone	44
Warner, Candice	2
Warner, David 'Cannon'	ix, 1-13, 64, 80
Warner, PF 'Plum'	143, 146-147, 151, 152, 155, 166, 174
Claims Jack Marsh is a thrower	173
Watson, Graeme	94
Watt, Tom	105
Waugh, Mark	26, 27, **35-43**
Four ducks in a row	28
Waugh, Steve 'Tugga'	26, 32

An Australian XI not to play Test cricket	139
Australians who also played Test cricket elsewhere	186
Ball tampering	6
Called for Throwing in a Test	107
Dean Jones' run blitz after being dropped	30
Jones in Tests Ground by Ground	31
Highest all-time Victorian run makers	21
Highest scores by Victorians since 1950	22
Most Victorian centuries/games	22
Rebel teams to South Africa 1981-90	52
Sid Barnes in grade cricket	126
How Barnes compares with the best	128
The amazing world of Sid Barnes	130-131